HISTORY OF THE OLD TESTAMENT

II

VOL. II

HISTORY OF THE
CLAUS SCHEDL

OLD TESTAMENT
GOD'S PEOPLE OF THE COVENANT

OT
3079
Sch

alba house
A DIVISION OF THE SOCIETY OF ST. PAUL
STATEN ISLAND, NEW YORK 10314

First published under the title: **Geschichte des Alten Testaments** by Tyrolia-Verlag, Innsbruck, Austria

Library of Congress Cataloging in Publication Data

Schedl, Claus.
   History of the Old Testament.

   Translation of Geschichte des Alten Testaments.
   Includes bibliographical references.
   CONTENTS: v. 1. The ancient Orient and ancient Biblical history.—
v. 2. God's people of the covenant.—v. 3. The golden age of David. [etc.]
   1. Bible.   O. T.—History of Biblical events.
I. Title.
BS1197.S3213   221.9   70-38990
ISBN 0-8189-0231-0 (set)
ISBN 0-8189-0229-9 (v. 2)

Nihil Obstat:
   Donald A. Panella, M.A., S.T.L., S.S.L.
   Censor Librorum

Imprimatur:
   James P. Mahoney
   Vicar General, Archdiocese of New York
   November 11, 1971

The nihil obstat and imprimatur are official declarations that a book or pamphlet is free of doctrinal or moral error. No implication is contained therein that those who have granted the nihil obstat and imprimatur agree with the contents, opinions or statements expressed.

Designed, printed and bound by the Fathers and Brothers of the Society of St. Paul as part of their communications apostolate.
Library of Congress Cataloging in Publication Data

THE THEOLOGIAN AND
THE OLD TESTAMENT

BY theologian we understand not merely the professional theologian who studies the Bible in connection with his vocation in order to qualify himself for the exercise of his office, but every believer for whom the Bible is an interesting and venerable document of the history of the ancient Eastern mind and religion. The Bible is not the private literature of a specially elect band of devotees, but the life book of God's people. It is in this book that the Word of God, binding on all men, has become flesh.

Just as the person of Christ "who, though he was in the form of God, did not count equality with God a thing to be grasped, but emptied himself, taking the form of a servant, being born in the likeness of men" (*Phil.* 2, 6-7) is the key to all theology, it is also the only approach to the Bible. Just as the God-man Jesus spans a mighty dichotomy in his person, by uniting what appear to be strictly disparate elements in one divine-human unity, so the word of the Bible is filled with a dynamism which surpasses human measurement. Are we now about to do away with this involvement in the sphere of human affairs by advancing a theology of the word of the Bible that concentrates too heavily on the overpowering splendor of that Word which was in the beginning with God and which is incapable of being incorporated into "the shards of letters"? [1]

Not at all. Just as the man who repudiates Christ's bodily

---

1. Origen, *Commentary on St. John,* Migne, PG 13, 29B-32B.

existence and ascribes only a phantom human existence to the Incarnate Word is guilty of seriously misinterpreting Christ, so the man who refuses to recognize the fact of the Incarnation entirely misses the mystery of Scripture. Just as Christ was a true man of his times, speaking the Galilean dialect and wearing the dress of his century, so every word in the Bible is spoken in a concrete, unique, and historical setting. This very fact determined its fate. The dust of centuries has grown heavy upon it. The Word has made its way into history, as every other, earlier or later, profane document of history.

If we mean to approach this word, we must face the difficult task of entering into all the stipulations of historical development and not rest comfortably in our secure position by pointing to the fact of inspiration. Whoever wishes to approach the Bible in a scientific manner necessarily takes on the total load of a profane exegesis. The Old Testament is a written document of the Ancient Near East, and it has undergone a development over the course of more than a thousand years before reaching its present form. For the most part it is written in the Hebrew language. A scientific examination of the Old Testament, therefore, becomes impossible without the study and knowledge of this language. The man who bases his approach only on translations is always something of a stranger to the concrete call of the revealed word; for every translation is, in some respects, a betrayal. Only the original text is inspired, and not the translations, no matter how venerable they might be.

The Old Testament is also a literary document. Thus we are also obliged (and it would be a serious error to omit this task) to approach the text in terms of the principles of philology and literary criticism in order to critically test every passage. But a literary criticism always runs the danger of being too removed from life and reality, unless it constantly keeps in sight the *Sitz im Leben* — its position in actuality.

The written document thus appeals to the mute witnesses of ancient history, which are made articulate by archaeological excavation. Philology, literary criticism, archaeology, and the history of the Ancient Near East are the guideposts for this profane exegesis; without them we are irrevocably lost in the realm of unreality, and we miss the full "incarnation of the Word." The personal religious conviction of the investigator plays no role in this. In fact, we might go so far as to claim that if there were one ideal technique for carrying out this methodology of examination, then the results of a study by an atheistic philologist and a believing theologian would be completely in agreement. And, in practice, to a large extent, this is exactly what happens.

But if we mean to rest content with this *profane exegesis,* we fail to recognize the inexhaustible reality of the Bible word. Profane exegesis must be enlarged upon, not only as a mere supplement, but as an ultimate fulfillment, by "pneumatic" exegesis. The primary source of Scripture is at once both human and divine. If one of the pillars is missing here, the whole construction collapses in ruin.

This is not the place to fully treat on the nature of inspiration,[2] although the study of Scripture wanders about blindly without a clear idea of it. Both Church and synagogue have always attested to the fact that the Bible contains God's word. Disagreements were only on questions concerning how the authorship of Scripture was to be ascribed to God, and how it was possible to speak of human authorship. The Patristic age [3] was fond of parables: the Holy Spirit, it was claimed, used the human author like a musical instrument (organ, flute, lyre, etc.). Though it is an attractive metaphor, it runs the risk of considering human cooperation too exclusively in terms of a dead "instrument," without any proper activity of its own. When God overshadows a human author, he does not extinguish human existence; he elevates it into greater light, into a freedom untrammeled by sin. Inspiration is the elevation of the human faculties. If God calls upon man to compose a book, he directs this call to a concrete, historically qualified man, who, under the divine impulse, takes up the historical source material available and forms it into a unity that has been revealed to him. In this process, it is only too easy

---

2. A. Merk, *De Inspiratione S. Scripturae,* Biblical Institute, Rome 1951.
3. Cf. J. Schildenberger, *Vom Geheimnis des Gotteswortes,* 1950, p. 17.

to recognize the awkward hand of the human author, who was obviously not always an accomplished literary artist. But it is from this very defect that God's power sounds its clearest note. Thus the word formed by man becomes the true "bounty of the divine Word." [4] We can then speak of personal literary style, power of poetic expression, artistic or faulty composition without thereby calling into question the divine reality of inspiration.

Once the divine origin of Scripture is properly grasped, there are some ponderable conclusions. The basic concept of this book is divine and grandiose. It lays bare the deepest abysses of sin and judgment; but it also discloses the glories of forgiveness and grace. There is nothing superficial or monotonous about this book. It sounds depths of such great dimensions that they shine like lightning "from the beginning to the end of days." This book was not composed without a plan; it storms along towards its goal. The "shards of the individual words" announce the irresistible and passionate arrival of the Eternal Word. The words are all oriented towards *the* Word. The Old Testament is the "educator towards Christ." Thus, if you tell how you look at Christ, I will tell you how you read the Old Testament. The ultimate understanding of Scripture comes only from faith and Spirit. Once a man has tasted the "sweetness of the word" (*Ps.* 34, 8), he is awake to the "passion of the divine." Since the Spirit who has inspired this book is passion and love, the man who has once experienced this "divine taste" can never again turn away. Even the mighty waters of boredom, which every study necessarily involves, will not be able to destroy this love. The final object of theological instruction does not consist in the imparting of knowledge, but in the development of the "theological eros." If this succeeds, the small spark becomes a conflagration which can inflame the entire world.

Thus we raise our voice in a complaint which is perhaps also an accusation: Why is there so much weakness and fragility in Christianity? Obviously, because the word has been dulled. We are taken up with New Testament exegesis and frequently

---

4. Origen, *Commentary on Jeremiah*, Migne, PG 13, 544C.

lose ourselves in spiritualistic conclusions. The bread of the Old Testament is not broken enough. And still the Catholic Church is, much more than we dare to realize, *the* Church of the Bible. The liturgical missal is almost exclusively Old Testament in its sung texts. If we would remove the Old Testament from our liturgy the Church would be without song. Take away the powerful readings from Law and Prophets from the liturgical year, and Christianity is made incomplete. The Old Testament is neither old nor ancient; it is a living reality in our midst. But how many of us recognize the power coming from this book? Today, more than ever, we must call upon the tidings of the Old Testament, in order to recognize the hand of Yahweh in a world on the verge of collapse. Yahweh is a God of history, and he directs the chaos of human history towards a goal and purpose he has set.

The concluding words of this introduction are taken from Origen, one of the greatest Scripture scholars and interpreters of the Greek Church, and for that matter, the whole Church: "If we have once admitted that these writings owe their origin to the creator of the world, we must be convinced that whatever is encountered by those who examine into the fundamental meaning of the world will also be met with in the study of Scripture. The further we progress in reading, the higher the mountain of mysteries towers above us. And just as a man who sets out upon the sea in a tiny ship is unafraid so long as he is close to the land but, when he gradually approaches the high seas and the waves begin to swell and he begins to be lifted high upon their crests or, when they gape open and he begins to be swarmed under into the abyss, it is then that his spirit is seized by a monstrous fear and anxiety for having entrusted such a tiny ship to such monstrous floods — this is the experience we seem to have when, from the smallness of our merit and the narrowness of our spirit we dare to approach so wide a sea of mysteries." [5]

---

5. Origen, *Homily on Genesis.*

CONTENTS

SECTION ONE
THE PATRIARCHS

SECTION TWO
MOSES AND THE COVENANT OF THE TWELVE TRIBES

ABBREVIATIONS

AASOR	Annual of the American School of Oriental Research
ABEL	F. M. Abel, *Géographie de la Palestine* (Études Bibliques), Paris, vol. I, 1933, vol. II, 1938
AfO	E. Weidner, *Archiv für Orientforschung*, Graz
AJA	American Journal of Archaeology
ANEP	J. P. Pritchard, *The Ancient Near East in Pictures relating to the Old Testament*, Princeton Univ. Press, 1954
ANET	J. P. Pritchard, *Ancient Near Eastern Texts relating to the Old Testament*, Princeton Univ. Press, 1955
AnglTR	Anglican Theological Review
Ann. PEF	Annual of the Palestine Exploration Fund, London
AnOr	Anacleta Orientalia, Rome
Ant.	Flavius Josephus, *Antiquitates Judaicae, Jüdische Altertümer*
AO	Alter Orient
AOB	H. Gressmann, *Altorientalische Bilder zum Alten Testament*, Berlin/Leipzig, 1927
AOT	H. Gressmann, *Altorientalische Texte zum Alten Testament*, 1926
APAW	Abhandlungen der Preussischen Akademie der Wissenschaften, Berlin
ARM	Archives Royales de Mari, Paris
Arch	Archaeology
ArOr	Archiv Orientálni
AT	Altes Testament
ATD	Hentrich and Weiser, *Das Alte Testament Deutsch*, Göttingen
BA	The Biblical Archaeologist
BASOR	Bulletin of the American Schools of Oriental Research

BB	Bonner Bibelkommentar
Bibl	Biblica
BiblArch	The Biblical Archaeologist
BibLex	H. Haag, *Bibellexicon*
BibLit	Bibel und Liturgie
BHK	R. Kittel, *Biblica Hebraica*, adapted by Stuttgart, 1954
BJRL	K. Galling, The Bulletin of the John Rylands Library
BK	M. Noth, *Biblischer Kommentar, Altes Testament*, Neukirchen
BRL	Biblisches Reallexicon
BZ	Biblische Zeitschrift, Neue Folge, Paderborn
BZAW	Beihefte zur ZAW
CalwK	Calwer Kommentar: Die Botschaft des Alten Testaments, Stuttgart
CBQ	The Catholic Biblical Quarterly
ClamB	Pirot-Clamer, *La Sainte Bible*, Latin and French text with both exegetical and theological comment, Paris
DB	Vigouroux, *Dictionaire de la Bible*, Paris, 1861-1912
DBS	Supplément au Dictionaire de la Bible, Paris, 1926
DOT	Winton-Thomas, *Documents to the Old Testament*
EB	Echter Bibel, Würzburg
EinlAT	O. Eissfeldt, Einleitung in das Alte Testament unter Einschluss der Apokryphen und pseudepigraphen sowie der apokryphen und pseudepigraphenartigen Qumrän-Schriften. Entstehungsgeschichte des Alten Testaments, Tubingen, 1956
EnchBibl	Enchiridion Biblicum. Documenta ecclesiastica Sacram Scripturam spectantia, Rome, 1956
EncMikr	Encyklopaedia Mikra'it. Encyclopaedia Biblica. Thesaurus rerum biblicarum, Hebrew University, Jerusalem, 1950
EphThLov (ETL)	Ephemerides Theologicae Lovanienses
ET	The Expository Times
EvT	Evangelische Theologie
FF	Forschungen und Fortschritte, Berlin
Fs	Festschrift
GAV	H. Schmökel, *Geschichte des Alten Vorderasien*, Leiden, 1957

GTT	J. Simons, *The Geographical and Topographical Texts of the Old Testament*, Leiden, 1959
GVA	A. Moortgat, *Geschichte Vorderasien bis zum Hellenismus*, Munchen, 1950
HAT	Handbuch zum Alten Testament
HistM (HM)	Fritz Kern, *Historia Mundi*, 1952
HUCA	Hebrew Union College Annual, Cincinnati
IEJ	Israel Exploration Journal, Jerusalem
IntBib	The Interpreters Bible. A Commentary in twelve volumes, New York
JAOS	The Journal of the American Oriental Society
JBL	The Journal of Biblical Literature
JEArch	Journal of Egyptian Archaeology
JerB	Jerusalem Bible
JNES	The Journal of Near Eastern Studies
JSS	The Journal of Semitic Studies
KAT	E. Sellin, *Kommentar zum Alten Testament*, Leipzig
KB	Keilschriftliche Bibliothek
LexVT	L. Koehler — W. Baumgartner, *Lexicon in Veteris Testamenti Libros*, Leiden, 1953
LXX	Septuaginta
Migne, PG	Migne, *Patres Greci*
Migne, PL	Migne, *Patres Latini*
MiscBibl	Mischellania Biblica
MT	R. Kittel, *Masoretischer Text nach der Biblica Hebraica*, 1954
NouvRevThéol	Nouvelle Revue Théologique
OLZ	Orientalische Literaturzeitung, Leipzig
Or	Orientalia, Rome
PEQ	Palestine Exploration Quarterly, London
PG	Migne, *Patres Greci*
PL	Migne, *Patres Latini*
RA	E. Eberling and Br. Meisnner, *Reallexicon der Assyriologie*
RB	Revue Biblique, École Biblique, Jerusalem
RCB	Rivista di Cultura Biblica
REHM	Die Bücher der Könige, Echter Bibel, Würzburg, 1949
RSR	Recherches de Science ...eligieuse

Rev HistRel	Revue de l'Histoire des Religions, Paris
SAT	Gunkel — Gressmann, *Die Schriften des Alten Testaments*, Göttingen
ST	Studia Theologica
TGI	K. Galling, *Textbuch zur Geschichte Israels*, Tubingen, 1950
ThLZ	Theologische Literaturzeitung, Leipzig
ThZ	Theologische Zeitschrift, Basel
TTZ	Trierer Theologische Zeitschrift
UM	C. H. Gordon, *Ugaritic Manual*, Rome, 1955
VD	Verbum Domini
VT	Vetus Testamentum
WTJ	Westminster Theological Journal
ZAW	Zeitschrift für Alttestamentliche Wissenschaft
ZDMG	Zeitschrift der Deutschen Morgenländischen Gesellschaft
ZDPV	Zeitschrift des Deutschen Palästinavereines
ZKT	Zeitschrift für Katholische Theologie, Innsbruck
ZTK	Zeitschrift für Theologie und Kirche

GOD'S PEOPLE OF THE COVENANT

A COMPLETE revision has turned the American translation of Volume I, *The Ancient Orient and Ancient Biblical History* into what might more properly be termed a 3rd edition. The sacral structural principles and formulae of the sacred text which are here examined into and explained have meantime been proven to be significant factors for the Rabbinic and Early Christian literatures as well — *Talmud-Evangelium-Synagoge* (Tyrolia, Innsbruck, Vienna, Munich: 1969).

In keeping with these new developments, Vol. II, which first appeared in 1956, would also have to be thoroughly revised. This project has been seriously hindered by severe illness. Still, I feel that the translation of this volume is very necessary in view of its contribution to the entire set. The direction has, after all, been clearly pointed out: the objectives are clearly set. And for the rest, there is something "incomplete" about everything we write: we learn as long as we live.

Graz. Dec. 6, 1970

SECTION ONE

THE PATRIARCHS

CHAPTER I

THE LITERARY GENRE
OF THE PATRIARCHAL NARRATIVES

IN THE history of the patriarchs we are faced with the same problem of historicity that confronts us in prehistory. The Bible does appear to make the claim that it is recounting events which actually occurred, but which took place long before the advent of written records. Between the event and its recording there are long, "dark" centuries, during which these accounts were passed on orally from generation to generation. It is certainly possible that elements of folklore and saga were gradually added to the historical events. The Biblical critic is once again faced with the difficult task of freeing the truths of revelation from the temporally determined historical concepts of the Ancient Near East.

Since the rise of Biblical criticism, critical judgment concerning the patriarchal era has embarked upon a variety of quite different approaches, many of them reasonably sound working hypotheses. Only the more important of these can be considered here.[1]

---

1. For a concise critical survey of the history of patriarchal exegesis, cf. de Vaux, RB 53 (1946), 321ff: *La Réalité historique des Patriarches.*

1) RETRO-PROJECTION

Wellhausen, in his *Prolegomena zur Geschichte Israels* (1886, p. 331), claims that we have no possible way to discover the truth about the patriarchal era. The only thing that can be controlled is the era in which the narratives themselves first developed. The patriarchs are a projection of thoughts and figures from the later history of Israel back into the era of pre-historic antiquity; hence their phantom and transparent appearance. Since these narratives were first developed in the ninth or eighth century, they can, according to Wellhausen's critical attitude, enlighten us only on the events of this period. Expressed in this strict form, Wellhausen's opinion has hardly any followers today, since the "night" in which the patriarchal figures are supposed to have been projected from historical times has now given way to the clear light of Ancient Near Eastern history, and the historical possibility of the patriarchal narratives appears more and more probable every day.

2) ASTRAL MYTHS

During the full blossom of Panbabylonianism, the patriarchal figures were interpreted as symbols of cosmic or astral phenomena. In the wanderings of Abraham from Ur to Haran — both of these being sites of a very ancient lunar cult — critics saw an incorporation of a lunar myth. In much the same way, the other characters of the patriarchal era, and especially Jacob with his twelve sons, were divested of their human and earthly character and transformed into mythical figures in the sky.[2]

The texts discovered at Ras-Shamra lent a new impetus to this position. Scholars claimed to have found the name of Abraham's father Terah, transformed, in these texts, into a lunar deity. They concluded on the basis of this evidence that the emigration of Abraham's descendants from Ur to Haran and Canaan represents a legend which was supposed to explain the

---

2. For a good treatment of the astral mythology, cf. A. Jeremias, *Das AT im Lichte des Alten Orients,* 4, (1930), 112ff. / H. Winckler, *Geschi-*

spread of the Babylonian lunar cult as far as southern Palestine. Further investigation, however, made it abundantly clear that this "Terah" has nothing to do with Abraham's father; it is either a noun that means something equivalent to "bride price" or a verb that means "to marry." [3]

3) THE PATRIARCHS AS CANAANITE GODS

In an effort to solve the historical problems, scholars have identified the patriarchal figures as ancient Canaanite gods. The Israelites, upon the conquest of Canaan, also took possession of the native sanctuaries. But since the Canaanite divinities had no places in their faith, they demoted them to the rank of ancestral heroes. Abraham and Sara are supposed to be gods of Hebron, more precisely, from Mamre and Machpelah, while Isaac is the genius (native deity) of Beersheba, and Jacob is a god from Transjordania.[4]

Such explanations, however, are too far removed from any historical foundation. What is more, they quickly lead to insoluble contradictions with the available facts. What would need to be proved in the very first place is the fact that such a cult of patriarchs as divinities actually did take place at the sites in question. One thing is certain: the religious centers during the occupation of the Holy Land do not coincide with the important sites mentioned in the patriarchal narratives. One might also point out that, whereas the study of religion history can amply illustrate the process whereby ancestors have been turned into gods, the reverse of this process is nowhere attested, the degradation of what are originally gods to the rank of illustrious ancestors. If there is still any room for doubt, we might

---

chte Israels, II (1900), 20ff. / E. Stucken, *Astralmythen,* 1896-1907.

3. R. Dussaud, *Les découvertes de Râs Shamra (Ugarit et l'Ancien Testament)* 1937, 108. / E. Dhorme, *La religion des Hébreux nomades,* (1937), 72, holds fast to the historicity of the patriarchal narratives, but claims that the spread of the moon cult is connected with migrations into which the story of Abraham must also have been drawn. Cf. C. H. Gordon, JBL 57 (1938), 407ff.
4. E. Meyer, *Die Israeliten und ihre Nachbarstämme,* (1906), 249.

turn, finally, to the sobering argument from philology. If the patriarchs were actually gods, then the formation of their names must necessarily betray their function as names of gods. But this is certainly not the case. The names of the patriarchs fit quite easily into the course of Ancient Near Eastern history as well-known human names.

Particularly conclusive in this respect are the business records dating from the time of the 3rd dynasty of Ur (2070 – 1963), the native city of Abraham. The imperial capital of Ur was almost completely uncovered in a systematic series of excavations from 1918 – 1932, with the result that we have learned practically everything we need to know about the city plan, the temples, administration buildings, residential areas, and cemeteries. The religious, social, and economic culture of this age is known in many details. This picture is further rounded out by the many thousands of business records on cuneiform tablets taken from the neighboring cities. All this documentary material makes it quite clear that the names of Terah's descendants were also borne by many other common citizens from the time of the 3rd dynasty of Ur, so that they are neither the names of gods nor the names of mythological heroes nor an import from the nomadic tribes.

The name Abraham is found in Mesopotamia from the beginning of the 2nd millennium in the form A-ba-am-ra-ma, A-ba-ra-ma, or A-ba-am-ra-am. The first element is the accusative form *Aba* or *Abam* (with or without mimation), *Ra-ma* and *Ra-am* is a verb form, derived from *Ramu-*, "to love"; it means: "He loves the father." Since Abraham emigrated from the territory of the eastern Semites into that of the western Semites, his name also undergoes a corresponding change. Since, in the western Semitic language (Hebrew), final consonants, and eventually even the case endings, all disappear, the form of the name can be essentially reproduced as Abram or Abra(h)am.[5]

The names of the patriarchs Isaac and Jacob are abbreviated theophoric names. The full form would be: *Yishaq-'el* and

5. Cf. N. Schneider, *Patriarchennamen in zeitgenössichen Keilschrifturkunden,* Bibl 33 (1952), 516-522. / de Vaux decides in favor of a

Ya'qob-'el, that is, a composite of an imperfect verb and the divine name. Such name formations which express the activity of God in behalf of mankind or describe an attribute or property of God are also a wish or a prayer. Jacob, on the basis of a verb root still attested in south Arabic, means "May God protect" ("'*aqaba* – protect"); *Yishaq-(el)* means "May God bring a smile, that is, may God be gracious." Such names are characteristic of the second great Semitic immigrations of the Amurru (or the eastern Canaanites or Proto-Arameans or "Hebrews," all names which have essentially the same meaning).[6]

The name Jacob has been discovered most recently in the form *Ya-ah-qu-ub-el*, in the excavations at Shagar-Basar in Upper Mesopotamia.[7] It dates from the eighth century B.C. As a place name, *Ya'qob-el* is known in Palestine from the fifteenth century and, in the geographic lists of the Egyptian Pharaoh Tutmose III and Ramses II. In its formation, it corresponds to the well-known geographical names Jezerel, Jabneel, and Iftahel.[8]

The name of Abraham's father Terah, his great-grandfather Serug, and his brother Haran, are also known from the Cappadocian tablets, the ancient Babylonian texts, and the Mari documents, as names of cities in Upper Mesopotamia.[9]

---

derivation from western Semitic: "He is big (*râm*) with respect to his father," that is, "he is of lofty origins." RB 53 (1946), 223ff. / W. F. Albright, JBL 54 (1935), 193.

---

6. M. Noth, *Die israelitischen Personennamen im Rahmen der gemeinsemitischen Namengebung*, (1928). A history of the semitic migrations can be established on the basis of the name formations. The words and the nominal sentence formations all point to the times of the earliest migrations (Akkad and Canaan), while the imperfect forms characterize the second wave of migrations, during which the origins of Israel are to be located.

7. C. J. Gadd, in Iraq Vii, (1940), 38.

8. De Vaux, RB 53 (1946), 324.

9. De Vaux, *op. cit.*, 323ff. Nahor identified as the name of a mountain in the vicinity of the mouth of the Balih; the name means either "volcano" (J. Lewy, *Studies in the Historic Geography of the Ancient Near East*. Or 21, 1952, 281-284) or "snorer" (N. Schneider, Bibl 33, 1952, 520).

The scanty philological material does not give much evidence, but it does illustrate one fact abundantly; these names all point to a territory and to an era from which, according to the Biblical tradition, the patriarchs themselves all come: the Semitic immigrations of the 2nd millennium and the locale of Upper Mesopotamia as a point of origin for the patriarchal immigrations.

In the names of the patriarchs we are thus standing on solid historical ground, and have no need to turn to the mythological world of gods and demi-gods.

4)   THE   PATRIARCHS   AS   CULT   HEROES

Still another opinion regards the patriarchs as cult heroes, legendary founders of Canaanite sanctuaries.[10] In order to give some historical foundation to their rule over Palestine, the Israelites are supposed to have invented legendary genealogies, thereby establishing family ties with the great heroes of Canaan. The patriarchal narratives would then be an after-the-fact justification of their illegal seizure of the country. This hypothesis suffers from the same weakness as the interpretation, discussed above, which identifies them with gods. From the time of their first entry into the Promised Land, to the establishment of the kingship in Jerusalem, no matter what period is supposed to have given rise to these legends, the primary sanctuaries of Israel were certainly Gilgal, Shiloh, Mishpa, and Gibeon. These cult sites, however, do not appear at all in the patriarchal history. Rather, the sites of Bethel, Hebron, and Beersheba, about which the lives of the patriarchs are centered, have an important role to play only since the time of David, that is to say, in the full light of history and not in the dark uncertainty of legend. The

---

10. R. Weill, *L'installation des Israelites en Palestine et la légende des Patriarches*, RHR 87 (1923), 69-120; 88 (1923), 1-44, is the chief proponent of the cultic myth. On the basis of the Ras-Shamra finds Weill once again defends his thesis, but involves himself in some untenable hypotheses: *Rev. des Études sémitiques*, (1937), 145-206: *La Légende des Patriarches et l'histoire*. Loisy represents a more moderate form of the cult myth: *La religion d'Israel*, (1933), 22-23.

patriarchal histories and the entry into the Promised Land are two such completely different entities that it could hardly appear credible that the one should have been invented as a justification for the other.

5) GENEALOGICAL INTERPRETATION

Whereas the theories discussed in the preceding chapters have hardly any followers today, the genealogical interpretation of the patriarchal histories is today more widespread than ever. According to this interpretation, the patriarchs are not to be considered persons, individuals, but rather personifications, names in which the collective tribal history has been reduced to a personal unity. The migration of Abraham, Isaac, and perhaps Jacob too, are thus meant to represent various waves of immigration. Marriages are to be interpreted as alliances between various tribes. According to this principle, it is possible to work out the actual historical course of events: the Jacob-tribe, which results from a mingling of the Hebrew Isaac-tribe and the Aramean Rebekah-tribe, is driven out of Palestine by the Esau-tribe. It returns to its original home in Aramea in order to recoup its energies; there it is strengthened by alliances with the Aramean tribes of Rachel and Lia, while it is attacked by the hostile tribe of Laban.[11]

This collective symbolism, however, when it is applied to individual details, quickly dissipates into improbable conclusions, although it is certainly possible that the hypothesis may be based on proper principles; for the Ancient Near East and the Bible are familiar enough with cases in which the fate of a people is indeed personified in the figure of an imaginary founder; it is generally a particular tribe which thus derives from a supposed primeval figure. But even granting the fact that legendary figures are within the realm of possibility, there are, in the case of the great patriarchs Abraham, Isaac, and Jacob,

---

11. C. Steuernagel, *Die Einwanderung der israelitischen Stämme in Kanaan,* (1901). / F. Schmidtke, *Die Einwanderung Israels in Kanaan,* (1933). / M. Noth, *Geschichte Israels* (1950).

serious arguments against this collectivization. The names Abraham and Isaac are used in a collective sense only in poetic texts (Micah 7, 20; Am 7, 9, 16); Jacob, on the other hand, is used more frequently, almost always as a national designation for the people of Israel. The patriarchal narratives, moreover, are unlikely grounds for such a collectivization process. They are full of personal freshness, concrete expression, evidence of historical activity that has taken place only once, and thus cannot either be repeated or material for a type.

6) LEGENDS ABOUT THE PATRIARCHS

It was primarily Gunkel and Gressmann [12] that introduced a new element in the interpretation of the patriarchal histories by examining the narratives not as a conflate composition, but rather dissolving them into their component elements, which, they claim, were circulated among the people independently of of each other. Various elements would thus correspond to homey popular stories with ordinary names for their heroes, for example, Hansel and Gretel. These popular fairy tales would then, in the course of time, have attracted cult legends and tribal narratives. Finally, the stories were localized at particular sites, and a wreath of legend began to form about them, handed down by word of mouth from generation to generation. In this process, historical events might also have made their way into the realm of legend and fairy tale.

The search for the *Sitz im Leben,* the source and origin of the individual narratives, has indeed brought to light some very valuable points of consideration and introduced some important new methodology into our understanding of the peculiarities of historical tradition in Israel, but the hypothesis always involves the danger of a too great subjectivism and, what is more, it takes us too far away from the sober reality of Ancient Near Eastern history, into the realm of the poetic

---

12. H. Gressmann, *Sage und Geschichte in den Patriarchenerzählungen,* ZATW 30 (1910), 1-34. / H. Gunkel, *Genesis* 3 (1910) — prehistory and the patriarchs: *Die Schriften des AT in Auswahl,* I, 1, 2 (1921).

and the fabled. The discoveries of Ancient Near Eastern archaeology always force us, in our consideration of the patriarchal
narratives, to abandon the realm of myth and saga and to take
a firm stand on the ground of actual history, which, although
it is not handed down in our modern critical sense as it stands
in the Bible, is nonetheless entirely credible and true to the
facts. In our presentation of the patriarchal era, we shall proceed on the basis of the Bible. We shall attempt to compare
the Biblical data with the results of excavation, and thus achieve
a more solid foundation for elaborating the contributions that
the patriarchal history has to make to the theology of the Bible.

CHAPTER II

THE PATRIARCH ABRAHAM

(Gn 12 — 25)

LITERATURE

E. Dhorme, *Abraham dans le cadre de l'histoire*, RB 37 (1928), 367-385; 481-511; 40 (1931), 364-374; 503-518. / L. Pirot, *Abraham*, DBS I (1928), 8-28 (Chronologically, surpassed; but the systematic organization still valuable). / F. Ceuppens, *De prophetiis messianicis*, in VT, Rome 1935, 43-61. / L. Woolley, *Abraham, Recent Discoveries and Hebrew Origins*, London 1936. (Described by Garofalo, Bibl 29 [1939], 109.) / A. Skrinjar, *De incolis Terrae promissae Abrahami aequalibus*, VD 17 (1937), 268-279. / R. Maritain, *Histoire d'Abraham ou les primières âges de la conscience morale*, Paris 1947. / J. Simons, *Two notes on the Problem of the Pentapolis (Gn 19, 24-26)*, OldTestSt (1948), 92-117. / J. De Fraine, *Clibanus fumans et lampas ignis (Gn 15-17)*, VD 26 (1948), 254. / For a compact over-all presentation, based on archaeology, cf. R. de Vaux, *Les Patriarches hébreux et les découvertes modernes*, RB 53 (1946), 321-348; 55 (1948), 321-347; 56 (1949), 5-36. Dem gleichen Zweck dient H. H. Rowley, *Recent discovery and the patriarchal age*, BRylL 32 (1949). / Over-all religious evaluation, cf. the special issue of Cahiers Sioniens, "Abraham, Père des Croyants," Paris 1951. Several collaborators: de Vaux — translation and literary analysis; Starcky — Ancient Near Eastern backgrounds; Guillet — significance of Abraham for N. T.; Danielou — Abraham's continuing role in the liturgy. / N. Schneider, *Patriarchennamen in zeitgenössischen Keilschrifturkunden*, Bibl 33 (1952), 516-522.

"THE history of Abraham is a magnificent fugue on the theme first sounded in chapter 12, 1-4a: land — seed — blessing — faith." [1]

> And Yahweh said to Abraham:
> Go from your country and your kindred and your father's house,
>
> to the land that I will show you.
>
> And I will make of you a great nation, and I will bless you, and make your name great,
> (so that you will be a blessing).
>
> I will bless those who bless you;
> and him who curses you I will curse;
> and by you all the families of the earth shall bless themselves.
>
> So Abraham went,
> as Yahweh had told him.

Just as this oracle is flanked on both sides by the name of Yahweh, so the entire life of Abraham plays its role under the protection and the commanding word of God, along a carefully predestined path, and at a stately tempo. At the age of 75, Abraham leaves his home country behind for the land promised to him by God. He wanders up and down this territory for 100 years, until he finally dies at the age of 175. In his 100th year, Isaac, the son of promise, is born to him. As we have already frequently pointed out, these numbers have a mystical and symbolic rather than a chronological value. The number 100 might be called the number of fulfillment; for the 100th year brings the son of promise, and in the course of 100 years, Abraham takes possession of the Promised Land.

---

1. W. Möller, *Bibl. Theologie des AT*, (1934), 163.

The idea that Canaan is the land promised by God, and thus the proper home of the people, is such a predominant concept in the patriarchal narratives that it is impossible to avoid the thought that it was this tradition which served as the psychological impetus for the Exodus from Egypt. For it hardly seems probable that Moses could have succeeded in convincing his contemporaries to attempt the Exodus if he had been able to offer them no other goal than refuge in the Sinai Peninsula. The Exodus becomes understandable only if Moses holds out to the Israelites as the final goal of their trek through the desert the land in which in ancient days their tribal fathers had lived in prosperity under the protection of their god. There is thus considerable probability to the hypothesis that Moses himself made some collection of the patriarchal narratives.[2] The patriarchal narratives current among the people were not collected into a single edition simply out of a typical interest in antiquity, simply to rescue them from oblivion; the entire collection pulses with the spirit of the national and religious enthusiasm that first gave direction and objective to the people in Egypt undertaking their battle for liberation in the sign of their fathers' god. The patriarchal narratives are an essential property of ancient Israel's national faith. Even though the present-day form of the patriarchal history is owing to a later editorial redaction, in which the various ancient elements were worked into a superimposed scheme of unity, this does nothing to alter the fundamental fact that we can follow in every section of the ancient narrative: with Abraham there is a grand and new beginning in the course of the national and salvation history of his people, a new impetus which continued its effect into another new beginning under Moses on Mount Sinai. Both events are intimately bound together by the reve-

---

2. Whereas pure textual criticism, left to its own resources, can promise little understanding for the true age of these narratives, form-historical interpretation shows that the patriarchal stories must date back to the time before the conquest of Canaan. "Israel must have possessed the basic elements of the sagas of Abraham, Isaac, and Jacob already prior to the immigration into Canaan" (Gunkel, *Genesis*).

lation of the god of their fathers, the god who determines the course of human history.

The outline of the Biblical narratives is immediately obvious from the text itself; it corresponds to the larger themes of the history of Abraham.

1) THE LAND OF PROMISE (12, 4b — 14, 24): Abraham wanders through the land of Canaan and erects his altars (12, 4b-8); he is forced by famine to withdraw from the land and make his way into Egypt (12, 9 — 13, 4); finally he divides the land with Lot (13, 5-18) and becomes the savior of his country against the invasion of the kings from the east (14, 1-24).

2) SON AND PEOPLE OF PROMISE (15, 1 — 18, 15): Abraham, on the occasion of a sacrifice, predicts the history of his people (15); Ishmael is born, according to the flesh (16); the seal of circumcision for the new people of God (17); Sarah's laughter at the promise of a son (18, 1-15).

3) THE BLESSING OF ABRAHAM (18, 16 — 21, 34): All mankind enters upon a new principle of distinction, as to whether they are friendly or hostile towards Abraham; those who wish him well will be blessed, those who oppose him will suffer punishment from God. During the destruction of Sodom, only those are saved who join with Abraham (18, 16 — 19, 38); Abimelech experiences the fact that mysterious forces are at work in Abraham (20, 1-18); Ishmael is banished, but still a special blessing is accorded to him because he too is a son of Abraham (21, 1-21); finally the princes of the southern country seek an alliance with Abraham because he is "blessed of God" (21, 22-34).

4) ABRAHAM'S FAITH (22, 1 — 25, 11): The great deeds of God are made possible only by Abraham's complete openness to God's call. The most powerful expression of this faith is the sacrifice of Isaac (22, 1-19); old and well advanced in years, Abraham acquires the field of Machpelah for his burial

(22, 20 — 23, 20), arranges for a bride for Isaac from the tribal relationships (24), and finally excludes all his other children in order to concentrate the blessing and the promise upon Isaac the son of promise, dies, and is buried beside his wife Sarah in the cave of Machpelah (25, 1-11).[3]

A) THE LAND OF PROMISE

(Gn 12, 4b — 14, 24)

Abraham's emigration from his home into Canaan is based upon the call of Yahweh: "Go from your country and your kindred and your father's house to the land that I will show you." The programmatic sentence suggests some problems for consideration: What was the original home country of Abraham? ("Your land!") — How is Abraham to be fitted into the ethnology of the Ancient Near East? ("Your kindred and your father's house!") — What was the cultural and social position of Canaan, when Abraham made his way there? ("To the land that I will show you!") — How is the lifespan of Abraham to be fitted into the historical background of Ancient Near Eastern history?

1) ABRAHAM'S ORIGINAL HOME: In three passages, Genesis refers to the city of Ur in Mesopotamia as the home country of Abraham's family. Genesis 11, 28: "Haran died before his father Terah in the land of his birth, in Ur of the Chaldeans (Ur Kasdim)"; Genesis 11, 31: "Terah took Abram his son and Lot the son of Haran, his grandson, and Sarai his daughter-in-law, his son Abram's wife, and they went forth together from Ur of the Chaldeans to go into the land of Canaan"; Genesis

---

3. The division represented here proceeds quite naturally from the text itself. Is there some form of number symbolism at work here? Since the object of the text is the land itself, the four cardinal directions, and the number four itself presents a logical system of arrangement. The above division of the Abraham story into four main sections, with four sub-divisions each, was first suggested by Bibl. Theol. des At: *Die Patriarchenerzählingen*, 129-165.

15, 7: "And Yahweh spoke to Abraham: 'I am Yahweh who brought you from Ur of the Chaldeans, to give you this land to possess.'"[4]

Even though these texts all clearly point to Ur as the point of departure for Abraham's emigration, there are some difficulties in the further identification of "Ur of the Chaldeans." The name Kaldu as a designation of southern Babylonia first appears in the eleventh century; the city itself could have carried the qualifying note "of the Chaldeans" only after the foundation of the new Babylonian empire in the seventh century. One might explain this difficulty by assuming that the name Chaldean is a later literary addition (marginal gloss) designed to provide a more precise identification for the city in whose territory the ancestors of Israel had lived long before the time of the Chaldean empire. Another possible conclusion is that the story of Abraham's sojourn in Ur of the Chaldeans is a tradition which developed among the Jews only during the time of the Babylonian Exile, an era, that is, in which relations between Ur of the Chaldeans and Haran in Upper Mesopotamia were particularly strong.[5] In this connection it is important to note that it is only in the text of Nehemiah, writing after the Exile, that we encounter once again this reference to Abraham's departure from "Ur of the Chaldeans" (Neh 9, 7), whereas the more ancient tradition in Joshua 24, 2, locates the patriarchs Terah, Abraham, and Nahor simply "across the river." Moreover, several passages in Genesis actually list the territory about Haran as the true home of Abraham and his family. According to Genesis 11, 32, God's command to leave his native country reaches Abraham when he is already in Haran. The man who is sent by Abraham to the land of his kindred, the land from which he himself emigrated, to select a wife for his son, goes to Haran (Gn 24, 4, 5, 7). Are these perhaps two contra-

---

4. The LXX translates Ur as *chôra*, "land," since for the Greek reader the name Ur no longer had any meaning.

5. Nabonidus (555-539) is from Haran. He has both the moon temple at Ur and the one at Haran restored. His father and his mother are priest and priestess of Sin in Haran, while his daughter is priestess of Sin in Ur. Cf. S. Smith, *Babylonian Historical Texts*, (1924), 36.

dictory traditions, one referring to Ur of the Chaldeans and the other two to Haran?

The difficulties are really only apparent difficulties. They can be explained by the rhythm of Ancient Near Eastern history. The most ancient cult centers of Mesopotamia are the Sumerian city states, among which the city of Ur, with what is even today the best preserved temple tower, surely played a most significant political and religious role. In the era of Akkadia, the Sumerian city states were incorporated into the Semitic world empire under Sargon. After the collapse of the Akkadian-Semitic central power there follows an era of Sumerian restoration, which historians refer to as Ur-III (2050 — 1950). The strong political power of the new Sumerian rulers surely had a disquieting effect upon the nomadic Beduin tribes that settled along the edges of the desert. When, in 1950 B.C., the Sumerian power began to collapse under the inroads of the western Semites, who created new centers of power in Larsa and Isin, the Beduin and semi-Beduin tribes in the surrounding territory were also stirred into action. They made their way up the Euphrates and established themselves along the territories of the upper river, from where Abraham and Lot made their way further into Canaan, and to which, in return, Abraham sent the man to select a wife for his son Isaac, and where, finally, Jacob lived for 20 years.

A whole series of passages refers to this territory collectively as Paddan Aram (the fields of Aram) or Aram Naharaim (Aram of the rivers) (Gn 24, 10).[6] The territory so designated is generally understood to be the country between the upper courses of the Euphrates and Tigris and the enclosed alluvial valleys of the Balih, Habur, and their tributaries.[7]

The primary memorial to the patriarchal era is intimately

---

6. Gn 25, 20; 28, 2, 5, 6, 7; — 31, 18; 33, 18; 35, 9, 26; 46, 15 — *Paddana* is the Aramaic word for "Plain, Fields." The corresponding Hebrew translation is to be found in Hoshea 12, 13: *sedê 'Aram,* perhaps best translated as "land, landscape of Aram."

7. *Naharaim* is a dual in form, but in meaning it is a geographical plural. *Nahrima,* in the Amarna Letters, and *Nhrn,* on the Thutmose Stele, refer to the Kingdom of the Mitanni in Upper Mesopotamia.

bound up with the city of Haran, whose name is preserved even today in the city of Eski-Harran on the upper Balih. The beginnings of this settlement go back into the earliest historical times. In the era of the Cappadocian tablets (nineteenth century) and the Mari texts (sixteenth century) Haran was an important commercial trade center between the Mesopotamian plains and the mountain peoples of the north and the west.

The Bible makes one reference to the city of Nahor (Gn 24, 10), a name borne by the grandfather and brother of Abraham. The Cappadocian tablets and an ancient Babylonian text reproduce this same name as an ancient city. In the royal archives of Mari, Na-hu-ur plays an important role. In the fourteenth century it is an administrative center in Upper Mesopotamia. After lying empty for some centuries, it once again appears in the seventh century under the name Til-Nahiri. It belongs to the district of Haran and must be located not far from that city. Nahor is also attested in the Assyrio-Babylonian lists as the name of a person. This parallel between geographical and personal names occurs once again in the case of Sarug, the great-grandfather of Abraham and also the name of a city half-way between the Euphrates and Haran; it is also true for Terah, the father of Abraham and the name of a city Til-ša-Turahri or Til-Turahi on the Balih. The excavations thus seem to confirm the Biblical tradition. According to the Bible, Abraham's tribal kindred established itself in Upper Mesopotamia, after emigrating from Ur; the Ancient Near Eastern texts attest to the same names as city names in a rather circumscribed geographical territory. Is this simply a chance equivalence in name or is there some further, perhaps causal, connection between the city names and the names of the tribal patriarchs? No matter how conservative our judgment, we can no longer seriously question the fact that Abraham's original home was in Upper Mesopotamia.

In Genesis 29, 1, Jacob does indeed return to Laban in the land of "the sons of the east," an expression which generally refers to Transjordania; but this does not mean that, on the basis of this passage, the original home of Abraham is to be located in the territories of Transjordania, on this side of the

Euphrates. From many geographical texts we are familiar with the fact that the word "east" (*qadmu*) is a regular designation for the upper right-hand territory of the Tigris, in order to distinguish between "the sons of the south" (*binu-yamina*) and "the sons of the north" (*binu-sim'al*).[8]

Abraham's emigration thus proceeds, under the leadership of his father, from Ur of the Chaldeans; the tribal groups next established themselves in Upper Mesopotamia, in the territory of the city Haran; Abraham then parted from his tribal kindred, out of religious motivations, and, together with his cousin Lot, made his way into Canaan.

Archaeological discoveries make it clear that the Canaan into which Abraham immigrated, in the era between 1900 — 1700 B.C., was in the throes of ethnic transformation. Northern tribal groups were pushing their way into Syria and Palestine, thereby lending new energies to the ancient city cultures; at the same time, the Beduin and semi-Beduin tribes were pushing into the territory from the edges of the desert. It is very probable that Abraham's emigration is to be fitted into the framework of these larger ethnic shifts. This is simply further proof of the fact that revelation always takes place within a definite historical area. Abraham's migration could, on the one hand, be explained in terms of purely human motivation; and yet it is clearly prompted by God's call.[9]

2) CAMPAIGNS OF THE KINGS OF THE EAST (Gn 14): In keeping with our modern ideas, we are perhaps very much tempted to portray the life of the patriarchs within the smaller framework of a family and to evaluate their fate as a small and personal thing. But the true extent of the life and circumstances of these patriarchs comes to the fore if we consider, for example, the campaigns launched by the kings of the east. Abra-

---

8. J. Lewy, *Studies in the Historic Geography of the Ancient Near East*, Or 21 (1952), 1-12.
9. Literature on Abraham's home: De Vaux, *Les patriarches hébreux et les découvertes modernes*, RB 55 (1948): *La migration d'Abraham*, 321-326.

ham here makes an unexpected appearance as a military hero and leader of a brave company of men, who do not hesitate, in a bold military stratagem, to attack a superior force.

This story has been taken by some as a post-Exilic literary invention, representing a later attempt to honor the patriarch of the people of Israel by attributing to him a glorious victory over the united kings of the east, an addition to the Bible phrased in a very archaic-sounding language, using words which are little used elsewhere in the Bible. Others have regarded it as actually a very ancient historical document which was taken over into the Biblical account and dates from an era which was very close to the events described, since the account refers to political situations which, in the course of Ancient Near Eastern history, played only a very small interlude.

At all events, this famous 14th chapter of Genesis recounts that for 12 years the cities along the Dead Sea (Sodom, Gomorrah, Adama, Zeboim, and Zoar) were subject to the Elamite king Kedor-laomer; but in the 13th year they rebelled against the foreign rule, and in the 14th year, the king of Elam, supported by Amraphel of Shinar, Ariok of Ellasar, and Tide'al of "Goim," organized a military campaign against the rebellious kings of the western countries. The troops forced their way through Transjordania, defeated the Amorite princes and the Horites, made their way as far as Cadesh, fought with the Amalekites in Negeb, overcame the Amorites at Hazazon-Thamar, and finally, concentrated their forces against the five cities along the Dead Sea. The five kings put up a stout resistance, but were eventually beaten and forced to flee. The victors carried off considerable plunder and captives. Among the captives was Lot, Abraham's nephew. When Abraham received news of this military disaster, he assembled the men under his command, appealed for assistance to the Amorites of Hebron who were friendly to him, and, with this rather small company, set out after the victors, overtaking them at Dan during the night, where he launched a sudden attack, freed Lot and his family, and pursued the fleeing enemy as far as the territory of Damascus. Upon his return he was met by Melchizedek, king of Salem, who approached him with bread and wine and blessed

Abraham in the name of the all-high God (Gn 14, 1-24).

This military account has been taken as the basis for fitting Abraham's life into the chronological pattern of Ancient Near Eastern history, simply by equivalating King Amraphel of Shinar with Hammurabi of Babel, thereby making Abraham a contemporary of the great Babylonian king. This identification, however, can no longer be defended today.[10]

The name Amraphel is composed of two elements: *Amra-phel*. The final syllable *phel* is equivalent to a form which is of frequent occurrence in Akkadian, the element *pi-ili* or *pi-El*, that is, "mouth or word of God." Thus, in the first Babylonian dynasty there is mention of a certain *I-tur-pi-ili; I-ba-al-pi-il* is a king of Eshnunna, *A-mu-ut-pi-il* is king of Qatna. The first element in the word *Amra-*, derived from the Akkadian, would mean "to see." The name *Amur-pi-el* would thus mean: "I have seen (or: see!) the mouth of God," that is, "I have seen the fulfillment of God's promise." But such an interpretation is quite without parallel. We turn, accordingly, with far greater probability, to the western Semitic language, in which, as in Hebrew too, the word *Amar* means "to speak"; *Amraphel* would then mean "the mouth of God has spoken."

Amraphel is called king of *Shinear*. Actually, in a later text in Daniel 1, 2, the Bible used the word *Shinear* as a reference to Babylonia. This would mean that *Shinear* is simply a general reference to Mesopotamia (Gn 10, 10; 11, 2; Josh 7, 21; Is 11, 11; Zech 5, 11). These texts would all tend to substantiate the Hammurabi thesis. The cuneiform documents, however, also speak of a country called *Sha-an-ha-ar*, which is quite distinct from Babylonia. The Egyptian texts also speak of a land of *Sngr*, which Tutmose III distinguishes from *Bbr* (Babylon). Finally, some Assyrian documents refer to a land called *Sin-gar* or *Sin-ga-ra*. In this last case the locale is closely determined. It is a territory in the district of Gebel Singar, west of Mossul. A Hittite text, finally, equivalates *Sha-an-ha-ra* with the Mitanni state of Hanigalbat. Whatever the case may be, all of these terms direct our attention to the territory of Upper Mesopotamia, between the Euphrates and the Tigris, and not into Babylonia proper. This identification seems to be confirmed by the names of the other kings and geographical sites.

The identification of King Ariok of Ellasar with Rim-Sin of Larsa rests on rather shaky foundations. This name, too, suggests Upper Mesopotamia rather than Babylonia. A son of Zimrilim of Mari is called *Ar-ri-wu-uk;* a tablet from Kirkuk refers to a king *A-ri-u-uk-ki*. The name is Hurrite. His city Ellasar might well be a city named in the Mari letters and in a Hittite text, Ilanzura, located between Carchemish and Haran.[11]

10. De Vaux, *op. cit.*, 331ff. / J. J. Stamm, *Die akkadische Namengebung*, (1939), 147ff.

The name of Tide'al, King of Goim, derives from the original form *Tudhalia*. This is the name of several Hittite kings. The oldest whose name we know, Tudhalias I, was approximately contemporary with Hammurabi. The title, "king of Goim," that is, "king of the peoples," is a vague reference to a distant people whose name is no longer current.

The most striking feature of the narrative is the fact that this campaign is supposed to have taken place under the leadership of Elam. Is this historically possible? The name of the king, *Chedor-la'omer*, is a genuine Elamite name. *Lagamar* or *Lagamal* is a goddess whose existence is attested by frequent texts and proper names. *Kudur* or *Kutir* ("servant") is also an element which occurs frequently in the formation of proper names. The name *Chedor-la'omer* is, however, attested by no text yet discovered. Nor does it appear on the Elamitic royal lists. This is no definite proof against the genuinity of the Biblical tradition, however, since the royal lists are not preserved in any complete form.[12]

The final result of our investigation is as follows:

a. None of the four kings named in Genesis 14 can be positively identified with any ruler known to us from the history of the Ancient Near East. This does not mean that the names are inventions. The campaign described certainly lies within the realm of historical possibility. In terms of archaeology, it is a well-known fact that, at the end of Middle Bronze Age I (2000 —1600), Transjordania experienced a powerful decline in settlement and city culture. The campaign, however, does presuppose a settled state of Transjordania. This would be one chronological point of departure for the dating of Abraham.[13]

b. Elam clearly has the lead in this war. This is also quite within the realm of historical possibility. According to the Mari texts, at the time of Hammurabi, Elam dispatched a strong military contingent to Subártu, Upper Mesopotamia. Somewhat later an Elamite, Kudur-Mabug, made himself master of Babylonia and established his two sons as kings of Larsa. He assumes the title "father of Amurru," that is, "father of the western lands." It was a treaty of Elam with the western Semites (Amurru) that led to the collapse of the 3rd dynasty of Ur (around 1950 B.C.). At a time in which the power of Amurru in Babylon was just beginning to consolidate (1st dynasty of Babel — 1930 B.C. — Hammurabi), and, at the same time, the Hurrites were making more and more insistent inroads from the south, historical probability is strongly in favor of a

---

11. M. Noth, *Arioch-Arriwuk*, VT 1 (1951), 91.

---

12. Albright's proposal (BASOR 88, Dec. 1942, 33ff) that *Kedor-la'omer* is to be identified with the Elamite King Kudur-Nahhunte, in the 17th century, has encountered too strong an opposition for us to discuss it seriously here. Cf. RB 55 (1948), 324.

13. N. Glueck, *The other side of the Jordan* (1940), 114.

campaign under the leadership of an Elamite king, fighting as an ally of Amraphel of the Amurru and Ariok of the Hurrites. *Abraham's migration must, accordingly, be fitted into the great ethnic upheavals of the Amurri and Hurrites between the years 1900 and 1700 B.C., and, preferably, towards the beginning of these migrations. Abraham might thus, with greatest probability, have settled at Hebron sometime around 1850 B.C., and it was from this base that he launched his attack against the kings from the east.*

c. If, finally, we pursue the route followed by this campaign, the names in Genesis 14, 5-7 all point to the "Royal Road," that is, the caravan route which travels diagonally through Transjordania, forming the essential link for commerce between Egypt and Mesopotamia. Seen in its broader outlines, the entire campaign was an attempt to secure this caravan route. From this larger framework of the whole undertaking, the Bible rivets our attention only on those elements that are significant for the history of the patriarchs. The account focuses more on the five cities along the Dead Sea because Lot and his family had settled there and thus had been drawn into the fate of this war. When Abraham summons his warriors and pursues the victors, this does not mean at all that he attempted to face the united powers of the kings from the east, but only that he fell upon the rear guard with its prisoners and liberated his kinsmen.

This chapter of Genesis, so solitary in its place in the Bible, and composed in such an archaic style and language, thus recounts a military campaign that is quite within the realm of historical possibility. In fact, the life of the great patriarch gains considerably in color and immediacy. His life is not a saga; it is an integral part of the Ancient Near Eastern history, a story, which, however, can only be approximately reconstructed with the means at our disposal today.

3) THE "SACRIFICE" OF MELCHIZEDEK (*Hebrew*: MALKISEDEK — KING OF JUSTICE): The campaign of the kings from the east ended with the encounter between Abraham and Melchizedek, Genesis 14, 17: "After his return from the defeat of Chedorlaomer and the kings who were with him, the king of Sodom went out to meet him at the valley of Shaveh (that is, the valley of the kings). And Melchizedek, King of Salem, brought out bread and wine; he was priest of God Most High ('El 'elyôn). And he blessed him and said, "Blessed be Abraham by God Most High, maker of heaven and earth...."

Abraham gives Melchizedek one tenth of all he has captured. He shows himself magnanimous towards the other kings, by returning everything that is theirs and claiming only what his men have used for provisions. Even his allies from Hebron are to have their share.

Where did this singular encounter take place? A marginal gloss explains the "Valley of Shaveh" as the "Royal Valley" in the neighborhood of Jerusalem (2 S 18, 18). The word "Shaveh" occurs only in this chapter 14, in verse 5 and verse 17. On the basis of Aramaic, Syrian, and Arabic parallels,[14] it can only mean "plateau," "great valley," and is, accordingly, insufficient evidence to determine the precise geographical location. Since the encounter is generally located in the neighborhood of Jerusalem, the royal city of Melchizedek, "Salem," is generally identified with Jerusalem.

Did Melchizedek sacrifice bread and wine? From the wording of the Biblical text this conclusion cannot be univocally drawn. What is written is simply that he "brought out bread and wine," apparently as an offering to the returning warriors. What is involved is thus primarily a meal. But since an ancient meal is unthinkable without some libation and prayer to the gods, it is perfectly proper to suppose that Melchizedek, who was also "priest of the Most High God," opened this meal with some sacrificial act which also included a blessing upon Abraham. There is no need to suppose that Melchizedek represents a religious orientation that is in any way at variance with the society of his time by calling upon the All-high God El. As we have already seen in the section that deals with the religion of Canaan, El was the proper name of the supreme god of the Canaanite pantheon. In this great hour of deliverance the priest-king calls upon not one of the subordinate gods, but rather the creator of heaven and earth himself, and thus testifies to the fact that faith in the one, Most High God, was still a living force in the Canaanite pantheon.

The priestly figure of King Melchizedek has given full rein to theological speculation. In Psalm 109/110, 4 the Messiah king is called "a priest forever according to the order of Melchizedek," who was both king and priest of the All-high God.

The speculation expressed in the Epistle to the Hebrews (7, 1ff)

14. RB 55 (1948), 329.

develops the thought that Melchizedek makes a very sudden appearance in the Bible, without any mention of genealogy: "For this Melchizedek, King of Salem, priest of the Most High God, met Abraham returning from the slaughter of the kings and blessed him .... He is without father or genealogy, and has neither beginnings of days nor end of life, but resembling the Son of God he continues a priest forever." In the Amarna letters the king *Puti-hepa* of Jerusalem also declines a genealogy, although in a quite different sense: "Behold, this land of Urusalim neither my father nor my mother gave to me, but rather the powerful hand of the king." *Puti-hepa* is king not by virtue of hereditary power, but owing to his installation by the pharaoh of Egypt.[15]

The narrative of the encounter between Abraham and the priest-king Melchizedek belongs among the most ancient traditions; at no time of Israelite history after the conquest of Canaan could such a legend have been created, a story in which Abraham, the tribal father of Israel and the "friend of God" (Is 41, 8), could have possibly received the blessing of a Canaanite, and also honored him as a priest by offering him a tithe. The antiquity of this military narrative is further corroborated by the marginal glosses: At the time of its recording, the ancient place names were no longer easily recognized: 14, 2: "That is Zoar"; 14: 3: "That is the Salt Sea"; 14, 7: "That is Cadesh"; 14, 17: "That is the King's Valley."

The military account of chapter 14 locates the life of Abraham squarely within the struggles and conquests of the Ancient Near East. His figure takes on force and color. Our original question, as to whether we are perhaps dealing with a later, post-Exilic invention instead of a genuine ancient historical tradition, must now be answered, on the basis of the facts adduced, in favor of historicity. This historicity is further corroborated by the fact that Abraham's life has now been solidly fitted into the framework of the Canaanite world in which he lived.[16]

4) THE PATRIARCHS IN THE CANAANITE WORLD AROUND THEM: When we assign Abraham's life to approximately the period around 1850, this dating locates us within the Middle Bronze Age (2000 − 1600 B.C., according to Albright). This is the era in which the western Semites were gaining control over Syria and Palestine, introducing a new golden age in the culture of these countries.[17] Trade relations with the north and south de-

---

15. Text in Knudtzon, *El-Amarna-Briefe* I, Nr. 287. / Galling, TGJ (1950), 24.
16. H. H. Rowley sees this narrative simply as an etiological saga from the time of David's accession to power. Cf. Ps 109/110. Fs. Bertholet 1950, 461-72.

manded a cultural as well as a commercial exchange between the countries of the Ancient Near East. As we know from the Cappadocian tablets (1850 — 1750), the people were able to move freely and without restraint from one country to another. In the whole territory of the Fertile Crescent there was no insurmountable linguistic barrier, since western Semitic was universally understood and Akkadian was the lingua franca, the language of diplomacy and commerce. There were particularly close political and cultural ties between Palestine and Egypt. Egyptian was understood in practically all the larger Palestinian cities, just as, conversely, western Semitic was spoken in large sections of the Nile Delta.

The Indo-Arian wave, with its mounted warriors and war chariots, had, in the Middle Bronze Age, not yet made its way into Palestine. In the patriarchal era there was not yet that clear distinction between sedentary and nomadic ways of life. In the winter, the population withdrew into the strongly fortified cities, while in summer, and particularly at the harvest time, the population would live outdoors, and outside the city, in simple huts and tents. The Bible portrays the patriarchs as semi-nomadic, sometimes following the annual migrations of their flocks from one pasture to another, and at other times engaged in the cultivation or harvest of their crops, as is illustrated in the dream of Joseph. They did indeed migrate with their flocks throughout the hilly country of Central Palestine as far south as the Negeb.[18] Excavations have shown that

---

17. Nelson Glueck, *Explorations in Eastern Palestine IV.* — New Haven (1951) 2 vols. Despite the war and the confusion following the war, in the years 1939/40 and 1942/47, he searched in Transjordania, in more than a thousand sites, for surface finds, thereby arriving at the conclusion that the flourishing Early Bronze Age culture (3200-2100 BC) in the Jordan trench and in Transjordania begins to die out at the end of this era, but that at the beginning of the Middle Bronze Age (2000-1600 BC) takes on a new burst of energy, perhaps as a result of cultural and ethnic immigrations from Syria. This new wave may well have carried Abraham into the country. ThL Z 77 (1952), 81.

---

18. N. Glueck, *The Age of Abraham in the Negeb,* Bibl Arch 18 (1955),

this territory contains hardly a single Bronze Age city settlement, and was thus a free and unsettled pastureland. Only during the Iron Age are there firm Israelite city settlements.

In the eighteenth century, the principal beast of burden was
the donkey. In the Cappadocian tablets and in the Mari correspondence we hear of donkey caravans, but never of camel
caravans. The identification of the patriarchs with the present-day
Beduin sheiks is, as a result, not entirely correct. The present-
day Beduins of Transjordania made their way into their territories only during the seventeenth century A.D. Their manner of
life is inseparably bound up with the camel. The tenacity of
this beast of burden allows them to freely cross the desert territories while the patriarchs, as cattle-herders, were never able
to penetrate very deeply into the desert, and, in their migrations
from Ur in Chaldea through Haran and into Canaan, always
moved in the steppe country, a territory which afforded sufficient
pasturage during the rainy season and a conveniently spaced
system of wells and natural springs. The present-day Beduin,
as a camel-breeder, is naturally a "man of the desert," to the
point that even today, in the black tents of their nomadic settlement, there is lively argument as to whether Allah created the
camel in order to nourish, clothe, and transport the Beduin
from one place to another, or whether he created the Beduin
in order to look after the camel and provide satisfactory pasturage, so intimate is the community of life between the two.
The life of the patriarchs takes on a quite different tone. It is
true that camels are mentioned in the history of the patriarchs:
the Pharaoh presents Abraham with camels (Gn 12, 16); Jacob
too has camels in his herd (Gn 30, 43); he presents his brother
Esau with 30 milch camels (Gn 32, 16); Abraham's servant
journeys into Mesopotamia with 10 camels (24, 10); Rachel sits
down on a camel saddle when her angered father comes to
search their camp for the stolen teraphim (Gn 31, 34). These
texts present something of a riddle. The proper domestication of
the camel is known only from a much later period, according

2-9. In Middle Bronze I the southern country was well settled. Around
1900 BC there is a break in the culture.

to Albright, not before the twelfth century.[19] The difficulty appears to be solved by assuming that, whereas the camel had been known both in Egypt and in Mesopotamia in their earlier history, it had then passed completely out of use, only to be rediscovered around the twelfth century. Since our sources are concerned only with the settled country, we cannot draw any conclusions as to what had happened meantime in the deserts of Arabia. The late date of the domestication of the camel is, accordingly, no argument against the genuinity of the patriarchal narratives.[20]

The clearest picture of the patriarchal era is afforded by the story of Beni-Hassan in Egypt, a narrative which is dated around the year 1892 B.C. A small Semitic Beduin tribe crosses the Egyptian frontier under the leadership of a tribal chief who bears the Semitic name *Abša* (*Abišai*) and is called "Prince of the foreign country" (*hk̓ .w h̓s.wt*, Hyksos). The family numbers 37 persons, men, women, and children. They come from Šutu in Transjordania. The Egyptian who is going out to meet them bears an inscription on which are written these words: "Year six under the majesty of King Sesostris II (1897 — 1879). List of the Beduins who are bringing cosmetics to the prince Hnumhotep. A total of 37 Beduins from the wilderness."

The clothing is distinctive, in most cases a half-length outer garment, made of a square piece of cloth, wrapped under one shoulder and above the other, and reaching to the knees. Some of the men are wearing only a loincloth. The dress of the women is distinguished from that of the men only by its greater length and more vivid colors. The men are wearing sandals, while the women are wearing dark brown shoes that come up over the ankles. The prince is bowing before the Egyptian official,

---

19. The question of the domestication of the camel is in a state of considerable flux today. Cf. De Vaux, RB 56 (1949), 5ff. / W. F. Albright, *The Archaeology of Palestine*, (1951), 206. — *From Stone Age to Christianity* (1949) 163ff. / R. Walz, *Zum Problem der Domestikation der altweltlichen Kameliden*, ZDMG 101 (1951), 29-51.
20. B. I. S. Isserlin, *On some possible early occurrences of the camel in Palestine*, PEQ 82 (1950), 50-53. / A. Pohl, *Das Kamel in Mesopotamien*, Or 19 (1950), 251; 21 (1952), 373.

who is not represented on the picture, and greeting him with
his right hand; with his left hand he is leading a tame ibex by
a rope. Between the horns there is a crooked staff, from whose
bark individual strips have been peeled off. This crook is such
a characteristic mark of the Beduin that the Egyptians, in their
hieroglyphic inscriptions, use it generically as the symbol for
"desert-dwellers." The weapons carried by the men are bows,
spears, and crooks which serve as clubs. There is also a musician
with an eight-stringed lyre.[21]

The episode described in Genesis 12, 9ff., in which Abraham
is forced by famine to make his way into Egypt, where, near
the Egyptian frontier, his wife Sara is taken into the harem
of the Pharaoh, could not be better illustrated than by this
painting in the tomb of Beni-hassan.

B) THE SON OF PROMISE

(Gn 15, 1 — 18, 15)

Together with the promise of the land, there is a second
central theme to the life of the patriarch Abraham: the promise
of a son who is destined to become a mighty people. Abraham
took possession of the land symbolically by erecting altars at
Shechem and Bethel and following his flocks from one district
to another, finally settling at Hebron where he acquired friends
and allies, with the result that he was in a position to take a
decisive part in the political struggle for power. In fact the
victorious outcome of his raid against the eastern kings could
well have been interpreted as the seal of God's promise made
to him. The fact that his flocks multiplied so rapidly that he
was forced to divide the pasture land with his cousin Lot was
also a sign of God's blessing. Abraham was actually well on
his way towards taking possession of the land of Canaan. Even
though the possession of the land was more or less attributable

---

21. Illustration and explanation in Gressmann, AOB (1927), Nr. 51 —
    Westminster Historical Atlas to the Bible: *The World of the Patriarchs*
    (1953), 23ff.

to the human sagacity of Abraham — such successful entries into the cultivated territory by wilderness tribes are a matter of frequent occurrence in the course of Ancient Near Eastern history — with respect to the promise of a son he was completely dependent upon the divine promise. This was a situation which could only be met by a test of faith. It is precisely by his faith in the son to be born that Abraham grows to the heroic stature of father of all the faithful. We thus enter into the mystical shadow of Abraham's encounter with God, an encounter which was to bind his life and the life of his people to come entirely with their God. It is not always a straight line of ascent and unqualified acquiescence to the divine will. Abraham does in fact strike a covenant with God (Gn 15) and receives the divine guarantee of posterity; but it is human and rational motivation that leads Abraham to choose a quicker and easier path: he takes a concubine (ch 16); God puts him back upon the right road by refusing to recognize the concubine's son as the bearer of the promised heritage. It is Sarah's son whom God promises once again and destines as the proper heir, at which Sarah can no longer contain her laughter (ch 18, 1-15). The wise plans of God seem ridiculous and unbelievable to the "reason" of mankind.

It is precisely this chapter from patriarchal life, in which the juridic questions of inheritance, marriage law, treaty alliances, etc., make their appearance, that demands a fuller treatment of the customs and practices of Ancient Near Eastern law, insofar as we understand it today on the basis of excavation.

THE PATRIARCHS AND THE LAW OF THE ANCIENT NEAR EAST

The patriarchs were semi-nomads and their legal customs were certainly dictated by the "nomadic law of the steppe," a system which, for lack of written documents, we are unfamiliar with. But since, as they followed their flocks, they came into regular contact with the sedentary populations, we are in a position to compare what we have discovered in the way of Ancient Near Eastern legislation with the details afforded by the patriarchal narratives. Seen against this background, the life of the patriarchs takes on new depth and significance, while their historical reality is considerably strengthened.

The historian of law assumes the existence of a fundamental system of law for the Ancient Near East, a system which spread to the north and to the west with the rise and expansion of the Babylonian culture. In the individual nations to whom it made its way it did, however, take on a very particular stamp, and it was constantly transformed and expanded by new immigrants and conquerors.

The discovery of the Code of Hammurabi [22] at the French excavations in Susa in the year 1902 greatly promoted our understanding of Biblical legal customs. At first it was presumed that the code furnished confirmation for the marriage practices current in the patriarchal narratives, particularly the custom of the concubine or second wife. Some scholars went so far as to claim that the lives of the patriarchs were directly under the influence of the legislation of Hammurabi. Our better knowledge of the Ancient Near East would prompt greater caution today. Just as Amraphel cannot simply be identified with Hammurabi, so neither can the lives of the patriarchs be forced into the narrower framework of the laws of Hammurabi. The differences are simply too great.

The Code of Hammurabi was legislated for a highly developed society, for the centralized kingdom of Babylonia with its many officials, with its various classes of society, its finely articulated commercial system and its very developed and extensive agriculture and irrigation. Such a society did indeed require a quite different law than did the shepherd tribe of Abraham and Jacob, who simply followed their flocks through the steppes of Mesopotamia and the hills of Palestine.

These interior difficulties are further aggravated by the problem of dating. Hammurabi promulgated his code only towards the end of his reign, approximately 1700 B.C., that is to say, later than the life of Abraham. The similarities between the law under Abraham and the Code of Hammurabi only prove the fact that Hammurabi did not create a new law, but simply reedited and reformed the already existing law of the Ancient Near East.

The aura surrounding the Code of Hammurabi has faded considerably now that we have discovered other sources of ancient legislation, such as the Code of Lipit-Istar, who was king in Larsa a century and a half before the time of Hammurabi, as well as the Code of Bilalama, King of Eshnuna, 40 years before Hammurabi.

The Assyrian law is, by and large, not so well known as the Babylonian. From the Cappadocian trade colony in the nineteenth century we are familiar with some legal provisions,[23] but what might more proper-

---

22. The discovery of the Hammurabi Stele is described in V. Scheil, *Mémoires de la Délégation en Perse*, IV (1902). / More recent studies and translations: W. Eilers, *Die Gesetzesstele Chammurabis* (Der Alte Orient XXXI, 3), 1932. / P. Cruveilheir, *Introduction au Code d'Hammurabi* (1939) — *Commentaire de Code d'Hammurabi* (1938).

ly be termed the Assyrian "lawbook" dates only from the time of Tiglath-
pilesar I, in the twelfth century. And yet it is precisely the Assyrian
law, particularly in the case of the levirate marriage, which exhibits
such a striking coincidence with the patriarchal usage, much more
markedly than do the Babylonian legal texts. What is the explanation
for this?

If we now examine the Nuzi texts, which were discovered in the
excavations at Jorgan-Tepe east of the Tigris, 1925 — 1931, we have
finally entered into the framework which properly illustrates the patriarchal
legal system. The Nuzi texts are not law documents in the proper sense
of the word; what they are is the archives of a merchant family with all
the colorful details of his business practice: commercial treaties, the
ordering of private family affairs, marriage, inheritance, and rent con-
tracts. They date from the time around 1500 B.C. and are written in a
barbaric form of Akkadian, since the population of Nuzi was, for the
most part, non-Semitic. Apparently they were Hurrites, that is, the same
ethnic block which, since the 2nd millennium, had been making their
way more and more successfully into Upper Mesopotamia, into the very
territory that the patriarchs regarded as their point of ancestral origin.
We are thus faced with the somewhat surprising fact that precisely
these texts, so removed in terms of geography and date of origin, have
cast such great light upon the patriarchal narratives.[24]

To complete the picture, it is necessary to briefly outline the Canaanite law as well, a system, which, despite the considerable evidence
excavated at Ras-Shamra, we know too little.

1) INHERITANCE LAW: In Genesis 15, 2, Abraham complains:
"O Lord God, what will you give me, for I continue childless,
and the heir of my house is Eliezer of Damascus." [25] Yahweh
answers: "This man shall not be your heir; your own son shall
be your heir." Thereupon he led him outside and showed him
the stars of the sky: "So numerous shall your descendants be."

The question has been raised as to why someone from the

---

23. Assyrian Law edited by G. R. Driver and J. C. Miles, *The Assyrian
    Laws* (1935), 376-379. / ANET (1950), 159-222.

---

24. For a selection of the Nuzi-Text: ANET: *Nuzi Akkadian, bearbeitet
    von Theophil* J. Meek, 3 adoption texts, 219-220. / F. R. Kraus, *Zum
    altbabylonischen Erbrecht.* Ar Or 17, 1, 406-412.
25. Has nothing to do with the city of Damascus. Cf. C. H. Gordon,
    "The Meaning of Damascus (Gn 15, 2) in Aramaic," Or 21 (1950),
    496. It is a common name, meaning "major-domo."

immediate kingship should not have been chosen for heir in the case of Abraham's dying without issue, perhaps his nephew Lot. The conclusion was reached, much too rapidly, that the tradition of Abraham was unfamiliar with the history of Lot. The question becomes considerably clearer if we think of adoption. Adoption is not provided for in the Mosaic Law, but it was customary in patriarchal times. Thus, Sarah, Liah, and Rachel all adopted the children of their slaves, and Jacob adopted his two grandsons (Gn 48, 5, 12, 16). In the Nuzi texts, adoption is a very frequent occurrence. A certain Tupkiya adopts his slave Pai-Tesup and leaves him all his property. Through this practice of adoption, childless couples hoped to secure a peaceful old age, an honorable burial, and the survival of their family name. If a natural son is then born, the adoptive heritage is null and void. There is an echo of these provisions in the patriarchal account: "Not the slave Eliezar born in your house shall be your heir; your own son shall be your heir" (Gn 15, 4).

This Ancient Near Eastern practice, is, however, in the case of Abraham, raised to a new theological importance, since this narrative ends with the theological commentary: "And Abraham believed the Lord; and he reckoned it to him as righteousness" (Gn 15, 6). The new creation that is here to come to pass will arise not from the power of blood, but from the unqualified submission of faith. It is only from this absolute acquiescence to the word of God, here spoken to alleviate an unfruitful human situation, that Abraham achieves that interior formation which alone can survive the demands of God: righteousness. This righteousness is far removed from a purely external or formal attention to the law; it is achieved, not in a context of law, but rather in the promise. Biblical "righteousness" must be understood and fulfilled from the act of faith.

2) ABRAHAM "CUTS THE COVENANT": The word of God's promise is also supposed to be fulfilled in a corresponding external ritual. Abraham is supposed to take a three-year-old heifer, a three-year-old goat, a three-year-old ram, a turtle-dove, and

a young pigeon. The three animals he is to divide in two, but not the birds. Abraham fulfills the command. Birds of prey sweep down to attack the dead carcasses. Abraham frightens them away. Then he is overcome by a mysterious sleep, *tardêma,* similar to what Adam experienced in Paradise, at the creation of Eve. During this sleep Abraham has a premonition of the heavy fate that lies in wait for his people, in a mysterious battle of soul. The sun set and darkness spread over the whole land. A smoking firepot and a flaming torch passed over the divided pieces of the animals. The ritual concluded with a renewal of the solemn promise to multiply Abraham's posterity and to give them the land that stretches from the Brook of Egypt as far as the great River as their inheritance (Gn 15, 7-20). This rather peculiar ceremony must be regarded as an official covenant striking between God and Abraham, and at the same time a sort of divine abjuration. The prophet Jeremiah is familiar with this same practice: "The men who transgressed my covenant and did not keep the terms of the covenant which they made before me, I will make like the calf which they cut in two and passed between its parts — the princes of Judah, the princes of Jerusalem, the eunuchs, the priests, and all the people of the land who passed between the parts of the calf, and I will give them into the hand of their enemies ..." (Jer 34, 18-20).

Passing between the cut parts of the animal is thus symbolic of the fate of those who are false to the treaty. Those who break the treaty shall be cut into pieces like the animal. The Hebrew expression for "make a covenant," *karat berît,* clearly refers to this ritual, since *"karat"* literally mean "to cut, to hack," and *"berît"* means "between the two." In the Mari texts the striking of a covenant is expressed by the formula "to slaughter the ass of the covenant" or simply "to slaughter the ass." [26] This practice is unknown in Akkadia, and points to the west. This practice also casts new light on the *benê-hamôr,* "the sons of the ass" of Shechem (Gn 33, 19; Josh 24, 32; Jg

---

26. RB 56 (1949), 24. / I. Henninger, *Was bedeutet die rituelle Teilung dines Tieres in zwei Hälften?* Bibl 34 (1953), 344-353.

9, 28), who venerate the *ba'al berît,* the Baal of the covenant (Jg 9, 4). The expression could refer only to parties to a covenant who had sealed their agreement by the ritual sacrifice of a donkey, the most valuable beast of burden and commerce of that day.

The ceremonial of the covenant between Abraham and Yahweh is not a unique occurrence; it is quite at home within the ambient of the Ancient Near East. What distinguishes it from the other treaty covenants is simply the partners. But God himself freely accepts the ratification of the covenant in the sign of burning fire between the animals. As a result, Abraham's life is bound up with God by a more powerful bond than mere words could ever have effected; and on the other hand God, too, if we might put it in these terms, binds himself to Abraham and to Abraham's posterity on the basis of fidelity to a covenant. But this binding agreement is not to be commemorated only in a unique ritual, an act that occurs but once; it is to abide "in the flesh" of Abraham. The covenant agreement leads immediately to the precept of circumcision, in which God's covenant is supposed to be constantly renewed and re-sealed in the "bearers of life," the male posterity of Abraham.

3) THE SEAL OF CIRCUMCISION: According to Herodotus (II, 37, 104), circumcision was practiced by the ancient Egyptians, Phoenicians, Syrians, Colchians, and Ethiopians. A tomb painting at Sakkarah has preserved the ancient Egyptian circumcision ritual. In ancient Egypt every man was circumcised. The portrayal exhibits two scenes from the actual circumcision of a young man. The ritual must have been extremely painful; behind the young man to be circumcised stands another man who is holding the candidate's hands fast over his head.[27]

---

27. Illustration in Gressmann, AOB (1927), 52, Ill. 158. In Egypt, circumcision of larger groups also took place. A stele from the first interregnum describes the circumcision of 120 men. ANET (1950), 326: "Circumcision in Egypt." / M. Pillet, *Les scènes de naissance et de circoncision dans le temple nord-eat de Mont à Karnak.* Annual Serv AntEg (1952), 77-104, dates the ritual into the third millennium.

Anthropology has ascertained the existence of circumcision as a tribal practice based on long tradition in a whole series of primitive tribes in Africa and Australia. Throughout Islam the ritual is still in practice today. In many tribes it is performed only after a young man's official entry to sexual maturity. As a result, many scholars have interpreted its original bearing as a sort of purification and preparation for marriage.[28]

Among the tribes in which it was practiced, circumcision might well serve as a tribal badge of recognition as opposed to those tribes who did not practice it and were thus regarded as "unclean." The Israelites looked down upon the Philistines with great contempt because they were uncircumcised and therefore unclean. Ancient Canaan also seems not to have known the rite of circumcision, as is witnessed by the case of Dinah, in Genesis 34, 14, where the sons of Jacob explain: "We cannot do this thing, to give our sister to one who is uncircumcised, for that would be a disgrace to us. Only on this condition will we consent to you: that you will become as we are and every male of you be circumcised."

Circumcision was thus not discovered by Abraham. The same law is at work here that we observed elsewhere in the history of revelation: an already existing ritual is taken up and filled with new significance. Circumcision in the tribe of Abraham becomes the sign of a covenant between God and this people. Since the covenant is primarily a promise of the blessing of fertility, circumcision becomes a very appropriate and significant symbol. It is a mark of possession by God, which all members of the "people of his possession" (Ex 19, 5) bore on their body as a symbol of their special privilege and election. As an external sign, it always involved the danger of externalization. The prophets wage a constant campaign for interiorization, interior awareness of the significance of circumcision; it is not a ritual accomplished in the flesh that makes Israel pleasing to God, but rather the "circumcision of the heart" (Jer 9, 24-25; 4, 4; 6, 10; Ez 44, 7, 9; Dt 10, 16; 30, 6).

---

28. Junker, *Genesis* (1949), 56.

4) THE PRUDENCE OF THE FLESH: Just as the rather high numbers assigned to the age of Abraham at the birth of Isaac, Abraham being 100 and Sarah 90, have no chronological value for determining the actual age of the couple, but must rather be understood on the basis of the numerical symbolism so prevalent in Genesis, they do, in terms of precisely this symbolism, make one very clear statement: Abraham and Sarah, from the point of view of all purely human resources, were barren and could never have children. This is the reason behind the choice of such high numbers.

But when Abraham nonetheless heard the repeated assurances from God that he would be presented with an heir from his own body, he must logically have considered the various alternatives available to him. One of these possibilities was the taking of a concubine or second wife, a practice sanctioned by law. The initiative here lay with the legal wife who, in this case, far from being evicted, is actually considered the primary agent, to the point that the children of her slave-girl are regarded as her own children.

It is with this thought that Sarah gives Abraham her Egyptian slave girl Hagar and tells him: "It may be that I shall obtain children by her" (Gn 16, 2). Rachel does the same thing with her slave Bilhah whom she brings to Jacob, and Liah also hopes to acquire children through her slave girl Zilpah (Gn 30, 3, 9). Let us consult the legal texts from the Ancient Near East.

The Code of Hammurabi, in sections 144 — 147, suggests one possible solution for the case of a childless marriage: what is involved is a childless marriage between a free man and a Naditu. When such a Naditu gives her man her own slave girl and the slave girl has children by him, the man is not free to take any Sugitu as a second wife or concubine. But if he has no children through her slave girl, then the man can take a Sugitu as concubine or second wife; but this person will not have the same rights as the Naditu. Now if the Subitu has children, she can then no longer be sold as a slave girl; if she has no children, then her mistress is free to sell her. The law is here concerned with a special case; for the Naditu is, apparently, a high-ranking priestess, who, while she is free to marry, is not allowed to have children, whereas the Subitu is a priestess of lesser rank who is allowed both to marry and to have children. This rather special case does not furnish a particularly apt point of comparison with the history of the patriarchs. It might be presumed, however, on the basis of paragraph 163, that the practice was a general one, and that a barren woman could have children in the above-mentioned manner.

One of the Nuzi texts confirms this legal practice, stipulating the manner in which a barren woman is to proceed: "If (the woman) Gilimininu gets children, (her husband) Sennima cannot take any other wife; but if Gilimininu is unfruitful, then she must give her husband a wife from the land of Lullu," that is, a land from which many slaves came.

The text continues: "The children of the slave girl shall not be driven out." If this were actually to happen, the law branded it as an injustice. When, accordingly, after the birth of Isaac, Sarah demands the expulsion of Ishmael, she has no legal foundation whatsoever; her only appeal is the understandable jealousy of her mother's heart, and her quite legitimate concern for protecting the heritage of her own natural son (Gn 21, 10ff.).

Even though the ancient law protected these half-children from being banished from the family, it does nonetheless exclude them from inheritance, unless the stipulations are made in a particular case. According to the Code of Hammurabi 170 − 171, such children can succeed to the inheritance only when their father recognizes them as natural sons. According to the Assyrian law they can succeed to the inheritance when the legal wife has no children; they are then considered as children of the wife. The Nuzi texts make similar provisions for this case.[29]

The various Ancient Near Eastern law systems thus all agree on one point. The children of the second wife or concubine are to be excluded from the inheritance unless there is some particular stipulation to the contrary. In Genesis 30, 6, we see a particularly realistic adoption arrangement, in which Rachel arranges to have her slave girl Bilhah give birth to her child on Rachel's knees while Rachel herself exclaims: "God has given me a son."

When, accordingly, the barren Sarah gives her Egyptian slave-girl Hagar to her husband, she is acting well within the limits of the law. In fact, she is using the law as a final attempt to achieve the blessing of motherhood, through her slave-girl. Such a slave-girl, however, did not enjoy the full rights and

---

29. *Hammurabi-Texts* in Gressmann, AOT (1926), 358ff. / *Nuzi-Texte* by E. M. Cassin, *L'adoption à Nuzi*, 285-287. − ANET (1950), 219. − Assyrian Laws in ANET: Assyr. Ges. §41, 183; Gressmann, AOT, 418.

privileges of a legal wife; she remained subject to the command of her mistress. "But if she made herself equal to her mistress," then, although her mistress was no longer free to sell her provided that she had borne children, still "she was free to put the mark of a slave upon her and number her among her handmaidens." Thus, by this course of action Sarah anticipates the possibility that Abraham could have had children by some independent concubine or secondary wife. She was free, should she so desire, to later adopt the children of the slave-girl, who just like their mother, were, from the legal point of view, her very own property.

But this very reasonable and perfectly legal "way out" proved to be an illusory solution. When Hagar became pregnant, she began to look down upon her mistress, so that Sarah acted very harshly against her, threw her out into the wilderness where she would have perished excepting that the angel of the Lord sent her back to her mistress with a properly humble attitude of subordination (Gn 16, 1-16).

The conflict occasioned by Ishmael, however, did not come to its full crisis until Isaac had already grown and been weaned. In Genesis 21, 8-21 what we have is not an arbitrary and cruel rejection of the concubine together with her grown son. Sarah is once again resorting to legal prerogatives in her effort to protect Isaac's threatened heritage. Given Abraham's clear preference for Ishmael, she could well predict that Ishmael would also receive a handsome inheritance; that is why she demands: "Cast out this slave woman with her son; for the son of this slave woman shall not be heir with my son Isaac." Hagar was thus legally released from her position as slave girl, thereby acquiring full freedom of movement. She did the most logical thing and returned to her own tribe. We perhaps find it difficult to absolve Sarah entirely from the charge of jealousy and cruelty, but nonetheless God's plans had reached their goal. Since Ishmael is so intimately bound up with Abraham, the bearer of God's blessing, he too is given a rich measure of divine blessing; he is destined to become the ancestor of a whole nation (Gn 21, 13).

5) THE PROMISED SON: The promise of an heir from his own body, a son destined to become a mighty people, runs through the entire Abraham narrative like a golden thread. Is it mere chance or the art of numerical symbolism in the narrative that the course of fulfillment of this promise involves seven stages? Seven is the holy number, the number of God; and thus it has a very deep significance when it is applied to the activity and promises of God. 1. On the other side of the River, God promises to Abraham that he will make him a great people (12, 2); 2. After his departure from his cousin Lot, this promise is renewed. His posterity will be as numerous as the dust of the earth (13, 15). 3. After the mystical conclusion of the covenant, with the animals cut in two parts and ratified by fire, God assumes a legal obligation to be true to his promise (15, 18). 4. When, at the age of 99, Abraham is at the turning point of his life, something quite paradoxical takes place: God demands that he change his name: instead of Abram he is now to be called Abraham, that is, "ancestor of a multitude of nations." That is, of course, an instance of popular interpretation. Philologically speaking, the two forms of the name occur side by side, as we have already explained. But our narrator now regards the longer form of the word as a compound with the Hebrew word *hâmôn* (multitude); this is a deliberate artistic embellishment by our narrator (17, 5). 5. At the same pivotal moment in their lives, Sarai's name is also changed, to Sarah, and this is explained by the fact that she is to be "the ancestress of nations" (17, 15); this is once again an artificial interpretation; for, philologically, the two forms mean the same thing, "princess," Sarai being the linguistically older form. 6. The promise reaches a climax with the apparition of the three angels in Mamre: "I shall return within a year and Sarah will have a son" (18, 10). 7. Finally the realization of the promise: "Yahweh did unto Sarah as he had promised."

This long course of preparation has a deeper theological import: it is to be made abundantly and inevitably clear that it is God's hand that is at work in the birth of Isaac. It is God who is responsible for this new and unheard of wonder: a

barren woman, advanced in years, gives birth to a son. It is
God who "has made laughter" for Sarah (21, 6).

C) ABRAHAM AS A BLESSING UPON THE NATIONS

Abraham's election is not a privilege of grace accorded
to him personally alone; his election is destined to redound to
the benefit of "many peoples." The patriarchal history is thus
supra-national and universal in its orientation, even though,
in terms of its external course of development, it focuses more
and more narrowly upon one national history. Blessing or
curse depends upon the position taken towards Abraham.

1) THE CATASTROPHE OF SODOM AND GOMORRAH: Since Abraham is called to be the father of nations, he must also be initiated into the events of history. The Sodom narrative adds a new
trait to the characterization of Abraham, that of prophet; according to the Israelite conception of things, the prophets are
those men whom God has initiated into his plans: "Surely the
Lord God does nothing, without revealing his secrets to his
servants the prophets" (Am 3, 7). God initiates Abraham into
his plans for judgment, so that even the most distant generations will tremble before the God of judgment (Gn 21, 25) who
wields right and justice upon earth (21, 19).

Abraham's famous bargaining with Yahweh over the fate
of Sodom must not be relegated to the position of being simply
a product of that haggling spirit and temperament which is not
awed even by the presence of God's mystery; it is rather to
be seen as the expression of that perfectly human tendency to
explore every conceivable possibility in behalf of one's fellow
men. This is, in itself, a sign of spiritual greatness.

The presentation is popular in form. God comes down for
a first-hand review of the situation. The two angels who come
as guests to Lot only underline the absolute depravity of those
men who paid no attention to the laws of hospitality that are
held in such high esteem and sacredness throughout the east,
demanding that the angels be surrendered to them. Caught

in this hopeless dilemma, Lot can find no other solution than to offer his own two daughters to satisfy the lustful passions of the citizens. This is a monstrous thing, and can be understood only as the last alternative of a desperate man who finds himself forced to do one evil in order to avoid a much greater one.

But the hour of judgment had come for Sodom; there are not ten just men to be found in the entire city. Only those men who are connected with Abraham are to be saved. Judgment will be withheld until these men have made their way into the city of Zoar. But then fire and brimstone will fall down from heaven upon the cities of Sodom and Gomorrah. "Yahweh overthrew those cities, and all the valley, and all the inhabitants of the cities, and what grew on the ground" (Gn 19, 25). Since Lot's wife hesitated in her flight, she too perished in the disaster. There is no need to assume the presence of any miracle in this account, when it is recorded that Lot's wife was turned into a pillar of salt (19, 26). The narrative has clothed the tradition of the destruction of this woman in a popular form, with the addition of local color drawn from the salt desert along the Dead Sea.

The further history of Lot and his daughters is closely bound up with the decline of the Jordan Valley. Lot went first to Zoar; but he was afraid to stay there because he felt insecure. Apparently the inhabitants of that city refused to extend to him the protection accorded to a fugitive (ger), and thus he fled into the wild mountain wilderness of Moab where he lived in a cave. He had thus cut himself off from all legal intercourse with the inhabitants of the country, and his daughters saw that they were deprived of any possibility of marriage, since marriages with the local population could only be arranged by treaty or custom. They were thus driven to a desperate expedient that can be understood only if we bear in mind the position of woman in the Ancient Near East. Her first obligation is to ensure the preservation of the tribe by bearing children. When they get their father drunk with wine and lie with him and conceive from him, this must not be regarded as "the immorality of lustful desire, but rather the immorality of a desperate and insoluble dilemma, a situation in which a person will turn to any alternatives; and this makes their action humanly comprehensible." [30]

The Mosaic Law itself recognizes, in the levirate marriage, one legitimate case which would otherwise be branded as incest: the childless widow is obligated to marry the brother of her deceased husband (Dt 25, 5). In the two children born of this incest, Moab and Ben-Ammi, the Hebrew ear would hear a play on the origin of the children: *Mo-ab*, "from the father," and *ben-'ammi* "son of my blood relative."

Where are the cities of Sodom and Gomorrah? Excavations in Tellilat-el-Gassul, on the northern end of the Dead Sea, have suggested the hypothesis that the two destroyed cities are to be found in this vicinity. But the further progress of the excavations there demonstrated the falsehood of this conclusion.[31] Today scholars are more inclined to consider the Valley of Siddim (Gn 14, 3), in the southern territory of the Dead Sea, south of the Peninsula of Lisan (tongue). What was once a verdant valley is today covered by the sea. The Dead Sea exhibits its greatest narrowness and shallowness at about the level of the Peninsula of Lisan, across from Masada. In Roman times, the water level was so low that it was possible to cross from the "tongue" to the western shore. Since that time the water level has risen and fallen again. Today it is certainly higher than it was 100 years ago, a fact evidenced by the sunken forests still visible at the southern end of the Dead Sea. The most probable hypothesis is, accordingly, that the cities of Sodom and Gomorrah, which perished in some great upheaval of the earth, are today covered by the waters of the Dead Sea. The Siddim Valley is, after all, a part of the great tectonic fault line which extends from Lebanon through the Jordan Trench and the Dead Sea into the Gulf of Aqabah in the Red Sea. Such territories are generally marked by earthquake activity, and are rich in asphalt, petroleum, and natural gases. The catastrophe of Sodom can be explained very easily in terms of the geographical data: earthquakes together with a volcanic eruption, so that "fire and brimstone rained down" (19, 24), followed by fires in the petroleum wells and the natural gas deposits, so that "the smoke of the land went up like the smoke of a furnace" (19, 28). The destruction of the cities is, accordingly, a divine judgment only in the eyes of the

---

30. Junker, *op. cit.,* 62.
31. Köppel, Bib 20 (1939), 51-63; A. Bea, Bib 22 (1941), 433-438. / J. Penrose Harland, *The Location of the Cities of the Plain,* BA 5 (1942), 17-32.

man who believes; for the unenlightened it is simply a natural catastrophe.[32]

2) ABRAHAM IN THE SOUTH: Abraham pursuing his semi-nomadic existence with his flocks, made his way into the coast territories of Palestine which, on the basis of excavation, have been shown to be little or not at all settled in the Middle Bronze Age, between 2000 and 1600 B.C., that is, into the middle Palestinian hill country, with the settlements of Shechem and Bethel, and into the south. Two events from these days are significant for determining the character of Abraham and the circumstances in which he lived.

As a semi-nomad, Abraham enjoys the freedom of the steppes, coming into occasional contact with the spheres of power established by the individual cities along the margin of the wilderness. From time to time, as in the case of Sarah's abduction by Abimelek, King of Gerar (Gn 20, 1ff.),[33] this leads to serious conflicts, which, in this case, Abraham attempts to avoid by claiming Sarah as his sister. The abduction by Abimelek has a parallel in the later abduction by the Egyptian Pharaoh (Gn 10 — 20). We need not consider the possibility of the same story being handed down in two different forms; it is just as possible that, given the similar conditions, the same thing should have happened on two occasions. For both the Egyptians and Abimelek Abraham is simply a semi-nomad and hence at a disadvantage. The more powerful relies upon his strength in order to take the weaker man's woman — whether it be sister or wife is a matter of lesser importance —and carry her off to the harem of the Pharaoh in Egypt or the royal harem at Gerar.

---

32. *Westminster Hist. Atlas,* map X, pp. 65-66.
33. In the years 1926/27, Flinders-Petrie made a very hasty excavation of the Tell Gemme located some 8 miles SSE of Gaza, which he identified as the patriarchal Gerar. There are remains from the Christian and Hellenistic era as far back as the time of Ramses III (1194 BC). Unfortunately the excavation was never completed. Gerar was an important trade center in grain and had extensive commercial connections with Egypt and the Aegean. Excavation report in Flinders-Petrie, GERAR. 1928.

Since this was an outrage against the prophetic dignity of Abraham, with whose fate God had bound up the promise of curse or blessing, God himself must make an active intervention. This he did by striking both Abimelek and the Pharaoh with a plague, so that each of them, in his turn, quickly returned Abraham's wife. In Genesis 20, 7, the return of Sarah is based on the fact that Abraham is a prophet. It is through the intercession of his prayer that the plague will be removed. The blessing promised to Abraham thus produces its effects outside the narrow circle of his family.

When the power of this blessing became known, the neighboring peoples entered into friendly relationships with Abraham, as is evidenced by the treaty with Abimelek (Gn 21, 22-34).

This treaty fits in perfectly with the cultural view of Abraham; the subject matter is the rights to the wells which, for the migratory nomads and their flocks, represents the very essential of life. Abraham digs a well in Beer-sheba and secures the right to this well by an oath, whence the well is called by the name "well of the oath." There would appear to be some difficulty in the treaty document, since Abimelek, in Genesis 26, 1, is called "king of the Philistines in Gerar," and, according to Genesis 21, 32, returns into "the land of the Philistines." Is it perhaps possible that later geographical and ethnic situations have been projected retroactively into an earlier era? The Philistines did not occupy their country until around the thirteenth or twelfth century, in connection with the great migrations of the sea peoples. A retroprojection of later circumstances is certainly quite in keeping with the nature of popular narrative, but it must not be appealed to here without qualification: we are in a better position to realize today that both Egypt and the Palestinian coast enjoyed close commercial relationships with the island of Crete, from which the Philistines first came. We must thus consider the possibility that, even before the invasions of the sea peoples, another Philistine tribe may have come to the Asiatic coast, settling not along the western coast of Palestine, but to the south. This hypothesis would seem to be confirmed by the non-Semitic name of Phikol, the leader of Abimelek's troops (Gn 21, 22). We might, accordingly, identify these men as a tribal group coming from the island of Crete, to whom the Canaanite prince Abimelek had given a place to settle on condition that they supply his military service.[34] The patriarchal narratives would, once again, be giving us a faithful picture of their time.

D) ABRAHAM'S FAITH

It is the sacrifice of Isaac that formed the religious climax of the Abraham story. It is here that the innermost depths of Abraham's soul are laid bare and his life is bound up with God in its innermost essence. It is this complete surrender, this total abandonment of human hopes and potential, that offers God his greatest opportunity to intervene in the world of history. Abraham's unqualified willingness to offer this sacrifice calls forth, in God, the willingness to bestow a blessing whose efficacy embraces not only the seed of Abraham, but all the nations of earth. The Abraham story might be described as a solemn song of praise to the great patriarch who, by his faith, constrained God himself. But despite this theological clarity, the narrative does involve some problems for the history of religion and the science of archaeology. First we shall have to examine more closely into the sacrifice of Isaac and Abraham's concept of God.

1) THE SACRIFICE OF ISAAC (Gn 22, 1-19): Verse 12 furnishes us with the key for interpretation: "Now I know that you fear God, seeing you have not withheld your son, your only son, from me." It is this fear of God, prepared to sacrifice everything for God, prepared to follow the inner voice to the utmost, that first makes Abraham susceptible to this proving, to this strange demand that he sacrifice his first-born son. There could surely be

---

34. Cf. in this connection 1 S 30, 14: "the Negeb of the Cherethites." According to Zeph 2, 5, the Cherethites are Philistines. In David's army there are "Cherethites and Peletites" serving as mercenaries (2 S 8, 18).

no greater way to prove his recognition of the God who had thus far been his leader. The Canaanite religion has some precedent for this manner of showing reverence to the divinity.

The thought of sacrificing his first-born comes to Abraham as a temptation. Temptation always offers a man the possibility of evil. It is true that the Bible refers the occasion of this sacrifice to a direct command by God's own voice. But the Bible's portrayal only abbreviates the psychological process, by attributing to God's direct command what is actually only the expression of an interior struggle, and thus always subject to the danger of error. In other contexts too, an evil which is only permitted by God is represented as having been caused by him: "An evil spirit from Yahweh fell upon Saul" (1 S 16, 14). In keeping with this usage, the Bible regularly represents an erroneous conscience as the voice of God.

God does not, therefore, demand the killing of the first-born son; yet he permits these thoughts as a temptation. A clear psychological parallel is to be found in the case of the prophet Micah (6, 6): "With what shall I come before the Lord, and bow myself before God on high?" The prophet is faced with an interior struggle as to how he shall give fullest expression to his reverence for God. Then, as the supreme human possibility, he suggests the thought of human sacrifice: "Shall I offer my first-born for my misdeeds, and the fruit of my body for the sin of my soul?"

Throughout the course of Old Testament history, in hours of supreme national or personal crisis, there is always some hint of human sacrifice. The King of Moab, besieged within his city, can find no other solution to his desperate situation than to take his first-born son, who is destined to be king after him, and sacrifice him as a holocaust of the city walls (2 K 3, 27). With the penetration of the Canaanite religion into Israel, there is fresh impetus to the practice of human sacrifice. Ahaz has his son passed through the fire (2 K 16, 3), and likewise Manasseh (2 K 17, 17). Hiel interred his first-born son when he laid the foundation stones for the reconstruction of Jericho, and his youngest son when the city walls had been completed. These Biblical accounts are confirmed by excavation, and, for that matter, not only for the Israelite kingdom, but also for the Bronze Age which preceded, the era to which the life of Abraham is to be assigned. In Megiddo a fifteen-year-old girl was interred in the foundations of the city defenses. In the excavations at Tell-el-Fara the skeletons of children have recently been discovered beneath the Bronze-Age city gates. Child sacrifice was, accordingly, a well established precedent as an act of religious supererogation throughout the history of the Old Testament. It is no wonder that a most god-fearing man should thus consider this sacrifice as the supreme expression of his religious sentiment, and that God's extraordinary intervention in the case of the patriarch of Israel should prove to be decisive for all generations to come. For this is the law which is clearly proclaimed in the narrative of the sacrifice of Isaac: the God of Abraham, Isaac, and Jacob does not want human sacrifice. God's intervention thus represents a correction of an erroneous conscience, an attitude which, in the darkness of temptation and trial, was prepared to submit itself to God to the point of paradox. This unreserved gift of self forces the very heart of God and makes Abraham into a powerful source of blessing for all coming generations.

According to Genesis 22, 2, Abraham was supposed to sacrifice his son "in the land of Moriah." Instead of this unknown proper name, the text most likely read originally: *'eres hâ'emoriyyah,* that is, "in Amorite territory," thus a very general geographical reference without any more specific location. The Jewish tradition which locates the site of the sacrifice on the mountain of the Temple at Jerusalem, has no support from the text. Most recently, L. H. Vincent has once again argued for the identification of Moriah as the citadel mountain of Zion.[35]

SALVATION HISTORY — PROSPECT

The figure of Abraham as patriarch of the chosen people is of such

---

35. L. H. Vincent, *Abraham à Jérusalem,* RB 58 (1951), 360-371: No Biblical text explicitly connects Abraham with Jerusalem. The author demonstrates that the Salem mentioned in Gn 14, 18 is a reference to Jerusalem. He also believes that Mt. Moriah in Gn 22, 1-19 is to be identified with Mt. Zion.

fundamental significance for the development of salvation that it is only
the fulfillment of salvation which supplies the proper framework for
evaluation.

Mary, the mother of Christ, sees the Incarnation of the Son of God
as the fulfillment of the great promise made to Abraham: "He has helped
his servant Israel, in remembrance of his mercy, as he spoke to our
fathers, to Abraham and to his posterity for ever" (Lk 1, 54). And
Zachary praises the mercy of God on the occasion of the birth of St.
John, a precursor of the Messiah: God has visited his people, mindful
of his holy covenant, of the oath which he swore to our father Abraham
(Lk 1, 72).

But it is primarily the theological thinking of Paul the Apostle
which seizes upon the figure of Abraham as the most serious argument
against the Jewish theology of his day. The wives of Abraham are, for
him, types for the relationship between Church and Synagogue (Gal
4, 22ff.). Now St. Paul claims that the Church is the genuine heiress
of the blessing and the promise, typified by Abraham's free-born wife
Sara. The Jewish religion, on the other hand, is incorporated by the
servile existence of Hagar and her son. It is understandable that such
assertions must necessarily fan the Jewish hatred to a glowing pitch,
so that Paul was cast out of the city, stoned, and flogged (Acts 14, 5).
Abraham's spiritual fatherhood over all peoples is, according to St.
Paul, already expressed by the fact that, even before his circumcision,
Abraham is acknowledged to have achieved "justice through faith" (Rm
4, 1ff.). The circumcision is a subsequent rite, and confers nothing
essentially new. It is, accordingly, faith which produces the child of
God, and not the rite of circumcision. St. Paul thus upsets another
important foundation of the Jewish theology, expanding the national
limitation of salvation to the proportions of the promise made to Abraham
as extending over all nations. Finally, in Romans 9, 1ff., St. Paul
openly declares that it is not descent from Abraham according to the
blood that is significant: "This means that it is not the children of the
flesh who are the children of God, but the children of the promise are
reckoned as descendants" (Rm 9, 8), and man must grow dumb in
deepest reverence before the mystery of God's free gift of grace and
election. Paul's polemical letters did not mean to completely undermine
the force of the Old Testament, but rather to put it in its true and
final light. What makes him the most powerful champion of Old
Testament theology is the very fact that he enlists the Old Testament
itself as his most convincing demonstration of the genuinity of the
Church's true messianic mission.[36]

---

36. J. Obersteiner, *Die Christusboschaft des Alten Testamentes.* "Die
    Verheissung an Abraham" 38-43 with reference to NT, Vienna (19-

2) THE GOD OF ABRAHAM: There are various possibilities for developing Abraham's concept of God. One obvious point of departure is the cult sites themselves. After Abraham, motivated by religious considerations, had departed from his tribal home in Haran and had already won other people for his new ideas, nonetheless, upon his arrival in Canaan, he made use of the sacred places already established in the land of his own religious ritual. He first stops at the "terebinth of the prophet" or "the oracle oak" (*'elon morê*) in Shechem, where Yahweh appears to him, whereupon Abraham erects an altar (Gn 12, 6). He then continues to Bethel, where he also builds an altar (Gn 12, 8). He makes a rather long sojourn at the "terebinths of Mamre, which are near Hebron. There too he built an altar for Yahweh" (Gn 13, 18). The terebinths are once again the site of a theophany by Yahweh (Gn 18, 1ff.). Finally, the fact that Melchizedek, the "priest of the Most High God" (*'el 'elyôn*) blessed Abraham (Gn 14, 19) clearly demonstrates the close similarities and interdependence in the religious conceptions of Abraham and the population of the land in which he found himself.[37] It is, accordingly, impossible to completely isolate Abraham from the religious circumstances of the world about him. He is both beholden to his origins and at the same time ripe for the development of something new.

Under what name does Abraham address his God? According to the present-day text, Abraham worships Yahweh; but this name has little information to offer in terms of the history of religion, since the name Yahweh has, since the time of Enosh (Gn 4, 26) been used of the true God, even though the actual name Yahweh certainly does not go back any further than the religious reformations of Moses, and it is certainly an anachronism in the patriarchal era. For Abraham, there are two characteristic names for God: *'el šadday* and *'el 'olam*. Whereas

---

47). / D. Lerch, *Isaaks Opferung christlich gadeutet. Eine auslegungsgeschichtliche Untersuchung.* Beiträge z. hist. Theol., Tübingen 12 (1950).

---

37. G. L. Della Vida, *El 'eljôn in Gn 14, 18-20*, JBL 63 (1944), 1-9. / H. G. May, *The Patriarchal idea of God*, JBL 66 (1947), 113-128.

the first shows clear relationship with the style of Aramaic paganism, the second appears to belong exclusively to Abraham's new religious creation.

a) *'El šadday*: The original meaning of the word *šadday* is still hotly contested today.[38] The traditional derivation is from "*šadad*," that is, "to be powerful"; *'el šadday* would thus mean "the almighty God." The Septuagint translates *šadday* as *Pantokrator;* later Biblical texts, moreover, such as Isaiah 13, 6, would tend to demonstrate the fact that the Hebrew word does in fact give some intimation of the concept of power.

God is called *'el šadday* at the moment of a new promise of blessings to Abraham (Gn 17, 1); again, when Isaac sends his son Jacob back into Haran: "May *'el šadday* bless you and make you fruitful..." (Gn 28, 3), upon his return, in Bethel, God once again reveals himself as *'el šadday* (35, 11). Jacob, as an old man in Egypt, refers to this apparition of *'el šadday,* when he adopts the children of Joseph (48, 3). If we also consider the fact that the Aramaic "prophet" Balaam calls upon God under the same name (Nb 24, 4, 16; 23, 7) and that the poet-author of the Book of Job frequently has his heroes use this name for God, and Job himself comes from the land of Hus, Aramaic territory, then we might consider as certain that the title *'el šadday* points to the Aramaic territory from which the patriarchs came.

Since the word *šadu* means "mountain" in Akkadian, and since there are many other divine names in which the concept of "rock" figures, such as the name "*pedâ-sûr*," that is, "may the mountain redeem me," many scholars are strongly in favor of interpreting *'el šadday* as a mountain deity: "The principal deity of the pre-Mosaic Hebrews was a mountain God or at least he was identified and combined with a mountain God. The mountain God in question is clearly the storm-god Hadad, whom the Canaanites refer to by the more general name Baal (master), while the Akkadians called upon him as the god Amurru, that is, the "western god," the storm god of the west, and frequently as "the great mountain" or some similar expression.[39]

If this derivation is correct, then the new element in Abraham's religious establishment does not lie in the fact that he discovered new names for his God, but rather that he retained the current names for the divinity but filled them with new content. His God *'el šadday* is not only the god of storm and thunder, who strides mightily over the mountains; he is also the God of eternity (*'el'ôlâm*) who strides beyond the paltry measure of time and space. There are serious philological

---

38. Albright, *From Stone Age to Christianity* (1949), 245. / O. Procksch, *Theologie des Alten Testaments* (1950), 50ff.
39. *Ibid.,* 246.

considerations against this derivation from *šadu* — mountain, however. *Šad-day* is regularly attested only in the form with *dd* so that the traditional derivation from "*šadad* — to overcome, to be powerful," has the greater claim to probability.

b) *'El 'ôlâm*: When Abraham plants a tamarisk at Beer-sheba and calls upon the name of Yahweh, the God of eternity (*'el 'ôlâm*), this title clearly represents the nucleus of the ancient belief (Gn 21, 33). God is bound neither to space nor time. He is present everywhere and at every time. There cannot be even the least shadow of thought but that God sees or hears it. He has the future in his hands; thus he can promise blessing for all generations to come. He is the God of the prophets, who unveils the future. This prophetic element already begins to break through in the case of Abraham and the other patriarchs. This supra-temporality of God's easily develops into the concept of the "God of the fathers," before whom past, present, and future lie open, the God who, finally and simply, "is there" (Yahweh). The Mosaic concept of God is already essentially expressed in the patriarchal era.

c) *Mal'ak Yahweh* — The angel of Yahweh: The life of the patriarchs is watched over and borne along by angels. But these angel narratives in the patriarchal histories present a certain degree of difficulty.

When Hagar flees into the wilderness, she is immediately met by an angel of Yahweh (*mal'ak Yahweh*). He addresses her as an envoy from God, commissioned to speak God's words: "Behold, you are with child, and shall bear a son; you shall call his name Ishmael, because the Lord has given heed to your affliction" (Gn 16, 7-16). Hagar herself interprets this encounter as a meeting with God: "Thou art a God of seeing" (17, 13). The same transition from the angel's word to God's own word occurs more boldly in the apparition of the three men to Abraham (Gn 18, 1ff.). The chapter is introduced by a reference to the theophany: "And the Lord appeared to Abraham by the oaks of Mamre . . . ." But in verse 2 the story reverts to "three men, who stood near him." During the remainder of the account, the presentation fluctuates between the plural of the angels and the singular of God. Verse 9: Then they said . . . . Verse 13: Then Yahweh said . . . . What is the solution to this problem?

a) The Trinitarian interpretation is quite foreign to the thought patterns of the Old Testament reader, and could thus hardly be the first and proper sense of the narrative.

b) But neither does the narrative mean to represent Yahweh accompanied by two angels, although a superficial reading of the text might suggest this conclusion. In 19, 18-21, Lot speaks to Yahweh himself in the guise of the two angels, just as Abraham in 18, 3, addresses Yahweh in the person of these three men and receives an answer from the person of God (19, 21). Yahweh is thus present in the apparition of both the two and the three angels or men. An identification of "the angel of Yahweh" with Yahweh himself (hypothesis of identity) fails to take into account the variety in the narrative, which fluctuates between two or three persons.

c) The representation hypothesis claims that the angel or the angels proclaim a message from God who is conceived of as being absent from the scene, and speaking through his representative. The angels are, accordingly, representatives of the absent ruler. This hypothesis offers too weak an explanation of the word of Yahweh which is directly and immediately bound up with the word of the angels.

d) The hypothesis of revelation does, perhaps, give most justice to the world-views of the Old Testament insofar as the "angel of Yahweh" functions as the escort and bearer of Yahweh's own glory and reveals the presence of God by his own visible form, God himself remaining mysteriously invisible. This would be a representation of "Yahweh, who makes his throne above the cherubim." [40] From the point of view of this conception of things, the narrator is free to fluctuate between the presentation of the external appearance of the angel and the invisible majesty of Yahweh. The Old Testament knows God not so much as a solitary being, existing only for himself, but rather as king, surrounded by his royal court. The God of Hosts, whom the prophets will proclaim, was already the God of the fathers.[41]

Abraham's life finally achieved its greatest ethnic spread not by the fact that Ishmael and Isaac are descended from him, but rather by the fact that through his marriage with Keturah (Gn 25, 1-6), a great number of other sons derived their descendency from him. The list of these sons is a catalogue of the tribes of the Arabian desert, whose leading elements all

---

40. Cf. the inaugural visions of Isaiah, Ezekiel, and Daniel.
41. The various hypotheses can be found in Junker, *Genesis* (1949), 63.

traced their ancestry back to Abraham.

But Abraham's true significance does not lie in the sons of the flesh, but solely in the son born of the promise, in Isaac, who is the bearer of revelation and protector of the religious impetus that stems from Abraham.

Ripe in years, Abraham dies at the age of 175 years — the number has a symbolic value — and is buried in the burial plot that he had purchased at Machpelah.[42]

---

42. This burial place is located in the vicinity of the city of *kiriath-'arba* (later Hebron), where Sarah died (Gn 23, 1). Kiriath Arba does not mean, on the basis of the Hebrew etymology, "four-city," a reference to its formation from four city quarters; it is a name that develops from the Hurrite tribe of Arba that lived there, just as Jerusalem is the city of the Jebusites (*'ir hayebûsî*: Judg 19, 11; Neh 11, 25). The inhabitants of the city are called Hittites. In their territory Abraham settled, at Mamre. The influence of Hittite law has been established by M. R. Lehman; *Abraham's Purchase of Machpelah and Hittite Law*, BASOR 129 (1953), 15-18; ANET (1950), 188. The negotiations over the burial caves and the purchase of the site have some parallels in the Nuzi texts. The agreement is valid only if it is set down in writing and proclaimed at the city gates (Gn 23, 18). Cf. De Vaux, *Patriarches hébreux et découvertes modernes,* RB (1949), 24-25. North of Hebron, modern Halil, on the route towards Bethlehem. In 1920-28, under auspices of the Görresgesellschaft, Mader excavated in the mounds at Ramet-el-Halil and uncovered large building sites from the Hadrianic and Herodian eras. Among them pottery and pavements from the 9th century B.C. Mader thought he had discovered the Mamre of the patriarchal stories. Bibl 9 (1928), 120-126; RB 39 (1930), 84-117; 199-225. / Galling, *Biblisches Reallexikon* (1937), 275.

CHAPTER III

THE PATRIARCH ISAAC AND HIS SONS ESAU AND JACOB

WHILE still alive, Abraham had taken every precaution that his son Isaac should take a bride from among his relatives in Haran and, to this end, he had sent his chief steward Eliezer back to his homeland. It has long been noted that the marriage arrangements were carried on between Laban, the brother of the bride-to-be Rebekah, and Eliezer. Even the mother of the bride had no voice in the matter. Still the final decision lay with the girl herself. This is particularly noteworthy in view of the other marriage customs familiar to our study, in which the women are not even asked for their consent. Liah and Rachel, for example, are married to Jacob by their father without having given any indication of their prior consent.

On the basis of our knowledge of Ancient Near Eastern law, scholars have concluded that at the time of the marriage arrangements Rebekah's father was already dead. In this case Laban, as Rebekah's brother, would represent the house. But he was not allowed to give his sister in marriage against her will. Her express consent was necessary for the validity of the marriage. From Nuzi we have a contract in which a brother gives his sister in marriage and she expressly declares: "It is with my full consent that my brother has given me to NN as wife." [1] This represents one step towards the emancipation of woman and the restriction of fraternal power after the death of the father. [2]

The man sent to find a bride in Haran is faced by the further problem of what to do in the event that the bride is unwilling to return to Canaan (Gn 24, 5, 8). This presupposes a custom known from the Assyrian and Babylonian laws, according to which the wife is free to choose her own residence and can, if she so desires, remain in her father's house. [3] Rebekah, however, courageously faces the prospect of moving into a foreign country, to meet an unknown bridegroom.

But their marriage was not blessed at first. Just as in the case of Abraham, in the story of Isaac we once again encounter the theme of the wife's barrenness. It is only by God's particular blessing that a child is given to them. The children of the promise are not primarily "children of the flesh," but children of a true promise. When Rebekah did finally conceive, she felt the full terror and pressure of motherhood. In her time of tribulation she went "to ask Yahweh" (Gn 25, 22). Since the answer is given in the form of a divine oracle, the questioning was apparently performed by a seer or a priest. Abraham's dealings with Melchizedek (Gn 14, 18-20) and the appearance of the non-Israelite prophet Balaam (22 — 24) show that the consultation of a non-Israelite "man of God" was certainly a possibility. It is precisely this detail that locates the patriarchal narratives immediately within the world of the Ancient Near East, and thereby makes them much more credible.

The man of God interprets the mother's tribulation as caused by the fact that the twins in her womb are struggling together, and then two peoples will emerge at birth (25, 23). In keeping with the custom of the people, the children are named after some particular circumstances of their birth. The first-born, since his skin is ruddy in color, receives the name Esau, that is,

---

1. H. Lewy, Or 10 (1941), 211.
2. P. Koschaker, ZA (1933), 33.
3. De Vaux, RB 56 (1949), 29.

the "ruddy one," while the second, Jacob, is so called because he was holding his brother's heel and thus, from the very moment of his birth, appeared to be fighting for the position of first-born. St. Paul sees this as a deeply theological insight into God's free election in grace, assigning to each person the measure of divine gifts that he will, independent of any previous merit (Rm 9, 10-13).

Externally, Isaac's life proceeded in practically the same manner as that of his father Abraham. He followed his flocks into the southern country, was forced to fight for water rights, concluded treaties with Abimelek of Gerar. In terms of salvation history, the most significant element in the struggle between his two sons, a struggle which is carried on and brought to a conclusion under his very eyes (Gn 26, 1ff.).

A) THE FIGHT FOR THE BIRTHRIGHT

"When the boys grew up, Esau was a skillful hunter, the man of the field, while Jacob was a quiet man, dwelling in tents. Isaac loved Esau, because he ate of his game; but Rebekah loved Jacob" (25, 27). When Jacob, seizing a favorable opportunity, did his brother out of his birthright for the price of a dish of red pottage, this is not simply a clever strategy on his part; it is quite within the possibilities of Ancient Near Eastern law.

The Assyrian law contains the following regulations: "If brothers are dividing the heritage of their father, the orchards and the wells in the country, the eldest son shall first choose a double portion of everything, and then each of the brothers shall have his share. The youngest son shall receive the cultivated land with all its products; then let the eldest choose and take his share and then cast lots with his brothers for the second share." [4] It is obvious that the first-born enjoyed considerable advantages. We also know, on the basis of texts from Nuzi, that the right of the first-born was alienable. In a similar contract a man renounces his right to the privileges of first-born

---

4. Assyrische Gesetze, table B, §1: ANET (1950), 185.

with respect to the inheritance from his father, in favor of a foreigner. In another text a man sold his first-born rights to a garden, for three sheep.[5] In Israel, the right of the first-born had consequences beyond the question of property. It was intimately bound up with the position of ruler in the tribe, and also with determining who should be the bearer of the promise, as witness the concern for the patriarchal blessing.

B)   JACOB'S SURREPTITIOUS BLESSING

Elsewhere in the Old Testament there is no mention of a special blessing for the first-born. But from the wording of the blessing pronounced by Isaac it is clear that his intention was to establish in the eyes of God Esau's special position as first-born in the generation of Abraham. But he had not reckoned with the love and intrigue of the children's mother, who had already been considerably vexed by the Hittite wives of Esau (26, 34). She does not shrink from outright deceit in order to win the privileges of the first-born for her favorite son. The words of the blessing make the situation clear:

"See, the smell of my son is as the smell of a field which
    the Lord has blessed.
May God give you of the dew of heaven,
    and of the fatness of the earth,
    and plenty of grain and wine.
Let people serve you,
    and nations bow down to you.
Be lord over your brothers,
    and may your mother's sons bow down to you.
Cursed be every one who curses you,
    and blessed be every one who blesses you!"
(Gn 27, 27-29)

The blessing formula clearly bears the stamp of the southern country, where there is very little rain and the fertility of

5. RB 56 (1949), 30.

the land is, for many months of the year, absolutely dependent upon sufficient dew. Moreover, the blessing establishes the "first-born" as chieftain in the tribe, with all his other brothers subordinate to him. At the same time it presents an outline picture of the future, which draws nations and peoples of the future into the fate of the brother who is blessed. Thus all the promises and blessings made to Abraham are, in Jacob, transmitted to the generations to come. The continuity of salvation is thus assured.

After Isaac is informed of the deception, he does not transform his blessing into a curse; he lets it stand. Perhaps he is motivated by the conviction that a blessing solemnly pronounced in the presence of God cannot be subsequently changed.[6] Upon Esau's repeated pleading, he does also pronounce a blessing upon him, which, in prophetic style, foretells the future fate of his son: "Behold, away from the fatness of the earth shall your dwelling be,[7] and away from the dew of heaven on high. By your sword you shall live, and you shall serve your brother; but when you break loose you shall break his yoke from your neck" (27, 39). Even though the Biblical account does not expressly condemn Jacob's behavior, there are still some indications in the text to support a very realistic and hard characterization. He himself shrinks before the prospect of "mocking his father" (27, 12); but his conscience does not keep him back from the deed. Still it is his mother who persuades him to use this intrigue; the Hebrew word here almost always bears the connotation of treachery and deceit. Finally, Esau interprets his brother's name as "deceiver" (27, 36), since the name Jacob can be derived from the Hebrew verb 'aqab, that is, "deceive."[8] The later prophetic literature, how-

6. Junker, *Genesis* (1949), 82.
7. The Vulgate translates: *in pinguedine terrae et in rore coeli desuper erit benedictio tua*: the translation takes the word *min* in the original Hebrew (*miššemannê* and *mittal*) in the partitive rather than the primitive sense, even though the latter is clearly suggested by both philological and exegetical considerations.
8. *'aqeb* also means "heel." Both are popular interpretations of the name. Philologically, the word *yaqub-el* means "May God protect."

ever, expressly condemns Jacob's behavior (Hos 12, 2; Jer 9, 4; Is 43, 27). Jacob is thus stamped as a sinner before God, but nonetheless he bears the seal of the promise. It is this contradiction which underlines the whole tension of the history of salvation.

C) JACOB IN MESOPOTAMIA

The patriarch Isaac, after giving his patriarchal blessing, withdraws from the arena of history, which is now concerned only with Jacob as the bearer of the blessing. There are two stages to be discerned in his life: 1. From his flight into Mesopotamia until his return into Canaan; 2. From his return to his death.

a) THE "HEAVENLY LADDER": In order to avoid Esau's revenge, and, at the same time, to find a wife from his own kinspeople, Jacob fled into Haran to his uncle Laban. The first stage of his flight carried him to Bethel, where he had a vision of the "heavenly ladder." At this time he appears more like a man cursed than a man blessed, but the experience of this night's vision strengthens him in the faith that God's blessing is still very much in effect. What he saw in his dream was not a ladder stretching from earth to heaven, with angels going up and down upon it, but rather a representation of a huge staircase, such as is familiar from the terraced temples of Mesopotamia.[9] On the height of the tower God is envisioned as dwelling. The angels going up and down upon the "sullam" is here not to be interpreted simply as a ritual celebration of the heavenly host, something after the manner of the processions which took place on the stairways that led up to the temple

---

After the loss of the theophoric element, only the verb stem remains, which is now subjected to various interpretations as the situation demands.

9. The Hebrew word that corresponds to "ladder" is sullam, which is best derived from salal: "to heap up"; hence sullam is a "mounded stairs" — Junker, Gn 85.

towers. The context suggests a quite different interpretation. The "heavenly host" which surrounds the throne of Yahweh in his heavenly dwelling place, prepared to do his will, are countless angels, who as the instruments and servants of the divine rule of the world, make their way up and down the *sullam* of the heavenly sanctuary. The vision is supposed to awaken in Jacob the comforting certainty that his life is entirely under the protection of God and his angels. In remembrance of this experience, Jacob erects a *massebah*, that is, a stone to serve as a religious monument. He anoints this stone with oil as a sign of Consecration (Gn 28, 10-22).

b) WOOING THE BRIDE: Jacob's sojourn in Mesopotamia has, thanks to recent discoveries, progressed more and more from the "darkness of legend" into the full light of history. Jacob asks his cousin for the hand of Rachel. On the wedding night, however, it is her dim-eyed sister Leah who is given to him instead. Marriage with two sisters is forbidden in Israel, on the basis of Leviticus 18, 18. The Code of Hammurabi, however, makes provision for this possibility.[10] In order to pay the bride price, he must oblige himself to work seven years for each wife; he must work for an additional six years, as it turns out, to provide an independent means for himself.

DID JACOB CONTRACT AN ERREBU MARRIAGE?

Normally, after her marriage, the woman would move into the house and family of her husband. But the opposite procedure was also a possibility, in which the man would "enter" into the family community of the wife. This is the meaning of the Akkadian word *errêbu*. The man is then adopted by the father of his bride. There is a record of such an adoption in the texts from Nuzi: "The tablet of adoption belonging to Nashwi, the son of Ar-shenni; he adopted Wullu, the son of Puhishenni. As long as Nashwi is alive, Wullu shall provide food and clothing: when Nashwi dies, Wullu shall become the heir. If Nashwi has a son of his own, he shall divide (the estate) equally with Wullu, but the son of Nashwi shall take the gods of Nashwi. However, if Nashwi does not

---

10. M. Schorr, *Urkunden des altbabylonischen zivil-und Prozessrechtes* (1913), Nrs. 4 and 5.

have a son of his own, then Wullu shall take the gods of Nashwi. Furthermore, he gave his daughter Nuhuya in marriage to Wullu, and if Wullu takes another wife he shall forfeit the lands and buildings of Nashwi. Whoever defaults shall make compensation with 1 mina of silver and 1 mina of gold."[11]

Scholars have noted many similarities with the Jacob story. Laban orders Jacob to take no other wives besides his daughters (Gn 31, 50). Since there is no mention of any sons of Laban, the story could be best explained by precisely this form of adoption. But, at the end of (Gn 30, 35); according to the first "adoption contract," Jacob and his two wives should have been heirs, but apparently sons were later born to Laban, so that Jacob realized that he would be deprived of the inheritance. The reaction of the two daughters woul fit in well with this interpretation: "Is there any portion or inheritance left to us in our father's house?" (Gn 31, 14). As adoptive son, Jacob is completely subject to the paternal powers of Laban, so that, upon the occasion of Jacob's flight, Laban is justified in complaining: "The daughters are my daughters, the children are my children, the flocks are my flocks and all that you see is mine" (Gn 31, 43).
Jacob's sojourn in Mesopotamia, some sons of Laban are also mentioned (Gn 30, 35); according to the first "adoption contract," Jacob and his two wives should have been heirs, but apparently sons were later born to Laban, so that Jacob realized that he would be deprived of the inheritance. The reaction of the two daughters would fit in well with this interpretation: "Is there any portion or inheritance left to us in our father's house?" (Gn 31, 14). As adoptive son, Jacob is completely subject to the paternal powers of Laban, so that, upon the occasion of Jacob's flight, Laban is justified in complaining: "The daughters are my daughters, the children are my children, the flocks are my flocks, and all that you see is mine" (Gn 31, 43).

Even though the concept of *errêbu* marriage seems to explain many difficulties, it remains only an hypothesis, since Jacob did not mean to bind himself to an alien existence, but left Palestine with the firm resolve and assurance that he would return. The whole situation can be even better explained simply by postulating a contract between Jacob and Laban. He would then be obligating himself to a corresponding number of years in the service of his cousin, with the intention of returning into the land of his fathers after the course of this service. The fact that this return eventually took the form of flight was the result of a rupture in the relationship between father-in-law and son-in-law. If Rachel, on this occasion, stole the household gods (teraphim) of Laban,

11. Text in ANET: Nuzi-Texte, p. 219.
12. De Vaux in RB 56 (1949), 35.

in order to secure a right of inheritance in her father's house, in keeping with the Nuzi law, this took place against Jacob's will. In his conception of things, he had acted with perfect legality towards his father-in-law, and it is in this respect that we are to interpret all the clever dealings on both sides. With respect to his wife and his secondary wives, Jacob is thus acting within the possibiliities of the then existing law, so that the entire Jacob narrative "breathes the social climate of the Ancient Near East."[12]

c) THE FIGHT WITH GOD AT THE JABBOK: On his return into Canaan, as he crosses the river Jabbok, Jacob is forced into a conflict with a mysterious being, an encounter which is of such fundamental importance for the further history of salvation that from that hour on Jacob receives the name Israel (Gn 32, 23-32). Jacob's adversary is introduced as "a man who wrestled with him" (32, 24). A comparison with the vocation of Gedeon (Jg 6, 11) and the miraculous promise of the birth of Samson (Jg 13, 3) makes it clear that this "man" who wrestles with Jacob is not to be understood simply as an angelic power, but God himself. The fact that Jacob is lamed in his hip serves as further confirmation for the reality of this encounter with God and the divine oracle that interprets his name: "Your name shall no more be called Jacob, but Israel, for you have striven with God and with men, and have prevailed" (32, 28). The content of the struggle has to do with a blessing; the pair struggle throughout the night; apparently the conflict will come to no clear decision; the dawn is already breaking when Jacob, by his perseverance, overcomes the divine being and receives the blessing.

Even though Jacob was prevented from learning the name of this mysterious being (32, 29), he named the location of the struggle *Peniel*, that is, "face of God." To look upon the face of God, in purely natural terms, always means death (Ex 33, 20), but in the dispensation of grace, it brings life which is now promised to Jacob-Israel. What we are dealing with here is not so much the revelation of a name as the revelation of God's being. His being comes to light in the blessing for which Jacob had wrestled and received. In this blessing he is promised the power of life which will stream upon him and his house. This archaic narrative makes it clear that the God of Israel originally conceals his name so that it is just as incorrect to refer to him as Yahweh as it is to call the God of the fathers by that name. The patriarchs refer to him only by the general Semitic name for God, El, but this word is continually being filled with new content.[13]

Under the influence of this theophany, Jacob gives the following command in Shechem: "To bury all the foreign gods that they had and the rings that were in their ears, under the oak that was near Shechem" (35, 2-4), in order to assume a new obligation to the God of revelation in Bethel (35, 7). Peniel is thus a climax and turning point in the development of the Old Testament religion.[14]

The name Israel, like a crystal prism caught by the sunlight, combines the entire meaning of salvation history in one bright focus. Israel, in keeping with the Biblical popular etymology, is generally interpreted as "God's warrior" — but this is impossible on philological grounds. In terms of its form, *Yisra'el* is a brief sentence with El (God) as subject and the imperfect of the verb *sarah* (to fight). Who, on the basis of this sober grammatical analysis, is really the fighter, Jacob or God? The preponderance of the activity lies with God: "God fights." Or, if we translate the imperfect as an optative form, along the pattern of other names formed with El, the word Israel is a prayer: "May God fight." [15] The fact that the history of salvation is ultimately bound up with the constant intervention of God

---

13. On the subject of the development of the divine image of God in the patriarchal era, there are some very stimulating problems in O. Procksch, *Theologie des AT* (1950), 59ff. / M. Schmidt, *Jakob kämpft um den Segen. Exegetische Besinnung zu Gn 32, 14-33.* In "Iudaica" 4 (1948). / A. Bentzen, *The Weeping of Jacob,* VT 1 (1951), 58.

14. For an explicit treatment of the "angel combat" in terms of the form-historical tradition, cf. H. Eising, *Formgeschichtliche Untersuchung Zur Jakobsüberlieferung der Genesis* (1940), 118-137: "Der Kampf am Jabbok." The Jacob stories are the work of a later author which was, in turn, reworked at a still later date; but they are not "fairy-tales

gives the believer a secure assurance of victorious outcome, no matter how difficult the individual stages of the battle.

Strengthened by this encounter with God, Jacob, as "blessed by God," makes bold to approach his brother Esau, who is willing to be reconciled. Jacob takes the same nomadic course that Abraham followed, across Shechem — where his daughter Dinah is violated and avenged by his two sons Simeon and Levi in a violent and precipitate attack upon the city — to Bethel, and Bethlehem, as far as Mamre, where he meets with his aged father Isaac, whom, in company with Esau, he buries in the family burial grounds (Gn 33 — 35). Chapter 36 continues the generations of Esau, whereupon Esau departs from the focus of salvation history. The interest of the author of Genesis now concentrates more and more upon Jacob and his sons.

---

or saga or fluctuating, impersonal popular narrative."

15. In addition to the derivations of the name Israel described above, two other interpretations might also be noted: a. derivation from the verb root *sarar*: "to light or shine," Israel thus meaning: "May God shine!" / H. Bauer, *Orientalistische Literaturzeitung*, 38 (1935), col. 477. b. derivation from the root *yasar*, which does not occur in Hebrew but means "to heal" in Arabic and Ethiopian. Israel would then mean: "May God heal." / W. F. Albright, *Journal of Biblical Literature*, 46 (1927), 154-158. — Further suggestions in DBS (1947), col. 730.

CHAPTER IV

THE PATRIARCHS JACOB AND JOSEPH

(Gn 37 — 50)

IN the second stage of his history, Jacob draws more and more into the background. The narratives focus more about his son Joseph, who far outshadows all three patriarchs to the degree that he achieves a higher secular position and thus directs the fate of Israel along an entirely different course. Whereas the preceding patriarchal history has concentrated on the bonds between Israel and Mesopotamia, the powerful and striking personality of Egyptian Joseph brings the chosen people into contact with Egypt. The historical credibility of the Joseph narratives is more and more confirmed by Egyptology; scholars have noted a genuine Egyptian milieu, elements of the Egyptian language, and a genuine Egyptian coloring throughout the whole narrative." [1] A. S. Yahuda goes so far as to suggest that, in the composition of the "Joseph legend," the Hebrew author had Egyptian sources at his disposal.[2]

Even though the historical incorporation of Egyptian Joseph

---

1. A. Jeremias, *Das Alte Testament im Lichte des Alten Orients* (1930), 372.
2. A. S. Yasuda, *Die Sprache des Pentateuch in ihren Beziehungen zum Ägyptischen*, I, (1929).

into the larger picture of Egyptian history may not be a perfectly clear and compatible picture, as we shall see from the various
scholarly opinions to be examined, still the religious figure of
Joseph, bearer of salvation, is a clear and compelling picture.
The picture is drawn with a vitality suggestive of the portrait.
Even though his personal fate involves him in the deepest
suffering and shadow, still, these elements too are suffused by
the divine providence that has sent Joseph into Egypt, so that
through his sojourn there, Israel will achieve redemption (Gn
45, 7) and the national survival of the people will be secured.
Like the patriarchal history in general, the life of Joseph is
characterized by the extraordinary influence of God himself,
so that, in the last analysis, it is God himself who has interwoven
this career, with the immediacy of grace, into the broader
outlines of ancient Egyptian history; the whole Joseph narrative is, as it were, permeated by a single motif: "Yahweh
was with him" (Gn 39, 2, 3, 21, 23 − 41, 39). The blessing promised to Abraham was at work even in a foreign country.

A) THE PRIVILEGED ONE

Joseph is the son of Rachel, Jacob's favorite wife. He was
born only after Rachel had been barren for a long time. It
is this circumstance that provides the interpretation of the
name Joseph: "May El add to this (another son)."[3] The name
was, accordingly, not given immediately, but interpreted only
in keeping with the situation. The full form of the name
Yoseph-'el occurs, together with Ya'kob-'el, in the catalogue of
Canaanite territories conquered by Thutmose III (ca. 1479).[4]
This does not prove that these names have anything to do with
the Biblical Jacob or Joseph, in the sense that we are to interpret them as the names of the original home or cult sites of
these patriarchs. As we have already noted, the names of the
patriarchs are not the names of original gods or heroes, but
rather invocations and prayer formulae such as are everywhere

---

3. Gn 30, 24.
4. ANET (1950), 242.

attested for the end of the Early Bronze Age (1600 B.C.) throughout the whole territory of the Fertile Crescent, as the names of both persons and places. The names thus belong to that great second wave of Semitic immigration which established an empire under the dynasty of Hammurabi and, in the western territory, provided the foundation for the later establishment of the Hyksos Empire in Egypt. It is no wonder that one of the Hyksos leaders bears the name *Ya'kob-'el,* a name for which, quite recently, Albright has suggested the reading "*Ja'kob-har,* that is, "May the mountain-god protect." [5] In connection with the Hyksos rule, it is quite possible to anticipate the spectacular success of a man who bears the name *Yoseph-'el* and is a son of *Ya'kob-'el.* His name and his career are certainly not surprising in this historical situation.

Jacob and his family lived, as had his fathers, as a seminomad in Canaan. On the one hand he established a solid foundation in Mamre, where he practiced agriculture, as is attested by Joseph's dream of the sheafs which bowed before him. But at the same time his sons followed their father's flocks across the hill country of Palestine as far as Shechem and Dothain. Excavations have confirmed the fact that this territory, in the Bronze Age (3000 — 1200 B.C.), was very sparsely settled and thus an ideal territory for wandering Beduins.

Joseph enjoyed a position of special privilege with respect to his brothers, signified by his cloak, *ketonet passim,* a garment which reached to his ankles (Gn 37, 3). Such a garment was worn only by privileged people (2 S 13, 18), whereas the garb of the normal people left arms and feet free for work. His position of special privilege required that he keep watch over the other brothers, a situation which could only lead to considerable unpopularity, and eventually outright hate,

---

5. W. F. Albright, *From Stone Age to Christianity* (1949), 243. On the subject of an earlier mention of the name of Joseph in the Egyptian Execration Texts and on the recent attempts to explain the name, cf. particularly H. H. Rowley, *From Joseph to Josue* (1951), 36ff. — Stock, *Studien zur Geschichte und Archäologie der 13-17. Dynastie Ägyptens* (1942), 67.

so that they soon refused to give him the *shalôm* — the greeting of peace (Gn 37, 4). Joseph's dreams further aggravated this catastrophic situation. His brothers' sheaves appeared to bow before him, as well as the sun, moon, and eleven stars, that is, his father, mother, and eleven brothers. These dreams could be interpreted as simple wish fulfillment on the part of a very ambitious and arrogant young man, and still they were prompted by God's special direction, enlisting all these "natural developments" in the service of his great plan of salvation.

The hatred of his brothers eventually casts Joseph into the cistern, but their troubled conscience quickly lights upon a solution: Joseph is sold to some transient Ishmaelites [6] and they then lie about the entire affair to their own father. For Joseph himself, the sudden plunge from his position of privilege into a servile existence must have been a fearful experience, but still he emerges from this terrible trial not as a broken and revengeful man, but rather as a man more and more conscious of a divine purpose and mission: for "Yahweh was with him" (Gn 39, 2).

B) JUDAH AND THAMAR

The story of Joseph is interrupted by a secondary account, the story of Judah and Thamar (Gn 38, 1-30). The background for understanding this peculiar narrative is the custom of "levirate marriage," (from the Latin word *levir* — brother-in-law). Judah had married his son Er with Thamar. After Er's death, the next eldest son Onan was obligated to take the childless widow

---

6. The narrative of the selling of Joseph does not seem to be a unified story. According to one version, the brothers sold him to Ishmaelites who were traveling through the country (37, 26). According to the other version, it was Midianite merchants that rescued him from the cistern and sold him in Egypt (37, 28). The contradiction can be explained by the fact that "Ishmaelite" was a general term for caravan merchants at the time of the story. That the brothers are really responsible for the selling is clear from Gn 37, 36 and 45, 4. Cf. Junker, *Genesis*, 10.

and give her children. But since Onan realized that these children would not belong to him, he frustrated his own sexual functions by spilling his seed upon the earth. The fact that Onan died shortly after this was interpreted as a judgment from God. Now Judah himself would have been obligated, on the basis of the levirate law, to give Thamar to his next son Selah. Instead of this, he sent Thamar back into her father's house, on the basis that Selah was still too young. Thamar, however, resorted to a strange deceit in order to have a child by her father-in-law himself: she pretended to be a common prostitute. From her union with Judah were born twin sons Perez and Zerah. Since the story of Thamar is mentioned further in the genealogy of Jesus, it merits some special consideration.

The law of the levirate marriage is codified in Deuteronomy 25, 5-10: "If brothers dwell together, and one of them dies and has no son, the wife of the dead shall not be married outside the family to a stranger; her husband's brother shall go in to her and take her as his wife, and perform the duties of a husband's brother to her. And the first son whom she bears shall succeed to the name of his brother who is dead." In later Jewish practice, this custom was observed only with reservation, and was completely repudiated .by many groups, apparently by the Sadducees (Mt 22, 23). In the Ancient Near East the law of the levirate marriage is not mentioned in the Code of Hammurabi, although it is known in Assyria. Still, the interpretation of the Assyrian laws is a contested issue. It seems that the childless widow was given to the brother of the dead man in order to assure some posterity. In Hittite law there is an explicit treatise on the levirate marriage, in which the father-in-law and also the uncles are obligated to perform this duty.

If we thus postulate the influence of Hittite law or Canaanite practice, then Thamar has simply resorted to trickery in order to secure the rights which were denied her, and could hardly be considered as a prostitute. Her conduct was dictated not simply by lust or passion, but rather by her tremendous desire for a child, which would seem to justify what she did. But a closer examination of the text reveals the fact that in Israel this extended practice of the levirate marriage, in which the father-in-law is himself obligated to perform the duties, did not exist. For Judah himself explains that he would never have acted as he did, if he had recognized Thamar; furthermore, the twins born of their union are not regarded as the sons of the deceased Er, but rather as sons of Judah. Thus, despite the great similarities in "juridic milieu," we cannot speak of levirate marriage in the proper sense of the word, but rather a desperate attempt on the part of a sorely tried and childless widow.[7]

C) JOSEPH IN EGYPT

The "Ishmaelites" sold Joseph to the Egyptian official Potiphar, who is referred to as captain of the guard (Gn 39, 1). This was a high official position at the Egyptian court, presumably in the immediate vicinity of the Pharaoh. On the occasion of a palace conspiracy, they formed one part of the tribunal which sat in judgment over the accused. The name Potiphar is generally explained as a variant of *Pôtî-phera* (Gn 41, 45), the transcription of the Egyptian written name *P'-dy-p'-r*, that is, "He whom the sun-god Re has bestowed," Heliodorus in Greek. Such names are common for the 20th dynasty (1200 — 1090 B. C.), but are also familiar in the 17th dynasty (1610 — 1570). Particular mention is made of the fact that Potiphar is "Egyptian," perhaps in order to distinguish him from a ruling caste that was non-Egyptian. Since he saw that Yahweh's special blessing rested upon Joseph (Gn 39, 5), Potiphar entrusted him with the full administration of his house, in order to completely free himself for the service of the Pharaoh. This show of confidence and trust was, however, for Joseph an occasion of greatest temptation, in the form of improper advances by Potiphar's wife. Joseph refused to be a party to her suggestions, and

---

7. The Levirat is discussed by De Vaux, *op. cit.*, RB 56 (1949); "Juda und Tamar," 30ff. Ancient Near East backgrounds in P. Koschaker, *Zum Levirat nach hethitischen Recht*, RHA II, fasc. 10 (1933), 77ff. Koschaker maintains that the Canaanite tribe to which Thamar belonged could have practiced the levirate law in the broader sense of the word, while Israel restricted the practice to the brothers of the deceased husband. This legal conflict would have determined the personal behavior of Thamar who was thus determined to win her rights by force. / J. Mittelmann, *Der altisraelitische Levirat* (1934). / N. Neufeld, *Ancient Marriage Laws* (1944), 35-36. / H. Eheloff, *Ein altassyrisches Rechtsbuch* (1922), 32. / H. Gressmann, AOT (1926): Hethitische Gesetze, § 93, 430. / A. Goetze, in ANET (1950): The Hittite Laws: §193, 196. Standard edition by F. Hrozny, *Code hittite provenant de l'Asie Mineure* (1922).

took refuge in his God: "How can I do this great wickedness, and sin against God" (39, 9). This faithfulness to his God proved to be his own undoing. The scorned woman's desire quickly turned to hate. The man whom she had just recently desired she now refers to as "this Hebrew slave" (39, 17). This expression betrays the Egyptian contempt for the foreign Apiru, who worked as prisoners of war or as slaves in the temples or mines.[8] Joseph was accordingly cast into prison, presumably under the guard of Potiphar himself.

Many scholars have attempted to explain the story of Joseph and Potiphar's wife in terms of the Egyptian story of the two brothers. But, apart from some traits common to both stories, the attempt of the clever woman to seduce the young man and her calumny against him when she is repulsed, everything else is so thoroughly different that a literary dependence is hardly to be considered.[9]

Joseph's interior uprightness, and the fact that he had learned in a time of crisis to place his whole life at the disposal of God, soon won him the respect and confidence not only of his fellow prisoners, but also the captain of the prison itself. Just as his faithfulness to the law of God had first brought him into prison, it is now God's wisdom, through the medium of

---

8. Cf. above the "Apiru" in the Egyptian texts.
9. Gressmann, AOT (1926): Geschichte von der Ehebrecherin, 69-71. / John A. Wilson, in ANET (1950): The Story of the two brothers: 23-25. Both brothers work in the field. The younger is unmarried. The older sends the younger home to get some fruit. The wife of the elder brother goes out to meet the younger man, thinking that her opportunity has come. But he rejects her advances. She then binds her head and lies down and falsely accuses the young man to her husband upon his return home. Inflamed with anger, he seizes a knife and attempts to kill his brother. But the young man has been warned by the cows, who begin to speak, and he flees, pursued by his brother. The sun god makes a lake appear between them. Then the younger brother explains the truth of the situation to the elder brother, whereupon he returns home and kills his unfaithful wife and mourns for his lost brother all the remaining days of his life. G. von Rad, Josefsgeschichte und ältere Chokma, Copenhagen (1953), 120-127 maintains that the Joseph story was composed in the court wisdom schools at the beginning of the monarchy.

dream interpretation, that once again frees him from prison: for "it is not in me; God alone will give Pharaoh a favorable answer" (41, 16).

The interpretation of dreams was a flourishing art both in Mesopotamia and in Egypt. New discoveries give us a much closer insight into the ancient Egyptian method of interpreting dreams. In one papyrus, for example, we find sample interpretations of four good dreams and four bad ones: "If a man sees himself in a dream, and somebody is offering him white bread, that is a good dream. It refers to things that will make his face bright . . . . If somebody sees his face in a mirror, in a dream, that is a bad dream; it means someone else's wife." [10] In order to distinguish between dreams, in the book on interpretation the words "good" or "bad" are written in red ink. When, accordingly, after his disturbing dream, the Pharaoh summoned the scribes and sages of his court, we today can form a fairly accurate picture of what their work consisted in. They examined all the dream books, but could not find the interpretation they sought. Then the chief butler remembered Joseph's interpretation of dreams in prison. Joseph was accordingly summoned and prepared for presentation to the Pharaoh; he was shaved and his clothes were changed.[11] After calling upon his God, who alone is able to interpret dreams (41, 16), Joseph explains the dreams of the seven ears and the seven cows and immediately offers Pharaoh his plan for saving the country. The Pharaoh's dream is genuinely Egyptian; the "seven cows" are familiar to Egyptian mythology. Osiris often appears ac-

---

10. John A. Wilson, in ANET (1950): *The Interpretation of Dreams,* 495. Apparently the manuscript comes from Thebes, 19th dynasty, about 1300 B.C.; the contents can be followed back as far as the 12th dynasty, around 2000 B.C.

11. In the Sinuhe story there is a similar investiture ceremony, section 285ff: "I was brought into the house of a prince. Glory and splendor were in it . . . a bath . . . I was shaven . . . . I was clothed in fine linen and anointed with fine oil." (K. Galling, *Textbuch zur Geschichte Israels* [1950], 11).

companied by seven cows who provide him with nourishment
in death. In like manner, the "seven ears" are symbolic of
Osiris, the giver of wonderful fertility. The east wind, which
destroys all this fruitfulness, is the much feared Hamsin, which
even today threatens vegetation from February to June.[12] No
matter how Egyptian the dream appears to be, as the Bible tells
the story, its interpretation is quite un-Egyptian, a clear and
open manifestation of God's hand in history.

In the course of its long history, Egypt frequently had to
reckon with famines which were caused by the failure of the
Nile inundations. Already from the time of the Old Kingdom
we have an inscription cut into stone on the island of Seheil in
the vicinity of the first cataract, which tells of a seven-years'
famine under the Pharaoh Choser (2650 — 2600 B.C.); it relates
how the Pharaoh consecrated the island to the god Hnum, in
order to secure the restoration of the Nile's waters and the
blessings they brought to Egypt.[13] Against occasions like this,
it was important to be prepared. These were times of powerful
interference by the central government. An official of Sesostris
(Middle Kingdom) makes this report: "There were years of
famine. Then I plowed all the land of the goat's field from its
northern to its southern boundary. I nourished all the subjects,
I took care of their food, so that there was no man hungry among
them . . . ." Even more strongly reminiscent of Joseph's position
as chief steward of the grain supply is the mention of a man
in the Amarna correspondence who bears the Semitic name
Ianhamu. He is the Egyptian plenipotentiary for Syria. He is
charged with administration of the granaries and reserve depots,
and charged with supplying Syria with grain. As plenipotentiary
of the king, he has unlimited power which he quickly abuses.
Silver and gold, sons and daughters must be sent to him in
order to guarantee the delivery of grain.[14] The position of

---

12. A. Jeremias, ATAO (1930), 378ff.
13. *Ibid.*, 380.
14. Amarnabriefe: Nrs. 83, 31, 40; Nrs. 85, 15, 22, 48ff. — ATAO, 380.

Egyptian Joseph does not seem to have been without precedence in Egyptian history. We have pictures of granaries and siloes, and helpless Beduins knocking at the gates of Egypt to beg for bread and grain.[15]

The investiture ritual through which Joseph passes in his installation as general administrator for the seven-year plan is quite in keeping with what we know elsewhere of Egyptian court ceremonial (Gn 41, 36ff.). The sage Rekh-mi-Re, from the time of Thutmose III (1502 − 1448), describes his formal investiture as follows: "I was a noble, second only to the Pharaoh .... It was my first meeting after my being called .... I made my way clad in fine linen .... When I came to the palace gate, the courtiers all bent their back before me .... My whole being of yesterday was transformed since I became the mouth of Maat (goddess of justice) .... He gave me judgment and full power .... There is no one to resist me." [16]

The investiture with this new official power is accompanied by a corresponding change in name: *Saphenat-pa'neah*, apparently a transliteration of the Egyptian *dd.p'.ntr ivef 'nh*, that is, "God speaks: he lives!" In order to elevate Joseph to a position of nobility in keeping with his rank, he is betrothed to a daughter of the priest of On, Asenat, a name which corresponds to the Egyptian Ivs NT − "She belongs to the goddess Neit." Joseph thus has access to the highest circles of Egyptian society. Among the viziers, however, we cannot find the name of Joseph. It is possible that he had yet a third name. (There are many parallels to suggest this. Perhaps something like "Supreme mouth of the land," a title which we actually find in the 18th to the 20th dynasties, and which would fit in well enough with the Biblical narrative.)[17]

---

15. ATAO (1930), 381.
16. J. A. Wilson, ANET (1950), 212ff.
17. Josef M. A. Janssen, *Fonctionaires sémites au service de l'Egypte*. In *Chronique d'Egypte*, Brussels, 26 (1951), 50-62, shows that the Ramessids entrusted especially the Asiatics with their high positions of special trust. According to Gn 41, 43, Pharaoh orders that Joseph be greeted with the cry: *abrek*. In the Karatepe inscription we find the word *auarakus* (Akkadian: *ABARAQQU*, Sumerian *LU-ABARAK-*

Equipped with this plenipotentiary power, Joseph now advances to his important work. The methods which he employs can be explained on the basis of the course of Egyptian history. As we have already explained, the Old Kingdom was a centralized bureaucracy. The sole owner of the land was the Pharaoh. In the first interregnum there were some significant changes in the ownership of the land. Side by side with the Pharaohs we find the district princes, who receive the land as a fief from the Pharaoh and administrate it independently. The Middle Kingdom is, accordingly, a sort of feudal state. The landowners of the New Kingdom are, once again, only the Pharaoh and the temples. The landed nobility has disappeared. We have very little information as to the manner in which this process took place. Many scholars think that the landed nobility had sided with the foreign Hyksos rulers and, after their expulsion, had been gradually dispossessed by the Pharaohs of the New Kingdom. This conclusion, however, is not convincing; it is not very probable that the whole of the Egyptian landed nobility should have sided with the foreign rulers. The transformation is rather to be explained by the fact that the Pharaohs of the New Kingdom, with their strongly reinforced central power, were in a good position to reestablish a sort of "juridic continuity" with the circumstances of the Old Kingdom. There is no doubt that Joseph had a very significant role to play in this process of economic transformation between the Middle and the New Kingdoms. When we read that during the famine Joseph bought all the land of Egypt for Pharaoh, "for all the Egyptians sold their fields because the famine was severe upon them" (Gn 47, 20), and that Joseph let the "people" into the cities, this does not mean that he made a proletariat of the free peasants, since there had never been such a class in Egypt in our sense of the word; this would be to misunderstand the Biblical text. "People," in this context, once again refers to the

---

KU) in the meaning of "high official." *Abrek* thus means something like major-domo, "vizier of the kingdom." Upon hearing this cry, all were ordered to bow before Joseph. Cf. J. Herrmann, in ZATW 62 (1949/50), 321.

landed nobility.[18] Their moving into the city was probably bound up with their formal entry into the service of the Pharaoh, so that he would have a firmer grasp upon his officials. The rent arrangement is nowhere precisely noted on the Egyptian monuments; but we are surely not far wrong in supposing that it must have been at least a fifth of the harvest, and this is a sum which cannot be considered inordinately high, since even the peasants who were bondsmen on the larger properties were enlisted in the work (47, 24). By this centralization of administration and agriculture Joseph attempted to gain the upper hand over the impending disaster.[19]

The famine, when it came, also devastated the neighboring territories of Palestine and Syria. Thus, after a time, the family of Jacob also made their way to the gates of Egypt (Gn 42, 1ff.).

D) THE IMMIGRATION OF JACOB'S FAMILY INTO EGYPT

The text, already quoted in connection with Abraham, from the burial of Beni-Hassan,[20] establishes the fact that Asiatic Beduins frequently came to Egypt in search of help or commerce. The records of the frontier posts from a later era afford a clearer perspective. Papyrus Anastasi VI, from the end of the 19th dynasty (1345 — 1200 B.C.) contains this message: "The scribe Inena informs his master: . . . I have completed the mission entrusted to me . . . and I did not delay. I have just attended to the transfer of the Beduin tribes from Edom at the fortress of Mer-ne-ptah in Hotep-hir-Maat — life, prosperity, and health! — to Per-Atum (probably the Biblical Pithom) . . . so that they and their flocks can stay alive through the grace

---

18. The word "people" (Hebrew 'am) also refers to the controlling Hittite ruling class in Hebron, Gn 23, 7, 11, 13; also in 2 S 16, 18; 2 K 11, 18-20; 14, 21; 23, 30, 35. / VD 12 (1932), 333-336; 371-373: Circa Hebraeorum in Aegypto commonatione. Joseph in Aegypto.
19. Junker, Genesis (1949), 134ff.
20. Ibid., 30.

of the great Ka of the Pharaoh — life, prosperity, and health! — the good sun of all lands ...." [21]

When Joseph's brothers make their way into Egypt in order to buy grain and when, finally, the whole family together with the aged Jacob immigrates into Egypt, this is only one small act in the drama that must have been played over and over again in times of famine and crisis along the Egyptian frontier. Other immigrations are known to us only through the brief notice taken by the frontier officers, but the Bible, in its masterful narrative, provides us with an insight into the family tragedy which is played against this Ancient Near Eastern background.

The noble character of Joseph appears against the background in its true grandeur. He is not thinking of vengeance; he forgives all that is past with the magnanimous words: "You meant evil against me, but God meant it for good, to bring it about that many people should be kept alive" (Gn 50, 20). Through Joseph's intercesssion with the Pharaoh, Israel is settled in the land of Goshen (Gn 47, 1), a territory that had, in previous times of crisis, also been put at the disposal of Asiatic Beduins, to serve both as pastureland [22] and dwelling. The location is most likely to be identified with Wadi Tumilat, [23] in the eastern

---

21. Selections in ANET (1950), 258: *The Journal of a Frontier Official;* 259: *The Report of a Frontier Official.*

22. ANET: records of Beduin settlement: 258ff.

23. The Land of Goshen is called the "Land of Ramses" (Gn 47, 11) from the point of view of a later era, since in the days of Joseph the city of Ramses, or Pi-Ramses, that is, "house of Ramses," did not yet exist. It was the residence city built by Ramses II (1301-1234) and called by his name in the Delta, the city the Israelites were forced to work at building. It must be located in the eastern Delta. Its position was first sought at Pelusium, later it was identified with the Hyksos capital of Tanis-Avaris-Zoan. T. Montet, *Le drama d'Avaris* (1940), 116ff. But since, according to an ancient Egyptian geographical document, Zoan is distinguished from Pi-Ramses and in Zoan no palace of Ramses II has been excavated, the city of Ramses is generally sought today some 15 miles south of Tanis-Avaris-Zoan, in the vicinity of modern Qantir. B. Couroyet, RB 53 (1946), 75ff. In the immediate and distant vicinity of this city we must, accordingly, locate the Land of Goshen, as far south as the Wadi Tumilat.

Nile Delta. The Israelites are settled here along the margin of the Egyptian territories, for shepherds are an abomination to the Egyptians (Gn 46, 34). Here we have an expression of the ancient Egyptian sense of superiority which looked upon these Asiatic sand-dwellers as cultureless barbarians. The family of Jacob was allowed to live in this territory during the time of the famine, but it remained there in Egypt even after the crisis had passed. Soon it grew into a mighty people, until a change in the political situation forced a violent withdrawal from Egypt.

E) JACOB'S BLESSING

After a rich life, in which Jacob had experienced God's special blessing, he became ill. He now proceeds to pass on to his own sons the blessing which he had received from Abraham through Isaac. In order to emphasize Joseph's preeminent position, he adopted his two sons Ephraim and Manasseh in such a way that it was not the first-born Manasseh, but the younger brother Ephraim, who received the privileged blessing. The succession of the blessing is not always bound up with the strict primogeniture (Gn 48, 1-22).

The "blessing of Jacob" upon his twelve sons is both a blessing and a judgment. "Chapter 49 of Genesis presents a picture of great magnitude and beauty: The aged patriarch Jacob has gathered his twelve sons around his deathbed in order to take leave of them and give them his final blessing. Carried away by his prophetic spirit, a prerogative that the dying are frequently held to possess in ancient belief, he announces the fate and destiny of his sons; the solemn oracle is the epilogue of his life and the prologue of the history of the people of the twelve tribes." [24]

The blessing was not spoken by the dying Jacob upon his twelve sons in the artistic and poetic form familiar from our modern Biblical text. An originally shorter and simpler tradition of the last twelve words of blessing for each of his sons

---

24. J. Obersteiner, *Die Christusbotschaft des AT* (1947), 43.

was later cast into poetic form and partially enlarged by references to the historical fate of each of the individual sons.[25]

The words spoken over the first three sons are a judgment: Reuben is declared to have lost his right as first-born because of his incest with Bilhah (Gn 35, 22). The double portion to which the first-born had a claim is given instead to Joseph by the adoption of his two sons. The next two brothers, Simeon and Levi, receive a curse instead of a blessing. In order to avenge their sister Dinah, they had acted treacherously towards the Shechemites and taken an inhuman revenge (Gn 34). Just as he had on the immediate occasion of their unwarranted violence, the patriarch once again, in his dying moments, refuses them any portion by denying the pair of them any claim to a definite territorial district of their own (Gn 49, 3-7).

Next the dying man's eye lights upon his fourth son Judah, who is destined to achieve dominion over his brothers. In the great posterity of Judah, in the Messiah, this dominion over the twelve tribes enlarges into a dominion over all the peoples of the world. Judah's position of rule is described in the figure of the lion:

"Judah, your brothers shall praise you;
Your hand shall be on the neck of your enemies;
Your father's sons shall bow down before you.
Judah is a lion's whelp;
From the prey, my son, you have gone up.
He stoops down, he couched as a lion,
And as a lioness; who dares rouse him up?"

The blessing on Judah begins with a play on words: The name Judah is compared with the verb hôdah, "to praise." The fullness of praise devolves upon him. Judah is like the lion who comes down to the stream where all the animals of the wilderness come to drink, takes the best portion for himself, and then

---

25. Cf. also the oracles on Simeon, Levi, Zebulun, Issachar, which already speak in terms of the territories occupied by these tribes after the conquest of Canaan.

returns into his den from which no one dares to disturb him. He alone, among all his brothers, is promised the uncontested position of ruler.

The fulfillment of this prophetic blessing was prepared for by the fact that the tribe of Judah had always taken on a privileged position and had also distinguished itself by deeds of bravery. In the arrangement of the camp and during the trek through the wilderness, Judah always occupied the van (Nb 2, 3; 10, 5, 14). Also, on the occasion of the sacrifice offered by the tribal heads after the consecration of the new tabernacle, Judah went first (Nb 7, 12). When, after the death of Joshua, the sons of Israel asked the Lord who was to go first and be their leader in war, the answer was that Judah shall go first because the land had been given into his hand (Jg 1, 1). This prophecy was first fulfilled in David, of the tribe of Judah, whom God called to rule over Israel, and with whose family he intimately bound up the world dominion of the Messiah to come (2 S 7, 16). It was David, too, who victoriously overcame the enemies of Israel, establishing peace for his kingdom from every side. But the true depth of meaning inherent in this promise is exhausted only by Revelation 5, 5: "The lion from Judah has conquered, the root of David." Through him the earlier victories over the surrounding hostile tribes have become a victory over death, sin and hell, and the allegiance of all mankind.

The dying patriarch gives Judah the assurance that his position of dominion will last forever and will introduce a period of paradise restored. The prince to come is also the bringer of paradise:

49, 10: "The scepter shall not depart from Judah,
        nor the ruler's staff from between his feet,
        until he comes to whom it belongs;
        and to him shall be the obedience of the peoples.
    11: Binding his foal to the vine
        and his ass' colt to the choice vine,
        he washes his garments in wine
        and his vesture in the blood of grapes;
    12: His eyes shall be red with wine,
        and his teeth white with milk" (Gn 49, 10-12).

In the history of Scriptural exegesis, verse 10b has been variously interpreted: "'ad ki-yâbô šiloh." The first three words are clear enough: "'ad ki-yâbô — until he comes." The controversy ranges round the word "šiloh."

a) "Until he comes." Does the use of the word "until" mean to designate a final terminus, in the sense that Judah's dominion must come to an end before the Messiah comes? This prophecy would then have been fulfilled by the fact that, on the one hand, the Romans had put an end to Judah's autonomy and given the royal power to Herod the Idumaean, and on the other hand, Christ was born four decades later. This interpretation cannot be substantiated on philological grounds; neither does it correspond to the actual course of history, and it is radically opposed to the Biblical conception of the eternal dominion of the royal house of David.

The Hebrew word *'ad* (until) means, in its temporal sense, not the boundary point at which a condition ceased, but the point of time up to which it will continue. Whether or not this is also the final point, the point at which the condition ceases, is to be determined on the basis of other criteria (cf. 2 S 6, 23; Ps 109, 1; Mt 1, 25).

The rule of Judah, seen from the vantage point of profane history, did not come to an end shortly before the birth of Christ, at the hands of the Romans, but some 600 years earlier, at the hands of Babylon. The later period of autonomy under the Hasmoneans cannot be appealed to in this question simply because these princes were not from the tribe of Judah, but rather from Levi.

From the vantage point of salvation history, the rule of the house of David has no end; God had assured David, through the prophet Nathan, that his throne would last forever, for all time. The prophet, in his speech to David (2 S 7, 15ff.), pointed to the subsequent unworthiness of the royal house of David and called attention to the punishment that was deserved. But even though this punishment is actually destined to result in the loss of political autonomy, Nathan nonetheless expressly declares that the rule is not to be taken from the family of David, that throne and kingdom alike are securely promised to his posterity forever; they will be chastised, however, in human measure. The loss of the rule is, accordingly, in the prophetic conception of things, simply a brief intermezzo which is destined entirely to disappear in comparison to the eternal duration of David's throne; the right to rule never departs from the family. Jacob's blessing oracle thus has a partially prophetic perspective which transcends space and time and focuses on the essence.

b) *"Šiloh"* — Whereas the reading of the first three words is definitely established, the interpretation of *"šiloh"* involves some controversy. Most improbable of all is the solution which takes *šiloh* for the name of a place: "Until he comes to Shiloh." Shiloh, a city in the Tribe of Ephraim, was, in the first period after the Israelite possession of the land, a focal point of the Israelite tribal federation and the honored repository of the Ark of the Covenant. The solution suggested by this interpretation is that Judah was to hold a position of rule over the tribes until after the conquest of the promised land had dissolved their federation. But this offers no explanation for the messianic and eschatological character of the rest of the verses. The Vulgate translates *qui mittendus est* which is based on an erroneous derivation from the Hebrew word *"šalah"* — to send: "Until he comes who is to be sent." More defensible, but still far from definite, is the claim that *šiloh* is a contraction of the word *še'ilô*: "his longed for one, his prayed for one" (that is, the Messiah). A more recent explanation derives the word from a Hebrew verb *šil* (ruler), which is a cognate of the Akkadian word *šêlu* (prince, splendid ruler), and, correspondingly, translates as follows: "Until his ruler comes, to whom the peoples give obedience."

Of the many textual emendations there is one that deserves particular attention because it is supported by the reading in many Hebrew and Samaritan manuscripts as well in the traditions of the Greek Septuagint, the Syriac translations and the Targum, and has a parallel in Ezekiel 21, 32. In this emendation we read *šellô* instead of *šiloh*, and translate: "Until he comes to whom it belongs" (or is fitting), that is, the sceptre or the ruling power, whose permanent duration in Judah is being promised. This manner of expression can be explained from the figure of the ruler on his throne whose mark of authority is not a short scepter such as we might be familiar with, but the long ruler's staff known to the Ancient Near East which was held in the hand while it rested on the ground "between the feet." [26]

The conclusion of this blessing oracle represents the paradise of the future which the messianic rule will bring to pass. The land pours forth its most precious gifts in prodigal abundance, the fruit of the vine and the blessing of the flocks, wine and milk in abundance, images which we will once again encounter in the later prophetic literature (Am 9, 13).

The oracle on Joseph, in its compass and significance, forms a counterpoint to the oracle on Judah, corresponding to the preeminent position of Joseph in the circle of the twelve brethren. At the same time, in his two sons, he is assured the double portion of the first-born; but the position of rule which is normally conferred together with the privilege of the first-born, remains with Judah. In Joseph's case, however, Jacob is not sparing with his prophetic blessings (Gn 49, 22, 26). Joseph is compared to a fruitful vineyard, whose "branches run over the wall." [27] Next comes the image of the archer and his arrow

---

26. Junker, *op. cit.*, 140.
27. The literal translation in the Vulgate: *"Filiae discurrerunt super murum"* would be unintelligible. It is not just "daughters" that the text refers to, but the vines that grow up over the walls. / J. M.

and the mighty warrior whose hands remain agile, because he receives his strength from "the strong one of Jacob," that is, from the God of Jacob. It is God himself who had established Joseph as "the shepherd and refuge of Israel." In all his degradation he had still felt the power of God's blessing which was at work within him by reason of his belonging to the patriarchal family:

"The blessings of your father are mighty
    beyond the blessings of the eternal mountains,
    the bounties of the everlasting hills.
May they be on the head of Joseph,
    and on the brow of him who is separate from his brothers."
                                   (Gn 49, 26)

The "desire (gifts and blessings) of the eternal mountains and the bounties of the everlasting hills" are a picturesque description of the bounty of the promised land. The reference is to wine as the gift of the mountains and the milk of the flocks as the gift of the hills rich in pastureland, just as in the oracle to Judah. These forms of expression are meant as a reference to the landscape of Palestine where the promised blessings have already proved effective for the fathers and are now promised to continue into the future through the posterity of Joseph. "The bounties of the everlasting hills" is an expression which thus departs from the mysterious ambiguity of the distant past into the full simplicity of typical Ancient Near Eastern expression.[28]

Allegro, *A Possible Mesopotamian background to the Joseph Blessing of Gn 49*, ZATW 64 (1952), 249-251.

---

28. "The longing of the everlasting hills" goes back to the literal but meaningless translation of the Vulgate: "*desiderium collium aeternorum*," which is, once again, dependent upon the Septuagint. A proper translation is possible only in the light of the full context. Verse 26 can be interpreted as a protasis-apodosis: "Just as your father experienced the fullness of blessing, so shall Joseph also experience blessing in rich measure." The protasis is a further resumé of the life experience of Jacob. "The blessings of your father" should be taken as meaning "the blessing given to your father," that is, the

It is precisely by this process that the expression takes on its true grandeur; it is the very best thing that the dying head of a semi-nomadic family can wish to the chosen son. With his dying eye Joseph looks once again at that land of longing that God had promised to Abraham and to his seed, a promise destined to become reality in his sons.

Jacob's blessing is characterized by its language rich in imagery, and the many comparisons taken from the world of animals. Judah is a lion (49, 9), Issachar is a strong ass (49, 14), Dan is a serpent along the way (49, 17), Benjamin is a ravenous wolf (49, 27). These animal images may not have been the product of his own free invention; perhaps they are a poetic explanation of later heraldic animals which served as an occasion to fire the imagination of the later writer who describes the patriarchal blessing, which, in its prophetic view of the future, already unveils the events of the end-time (49, 1).

After Jacob had thus passed on the blessing of his fathers upon his sons, he requested that his remains be not buried in foreign soil, but in the patriarchal grave at Hebron (Gn 49, 29 — 50, 26). This same request is later addressed by Joseph to his brothers; upon their return into the land of their fathers they are to bring along his remains and inter them in his native

---

blessing of Isaac and Abraham (cf. Ex 3, 6). This blessing was not simply a ceremonial without any power; it contained an inherent power which is expressed in the Hebrew word *gabar,* "to be strong, powerful, mighty," just as in Ps 116/117, 2 the grace of the Lord is shown as powerful (*gabar*) (*quoniam confirmata est super nos misericordia eius*). The blessing of the fathers was primarily a blessing of fertility upon the land (Gn 27, 28). It is along this same line of thought that we must interpret the mysterious longing of the everlasting hills. — The "longing" is the second part of a Hebrew parallelism, corresponding to the "blessings" in the first half of the verse, and thus it is to be understood as a more precise statement of essentially the same thing. *Ta'awâh,* however, does not mean only "longing," but also "that which is longed for, something precious." The "longing of the everlasting hills" thus means, literally, nothing more than "the precious objects, the rich bounty" of the Palestinian mountain country, a figure in which the words "eternal and of old" are

soil (50, 25). "So Joseph died, being a hundred and ten years old; and they embalmed him, and he was put into a coffin in Egypt" (50, 26). Despite their privileged position in Egypt, Israel's whole longing is for Canaan where alone God has promised them the security of a country of their own.

---

not be pressed. In a logical progression of this prophetic symbolism and language, we can certainly look beneath the earthly blessing and its gifts to discover the fullness of the messianic bounties and salvation.

CHAPTER V

THE CHRONOLOGY OF THE PATRIARCHAL ERA

1) *Numerical symbolism*: The Bible appears to give a precise date for Israel's entry into Egypt. The point of departure for the reckoning is the building of the Temple under Solomon, 969 B.C. Now the Bible, in 1 Kings 6, 1, states that the building of the Temple began 480 years after the Exodus from Egypt; according to Exodus 12, 40, however, "the time that the people of Israel dwelt in Egypt was 430 years." In the prophetic promise made to Abraham (Gn 15, 13), we learn that "his descendants will be sojourners in a land that is not theirs, and will be slaves there, and they will be oppressed for 400 years." But this is certainly not a contradiction of the number 430, since it is only a question of round numbers. If we take the death of the patriarch Jacob as the beginning of the 430 years of Israel's sojourn in Egypt, so that from that date until the building of the Temple 480 + 430 = 910 years must have passed, then Jacob's death must have taken place in the year 1879 B.C.

From this point of reckoning the rest of the patriarchal era can easily be controlled. Jacob was 147 years old at his death (Gn 47, 28); Isaac was 60 years old when Jacob was born (Gn 25, 26) and Abraham was 100 years old at the birth of Isaac.

The date of Abraham's birth would thus be (147 + 60
+ 100) 307 years before the death of Jacob, that is 1879
+307) the year 2187 B.C. Since according to Genesis 12, 4,
Abraham was 75 years old when he went from Haran into
Canaan, Abraham's immigration into Canaan must have taken
place in 2111 B.C. This year must, accordingly, serve as the
beginning of the patriarchal era, which would then have lasted
from 2111 to 1879 B.C. Since Jacob was 130 years old when
the family settled in Egypt (Gn 47, 9), Israel's immigration
into Egypt would have to be dated in the year 1896 B.C.

These facts involve serious and insoluble contradictions
with the data of profane history and archaeology unless the
scholar recognizes the symbolic character of these numbers.
For this grand outline of Biblical chronology, it seems that
the Temple of Solomon is the point of reference. Corresponding
to the 12 tribes of Israel, who had made a special covenant with
Yahweh and worshipped him in the Temple of Jerusalem, the
number 12 seems to determine the whole structure of the chronology. This structure is clearly enough evidence if we set up
our dates, not in terms of BC dating as we have above, but
on the basis of the information furnished by the Bible itself.
If we count as our first year the creation of Adam in Paradise,
we get the following outline,

987: Henoch taken up into heaven.
1974 (= 2 x 987): Tower of Babel and Call of Abraham.
2454 (1974 + 480): Exodus and Building of Tabernacle.
2934 (2454 + 480): Building of Temple under Solomon.
3414 (2934 + 480): Building of Second Temple.[1]

Since the call of Abraham the history of the world proceeds

1. A. Jeremias, ATAO (1930), 125: The number 480 at the Exodus
   is arrived at by taking the 50 years in Haran together with the 430
   years of the sojourn in Egypt as the first unit of twelve 12 x 40 =
   480. This interpretation seems to be supported by the fact that the
   215 years since Abraham's entry into Canaan until the entry of Jacob
   into Egypt are precisely one half the sojourn in Egypt, 430 years.
   This conclusion is certainly not forcing; but it is very possible.

along a rhythm of 480 years, with the individual epochs clearly marked off. This number can be resolved into 12 x 40 = 480; since 40 is the number of a generation, we are dealing with 12 generations each time, as comprising an entire epoch. At the beginning of each individual epoch stands some particular intervention on the part of God: Paradise — the taking up of Henoch — the call of Abraham — Ark of the Covenant — first and second Temple. It is also possible that this rhythm based on the number 12 has been suggested by the primordial rhythm of the stars themselves, by the 12 months in the solar year. The essential point of view of this artistic construction of numerical values would thus seem to lie not so much in the individual datings, but rather in the great mystery that the course of world history lies in the hands of God, who, after the conclusion of each epoch, inaugurates the beginning of a new world-year through a new revelation. This fact, and the obviously symbolic character of the numbers, makes it abundantly clear that the figures have no possible bearing upon the chronological structure of history. We are forced to turn elsewhere for a chronological control.

2) TRIBAL HISTORY AS AN INTERPRETATION: This interpretation is in no better position to reckon with the actual numbers supplied by Scripture. It is true that Noth [2] ascribes a certain measure of historicity to the "patriarchs" insofar as he recognizes that, at sacred cult places, they were the recipients of divine promises regarding the future possession of a country of their own. This was already in the era in which the Israelite "tribes," which were established as such only in Canaan, were still nomadic Beduins in the Syrian and Arabian steppe. "Patriarchal figures" also traveled with the tribes and the revelations made to them were later localized at Palestinian sanctuaries. But this explanation deprives us of every conceivable chronological control over the patriarchal figures, who have now vanished into the dim light of pre-history. For the sojourn in Egypt there would be one approximate chronological fix, since the Hebrews

2. M. Noth, *Geschichte Israels* (1950): *Die Erzväter*, 105ff.

were forced to work on the construction of the cities of Pithom and Ramses, whereupon they left the country; but only a very brief portion of the Israelite tribes would have been in Egypt. According to Rowley, the tribes of Simeon and Levi came into Egypt after their earlier attempt to establish themselves in Palestine had proved a failure at Shechem (Gn 34). It would be shortly prior to this time that Joseph rose to his position of power and prominence under Pharaoh Ikhnaton (1377 — 1358) during the Amarna era.[3] Both authors deny any connection with the Hyksos invasions.[4]

3) ABRAHAM A CONTEMPORARY OF HAMMURABI?: Heinisch, in his *Geschichte des Alten Testaments*[5] argues for the hypothesis that Abraham was a contemporary of the famous Hammurabi, who is supposed to have reigned in the eighteenth century. Accordingly, Joseph would have made his way into Egypt at a time when the Hyksos had already established themselves there and risen to a position of power. Potiphar's wife speaks contemptuously of the "Hebrew" (Gn 39, 14, 17) as of a foreigner who had been brought into the country.

Since, according to the more recent chronology,[6] Hammurabi must be dated around 1728 — 1686 B.C., and the immigration into Egypt took place only in the 4th generation after Abraham, we would thus be forced to accept the very low date of 1550 B.C. But this would be clearly in contradiction with the already established facts of Abraham's history. Today, moreover, the identification Amraphel — Hammurabi has been completely given up,[7] as we have already discussed.[8] The chronology of the patriarchal era is thus left entirely to its own resources, since it cannot possibly be controlled by the regnal dates of the famous Babylonian ruler Hammurabi. But even though there are no fixed years and dates for the

---

3. H. H. Rowley, *From Joseph to Joshua* (1950), 116.
4. M. Noth, *Geschichte des AT* (1950), 72ff.
5. P. Heinisch, *Geschichte des AT* (1949), 53ff.
6. A. Moortgat, *Vorderasien bis zum Hellenismus* (1950), 493.
7. DBS (1947), fasc. XX, 733.
8. Cf. above: campaign against the kings from the east.

patriarchal era, the Biblical narrative itself, together with the results of Ancient Near Eastern archaeology and history, does provide sufficient points of reference to arrive at some reliable approximations.

If we take 1850 B.C. as an approximate date for Abraham, then the immigration into Egypt, after four generations, would fall in the era around 1700 B.C., an era in which the Hyksos sovereignty in Egypt was being established by peaceful Semitic immigrations. It is in connection with this Hyksos sovereignty that we can most easily explain the rapid rise of a Semitic "Hebrew" as imperial vizier; this hypothesis is also favored by the immediate vicinity of the Pharaoh's capitol city Avaris in the Nile Delta, so that Joseph's brothers could be admitted to audience (Gn 47, 1ff.) without first having to make their way to Thebes, the capital of the New Kingdom from about the year 1600 B.C., or to Amarna, the capitol city of Ikhnaton (1377 − 1358), up the Nile. The fact that Joseph is married to the daughter of a priest from Heliopolis, whereas the Hyksos worshipped not the sun god Re, but the Semitic god Seth (*suteh*), cannot be advanced as an argument against the Hyksos era,[9] since all usurpers make an effort to strengthen their position by marriage bonds with the older native nobility.[10] The fact that Joseph assumes an Egyptian name is further confirmed by the tendencies of the Hyksos rulers who certainly felt themselves to be native Egyptian Pharaohs. When, finally, the Israelites, upon the collapse of the Hyksos sovereignty, continue to remain in Egypt, this too is not a forcing argument against their original immigration to Egypt in connection with the Hyksos rise to power; for the Pharaohs of the New Kingdom were content to break the power of the ruling class without necessarily expelling all the Semitic elements from Egyptian territory. They considered themselves the legitimate successors of the Hyksos in the Asiatic spheres of influence and gradually began to incorporate the entire Semitic territory, from the borders of Egypt all the way to the Euphrates, by a series of vigorous wars.

9. H. H. Rowley, *op. cit.*, 26.
10. Cf. Napoleon's marriage with an Austrian princess.

The small Semitic tribe of the family of Jacob thus posed no threat to the plans for world sovereignty entertained by the Pharaohs of the New Kingdom. They were free to settle as they had in the land of Goshen, while the Pharaohs built their world capital in Upper Egypt, in Thebes. The turning point in this history occurs only when the center of power is once again concentrated on the Nile Delta, a project which involved the Israelites in forced labor at building the great cities; but this is a process which took place only in the era of the Ramessids (19th dynasty: 1345 − 1200 B.C.).

Meantime the family of Jacob was left in peace to continue its nomadic and pastoral existence, as it had done in Canaan, and to grow to considerable proportions. It is certainly most probable that throughout this long interval between their first entry into Egypt and their exodus from the country their ties with Canaan, the land of their origin, had never been entirely broken, that some connection had always been preserved with those members of the family who had been left behind,[11] especially if we recall that Jacob and Joseph each desired to be buried in the family plot at Hebron. Even if we assign only symbolic value to the Biblical number 430 years (Ex 12, 40), still the time of the sojourn in Egypt must comprise approximately 400 years.[12] The fact that we have no precise data for this long span of time is quite in keeping with the character

---

11. De Vaux, DBS (1947), fasc. XX, 735.
12. The "400 year stele" which dates from the time of Ramses I (1318-1317), first discovered by Marietta, then disappeared, and subsequently rediscovered by Montet in Tanis-Avaris, mentions the foundation of the city "400 years before Ramses I." Accordingly, the Hyksos capital in Egypt would have been founded around 1720 B.C. On the basis of this discovery, Albright (*The Archaeology of Palestine and the Bible* 1932, p. 143) postulates a specific Tanis Era some traces of which are to be found in the Bible; for according to Nb 13, 22, Hebron was founded seven years before Tanis. The 430 years of Ex 12, 40 must at all events be reckoned as coming after the Tanis Era. Israel's entry into Egypt would thus fall in the year 1720, and the Exodus would be dated 1290 B.C. Cf. Stock, *Studien zur Geschichte und Archäologie der 13-17, Dynastie Ägypten* (1942), 70. / For the use of the Tanis Era in biblical exegesis, cf. H. H. Rowley, *op. cit.*, 74ff.

of the Bible, which is a book of revelation and concerned only with religiously decisive moments in the course of history without making any attempt to present a more precise description in terms of profane history. Long intervals of time can thus be spanned without further concern, provided that they were without significance for the history of religion.

4) THE SIGNIFICANCE OF THE PATRIARCHAL ERA FOR BIBLICAL THEOLOGY: Our presentation has made it clear that the patriarchal era, in its entirety, can be neatly fitted into the course of Ancient Near Eastern history. Abraham's migration from Ur to Haran and from there into Canaan takes place in connection with the great Semitic wave of migrations which begins after the collapse of the 3rd dynasty of Ur (c. 1950) and includes the entire Fertile Crescent; similarly, the migration to Egypt takes place in perfect rhythm with the migrations of the Hyksos. What is new and exciting in the sphere of religion is simply the fact that, within this Semitic migration, Abraham's family is singled out and begins to embark upon a path exclusively its own. This special direction, moreover, is not to be explained by any consideration of contemporary economics; it is simply and solely a new religious foundation. It was not caused by any human deliberation, but solely and simply by the will of God which makes its own deliberate intervention into the course of human history. The patriarchal era is thus, in the last analysis, an institution, a testament of God.

At the beginning, this new element is hardly noticeable. Abraham does not give God any new name; he does not call upon him at any new site. Externally, there seems to be nothing essentially new. He sacrifices and prays at the Canaanite holy places, worships the supreme god El just as Melchizedek, and is even prepared to undertake the heroic act of child sacrifice, a ritual known to us from the Canaanite religion. Still there is evidence of something new. Abraham recognizes only the "almighty, eternal God," beside whom there is no other God. Jacob, upon his return from Mesopotamia, purges his family of every trace of idolatry and demonic cult by ordering all pagan amulets to be buried under the oak at Shechem. As this

faith in God develops in an increasingly pure form in the midst
of a paganism which is overgrown with mythology, the under-
lying concept and image of the divinity is, from the very outset,
intimately bound up with the faith in two great promises: the
possession of the land of Canaan and a posterity in which all
peoples of the earth are to be blessed. The one God of the
fathers thus becomes the God of promises. The patriarchal faith
is, accordingly, borne along by the impetus of its sense of
mission to the entire world. From the very beginning, the
patriarchal era is directed towards a universal relevance, leaving
every purely national consideration far behind.

And yet together with this world-wide character there is
also a progressively developing formation of the national individuality of Israel. Since Israel has a mission to the peoples,
she must first become "Israel." This concretization of universality
is a constantly developing concept from the call of Abraham
to the striking of the covenant, with circumcision as its external
sign. Following simply the line of blood descendance, the line
of Ishmael, Esau, etc., follows a separate development, while
the narrative concentrates solely on the bearers of the blessing.
Among the twelve, the blessing of leadership falls upon the
tribe of Judah, from whose blood is to be born the ruler of the
end-time, Christ. Thus we are justified in saying that the entire
patriarchal era develops towards Christ. Or, in other words,
we might say that the patriarchal era is a preparation for the
coming of Christ. Even though there is a veil lying heavy
upon these great figures of the inaugural era of Old Testament
religion, so that they never beheld the Christ, still each new
generation meant one step further along the road to the Incarnation of the great son of Abraham whose "day Abraham
saw and rejoiced in the spirit" (Jn 8, 56).

Investigations along the lines of form history have made
it progressively clearer that in this interpretation we are involved not so much with a retrospection of later theological
speculation, but rather the essential development of an original
idea.[13] The faith of the fathers belongs to the foundation of

---

13. Cf. H. Eising, *Formgeschichtliche Untersuchung zur Jakobserzählung*

the Old Testament religion. When Moses, acting upon a new impulse of divine revelation, proceeds to organize God's people upon Mount Sinai, this is not something essentially new; it is rather a further building on an old foundation which God had established in the person of the fathers; for Yahweh is none other than "the God of the fathers" (Ex 3, 13).

Finally, St. Paul draws his strongest arguments for the genuinity of Christianity from this patriarchal era, by demonstrating that the promises given to the fathers have been fulfilled in Jesus of Nazareth (Rm 4, 1ff.). Thus the divine activity described in the patriarchal era forms not only the foundation for the Old Testament religion, but also serves as basis for the religion of the New Testament. Both Testaments belong inseparably together. If we attempt to honor only one, we essentially lose both, because we have failed to recognize the bonds of salvation history that join the two together.[14] In our presentation of this era we have made every effort to present the patriarchs within the framework of Ancient Near Eastern history, and thus to cast whatever light we could upon the contemporary influences upon their lives and times. The patriarchs were men of the Ancient Near East, with all their strengths and weaknesses. But their transcendental greatness is achieved by the fact that God's call was upon them, transforming them into a new beginning of salvation history for all mankind.

---

der Genesis (1940): The patriarchal narratives are not the product of imaginary "collective powers"; they have been given shape and form by an individual author, who was not very far removed from the facts and events themselves. In unessential points his work was later reedited: in essential points, however, the Bible, even considered purely from the point of view of profane history, presents a genuine and trustworthy picture of the time it portrays (pp. 428ff).

---

14. On the internal connection and interdependence of Old and New Testaments, cf. Claus Schedl: *Sieben Thesen wider des Alten Testaments Verächter*, Vienna (1948). Vierte These: *Das Alte Testament ist Heilsgeschichte;* Fünfte These: *Das Alte Testament ist vom Neuen nicht zu trennen.*

MOSES AND THE COVENANT
OF THE TWELVE TRIBES

CHAPTER VI

THE EXODUS FROM EGYPT

LITERATURE

Martin Buber, *Moses*, 1948. / W. F. Albright, *From Stone Age to Christianity*, "The Religion of Moses" (1949), 249-272. / M. Noth, *Geschichte Israels*, 1950, "Der Bund von Sinai," 110ff. / H. H. Rowley, *From Joseph to Joshua*, 1950. / P. Montet, *Le Drame d'Avaris*, 1940.

Commentaries: P. Heinisch, *Das Buch Exodus*, 1934 (BB). *Das Buch Numeri*, 1936. / G. Beer, *Exodus*, 1939 (HAT).

A) ISRAEL IN EGYPT

Israel had made its way into Egypt as a small Beduin tribe of 70 men[1] (Ex 1, 5) and grew there, in an era of peace, to the proportions of a nation. Its spread had reached proportions that made it a source of anxiety to the new Pharaoh, who no

---

1. LXX, in Ex 1, 5; Gn 46, 27 and (depending on these texts) Acts 7, 14, gives the number as 75, counting a son and a grandson of Manasseh and two sons and one grandson of Ephraim together with Joseph. The number 70 clearly has a symbolic value and must not be pressed. The small number is, however, quite credible, since in the Semitic caravan of Beni Hassan (AOB 1927, no. 51) only 37 persons are counted. The domestics and followers are apparently not included in the court.

longer knew Joseph (Ex 1, 8). They were afraid that, in the event of war, Israel would go over to the enemy. In order to keep Israel in subjection, they began a deliberate policy of repression. The Israelites were forced to labor in the construction of the provisions' cities of Pithom and Ramses. When this failed to accomplish the desired results, the next step was the direct murder of newborn life. In this time of great national crisis there arose for the enslaved people a savior in the person of Moses, a man chosen to lead them from the bondage of Egypt, to take them to the very borders of the land of Canaan promised of old to their fathers. How are these Biblical narratives to be fitted into the framework of ancient Egyptian history?

Up to the present time, we have had no explicit testimony regarding the subject of Israel's being reduced to a position of forced laborers. This, however, is certainly not an argument against the historicity of this story. In the course of the dramatic history which was played along the Nile Delta, the case of Israel seems to have been only a small intermezzo.[2] At the time of the Middle Kingdom (2052 – 1778 B.C.), the era into which the patriarchal stories must be fitted, the eastern delta was a flourishing province with numerous towns and cities. The Hyksos era and the subsequent wars of liberation had reduced it to a desert solitude. The Pharaohs of the beginning New Kingdom (c. 1610 B.C.) looked upon the eastern delta primarily as a territory through which to direct their military campaigns against the lands of Asia Minor. Their center of power lay in the south, in the capital city of Thebes.

The Israelites were not the only Semites who knocked upon the gates of Egypt for help and food, were admitted, and continued to live after the manner of their fathers, in the Nile Delta. In the Middle Kingdom, even the Amu found a welcome in Egypt; they passed the Egyptian frontier walls (the royal walls) together with their herds. In the more recent era of the 18th dynasty (1570 – 1345 B. C.) a tribe pursued by its

---

2. For the history of the eastern Delta, cf. Montet, *Le drame d'Avaris*, Paris (1940).

enemies, a tribe already conquered and deprived of its weapons, reached the Egyptian frontier. They were given a place to settle with their wives, children, and flocks. Even later, under Seti II (1220) we have a record of a frontier official on the subject of the immigration of a tribe of Sasu.[3] The delta territory was thus a logical point of mustering for nomads from the bordering Asiatic lands who came to Egypt in search of bread and refuge.

When the Egyptian war of liberation against the Hyksos first began (c. 1570), not all the Semitic elements who had meantime settled in Egypt were driven out together with the Hyksos. The Pharaohs rested content with simply breaking the power of the "foreign rulers," but many Semitic characteristics continue to assert themselves in the New Kingdom. Most striking of all is the continuing and increasing cult of the god Seth, whose closest similarities are to the Semitic god Baal. The Pharaohs showed little interest in expelling the Beduins, and among them the Israelites who had come into Egypt with any warlike intentions. Texts from the time of Harmhab and Seti II (19th dynasty: 1345 − 1200) would suggest the hypothesis that the land of Goshen was made available to these immigrants by royal decree.[4]

The situation in the delta was changed only when the Pharaohs began to build up the eastern delta as the center of their kingdom. They were forced to erect new cities from the bare ground in a desolated land of ruins. Architects, masons, and stone cutters were in great supply in ancient Egypt; what was needed here was a supply of unskilled labor to prepare the building materials, and to supply the bricks that were necessary for the magnificent royal buildings. In this historical situation, it is easy enough to explain the use of the Israelites as forced laborers.

The Pharaoh under whom the policy towards the Hebrew settlers underwent such significant changes is to be identified

---

3. "Tagebuch eines Grenzbeamten" in TGI, 32ff. − And in ANET: "The Journal of a Frontier Official" and "The Report of a Frontier Official," 258ff.

4. P. Montet, *Le drame d'Avaris* (1940), 143-145.

as Ramses II (1301 — 1234), builder of the supply cities of Pithom and Ramses. The first official measures reduce the formerly free Israelites to the position of serfs and, like the Canaanites under King Solomon (1 K 9, 20), were put to work as forced laborers on the public buildings. Of the two cities at which the Israelites were forced to work, Pithom (house of the god Tum — Atum) has been identified as Tell Retabe in the Wadi Tumilat [5] and Ramses (the full form is *Per-Re'emasese* — "house of the Ramessids") has been identified as modern Qantir, both sites which were either built or rebuilt by Ramses II. These "cities of Ramses" flourished for two centuries (1300 — 1100 B.C.). In a panegyric on the glories of this new residence for the Pharaohs, it is called "great in victory," "victorious," a name which even the modern capital of Egypt still bears: Cairo, Arabic *Kahira,* that is, "the victorious one." [6]

The building material was the black mud of the Nile, which, after being thoroughly worked and mixed with straw or sand and molded in forms, was dried in the sun. The statement that Pithom and Ramses were planned as store-cities (Ex 1, 11) seems perfectly credible. For during the battles for world dominion which were carried on in Syria and Palestine by the Pharaohs of the 18th and 19th dynasties, the cities situated in the Delta had an important role to play in maintaining the Egyptian armies.

In addition to their work in building the cities, the Israelites were forced to work in the fields, particularly the monotonous and laborious task of irrigating the soil through a series of

5. Albright, *From Stone Age to Christianity* (1949), 255. / The earlier view represented by Naville, that Pitnom is the ruins excavated in the Wadi Tumilat, the site of El Mashuta, has been abandoned today, in favor of an identification with Succoth.
6. Songs for the City of Ramses by Erman, *Literatur der Ägypter,* 261ff, 337ff. / Gressmann, AOT (1926), 106. / J. Wilson, ANET (1960), 470ff. — Mummified head of Ramses II in AOB (1927), 99-100. Store building in Pitom in AOT (1930), S. 383. / P. Montet, *Les énigmes de Tanis* (1952), (Tanis = Avaris = Ramsesstadt). / B. Couroyer, *La résidence ramesside du Delta et le Ramses biblique* (Ramsesstadt = Qantir, 15 mi. S of Tanis). RB 53 (1946), 75-98.

water wheels that were operated by foot (Dt 11, 10). Perhaps the notice in Exodus 1, 13: "So they made the people of Israel serve with rigor" is to be understood as a degradation of the Israelites not only to the position of forced laborers, but actually slaves. But the attempt to break the national strength of Israel by forced labor was not a success. The more their slavery was increased the more powerful the nation grew. There was some sort of power bound up with this foreign people that far surpassed the capacities of the native deities, and the Egyptians came to fear it.[7] The oppression, moreover, also served to rekindle Israel's longing for the land of promise prophesied to the patriarchs. This "faith of the fathers," to which Moses solemnly appeals, reawakens, in this crisis, to a new pitch of fervor and becomes the true motive impulse behind the Exodus.

B) THE CALL OF MOSES
(Ex 2, 1 — 7, 7)

Moses, the specially called leader of the people, was providentially prepared by God for his work of liberation. His youth falls in a time of intense national oppression. In order to save his life, his mother exposes him in a basket on the Nile. He is rescued by the daughter of the Pharaoh, adopted by her, and educated in all the wisdom of the Egyptians.[8]

---

7. Beer-Galling, *Exodus* (1939), S. 16ff.
8. There is a striking parallel to the story of Moses' childhood in the childhood of Sargon I of Akkad (c. 2350). It is preserved in two Assyrian and one Babylonian recensions: "Sargon, the mighty king, king of Agade, am I. My mother was a changeling (a pauper), my father I knew not. The brothers of my father loved the hills. My city is Azupiranu, which is situated on the banks of the Euphrates. My changeling mother conceived me, in secret she bore me. She set me in a basket of rushes, with bitumen she sealed my lid. She cast me into the river which rose not over me. The river bore me up and carried me to Akki, the drawer of water. Akki, the drawer of water, lifted me out as he dipped his ewer. Akki, the drawer of water, took me as his son and reared me. Akki, the drawer of water, appointed me as his gardener. While I was a gardener, Ishtar granted me her

The Bible derives the name Moses in terms of popular etymology from the Hebrew verb *mašah* — "to draw out." The princess says: "I have drawn him out from the water" (*mešitihû*). *Môšeh* is an active participle and therefore means not "the one drawn out," but rather "the one who draws out"; it may well be that the Hebrew speaker heard an echo of the words "liberator." At all events, what we are facing here is the impossibility of explaining what was originally an Egyptian name in terms of some possible Hebrew meaning.

Even in antiquity some attempts were made to derive the name of Moses from the ancient Egyptian. Flavius Josephus (Ant. 2, 9, 6; Cont. Ap. 1, 31) and Philo (Life of Moses) divide the word into two elements: *Mô* (water) and *yses* (saved, preserved); this solution has little philological justification. The most probable derivations are the following: a. Moses is compounded from *Mô* (water) and *še* (stream, sea), with *Mô* having the transferred sense of "seed, child," and *še* referring to the Nile. Moses is thus simply "child of the Nile."[9] — b. There is greater probability for the derivation from *Ms(w)* or *mesu* (son) which occurs frequently as an element in the names of the Pharaohs: Ptah-mose, Tuth-Mose, Ra-mose, that is, son of the god Ptah, Tuth, Ra. In common usage, accordingly, the abbreviated form was more common, with the divine name being dropped. In the case of Moses, the full form of the name would involve the river god Nile.[10]

Since he was reared at the Pharaoh's court, Moses was spared the forced labor. Still he does not lose his close ties with his enslaved fellow citizens. It is an insight into his character that, in the grips of a righteous anger, he kills an Egyptian overseer who had just killed a Hebrew worker, thereby avenging his death with death (Ex 2, 12; 21, 23). Nobody would have dared to rebel against the all-powerful knout of the Pharaoh. That is why Moses' act is misunderstood even by his own countrymen.

---

love, and for four and (. . . .) years I exercised kingship. The black-headed people I ruled . . . ." ANET (1950), 119, "The Legend of Sargon."

---

9. A. S. Yasuda, *Die Sprache des Pentateuch*, I, 251-254.
10. Montet, *Le drame d'drame d'Avaris* (1940), 148ff. / Papyrus Anastasi I, 18, 2, contains the statement: "It is not good for Mose to hear this; he will punish you." Pap. Salt 124, 2, 17: "He lodged a complaint against the vizier before Mose who had removed him from his vizier's office." The texts date from the Ramessid era. Mose is the shorter form of the name of the Pharaoh.

The time for revolt is not yet. He is forced to flee. His deed shines out like the distant lightning of a threatening storm. At the very beginning of his career, Moses performs an act with important social consequences for his people; it will prove to be characteristic for his entire life.[11]

Moses flees across the Egyptian frontier, following the same path that many a political refugee before him had been forced to take, as we can see in the story of the flight of Sinuhe. He finds temporary refuge with the Midianites, where he marries Zipporah, daughter of the priest Reuel (Ex 2, 18), who, in Exodus 3, 1, is also called Jethro. Both names refer to the same person, the one apparently being his official name as a priest, while the other is his personal name (re'u-'el — friend of God; Yitro, Arabic watrun — excellency). In Midian Moses leads the life of the nomadic Beduins, driving his flocks from one pasture to another. On one such journey the call and mission of God overtakes him in the vicinity of Mount Sinai. He could not possibly have been, at that time, a man of 80 years, since the life of Moses is compressed within the symbolic generation scheme of 40 years. His actual age is better determined by some further evidence furnished by the text. Upon his return into Egypt he wants to bring his wife and children with him (Ex 4, 24), but is forced to leave them behind with his father-in-law, who brings them back to him after the Exodus from Egypt (Ex 18, 1). This would mean that they had not yet grown, but were still children. Moses' sojourn in Midian could, accordingly, have lasted for 10 years at the very most. His violent murder of the Egyptian overseer is more reasonably explained as the deed of a young man caught up in a fit of anger. Moses enters upon his great mission at full maturity, rather than at the approach of old age.

The decisive impulse which prompts the beginning of this new phase in the life of Moses is something that we find repeated again and again in the life of political refugees. The death of the old ruler and a change in the political power have always afforded the refugee a new hope for his return. The same thing

11. Beer-Galling, Ex 22.

happened in the case of Moses. "After many days that Pharaoh died" (Ex 2, 23); the Israelites began to hope for a lessening of their oppression. Moses too may have entertained some notion of returning and once again taking up the work of liberation he had begun. This was the moment at which he, in purely human terms, was prepared for the encounter with the divine. God meets with this man and opens up some unheard of horizons for his future.

Fire suddenly emanates from a thorn bush, without the bush itself being consumed. Moses boldly attempts to get a closer view of the marvel, but is warned by a mysterious voice that it is a holy place. Moses is struck with awe at the closeness of the divinity. He takes his shoes from his feet. The *Mal'ak Yahweh* appears to him in the form of fire (Ex 3, 2) and speaks in the name and person of Yahweh himself (Ex 3, 4ff.). Moses hears himself called: "Moses, Moses!" He answers: "Here I am" (Ex 3, 4ff.). Now the divine voice unfolds the plan of liberation: "I will come down to deliver them out of the hand of the Egyptians, and to bring them up out of that land to a good and broad land, a land flowing with milk and honey." The ancient faith of the fathers is rekindled; for the God who speaks here is none other than the God of Abraham, Isaac, and Jacob (Ex 3, 15), who, in the time of remotest antiquity, had promised the possession of Canaan to the people yet to come. Apart from that, the divine revelation has nothing essentially new to offer. The only new element is the fact that the God of the fathers, in this hour of national crisis, acknowledges the oath he had given and, in Moses, selects the instrument that will bring the divine word to fulfillment.

In order to be in a position to demonstrate the genuinity of his mission, Moses, like an experienced man who means to safeguard himself against illusion even from the divinity, boldly demands the name of the speaker. And God said to Moses: "I am who is.[12] This is what you shall say to the Israelites: The

---

12. For a more explicit treatment cf. E. Schild, *On Ex 3, 14 — I AM THAT I AM*, VT 4 (1954), 296-302.

'I am' has sent me to you . . . the God of your fathers" (Ex 3, 14).

What is new in this revelation of the divine name? Is the name Yahweh here spoken for the very first time or does it have some linguistic predecessors, which are now filled with a new theological meaning? The most important attempts at interpretation can be briefly described.

a) *Derivation from Hayah* (older form: *hawah*) — "to be, to exist." In terms of grammatical form, *Yahweh* is an imperfect. Names formed with the imperfect are common for this era; for example, the names Jacob, Isaac, Joseph, etc. (May God protect, smile, increase). The Semitic imperfect is not an expression of tense; rather it expresses an aspect of being, whether an activity is closed in itself or open. It generally expresses the beginning of an activity, a new period in what is being done. In terms of its form, Yahweh could be an old perfect Qal and, accordingly, Yahweh would mean the God who exists, in order to make a salvific intervention, the God of history who is already active in relationship to the fathers, who existed for them. The apocalyptic formula of God who "is, was, and will be" (Rev 1, 4) is only a logical further interpretation of the name of Yahweh. There is something dynamic in Yahweh: he exists, he is here, primarily in order to intervene in the world of history from without, to promote the interests of his people. The miracles which follow upon his appearance are at the same time the seal upon his name.

In terms of grammatical form, Yahweh could also be the causative form (Hiphil-causative); as such it could be either imperfect (he brings into being) or, following the form of the new Karatape inscriptions, even an old participle ("He who brings into existence," that is, the creator God).[13]

b) *Other derivations* connect the word Yahweh with the Semitic roots which mean basically "to fall" or "to blow" and thus explain Yahweh as the "falling one" (meteor), the lightening-hurler, the one who makes the winds to blow, the storm god. These proposals are too heavily loaded with negative religious criticism to command our attention. Equally questionable is the derivation from the Egyptian, in which *Yah-we* is supposed to mean "the moon god Yah is the only god." [14]

---

13. Albright, *From Stone Age to Christianity* (1949), 259. / J. Obermann, *Survival of old Canaanite participle and its import on biblical exegesis* (JHWH = the Sustainer, the Maintainer, the Life Giver).

c) *Side by side* with the full form of the name Yahweh, which can already be verified on the Mesha inscription (9th century) and in the Lachish letters (c. 589 B.C.), to turn to extra-Biblical sources, we also find the abbreviated form *YAHU, YAH, YO*, which many scholars believe they can date in the pre-Mosaic era. Theologically there can be no argument against this position, since, in the course of our investigation, we have frequently seen that revelation is generally intimately bound up with the normal course of human affairs.

Moses' mother is called *Jochebed*, "Yahweh is mighty" (Ex 6, 20). Procksch [15] maintains that the Yahweh name was popular long before the time of Moses among the central Semites, the Hebrews, Arameans, and Arabs. To this group must be added also the Amurru, whose home, based on evidence from the famous stele of Hammurabi, must be located in Upper Mesopotamia, the home country of the patriarchs. On their migrations towards the south, the patriarchs would then have brought their names for God along with them. When we encounter names like *Ya-pi-ilu, Ya-um-ilu* in the Babylonian and Syrian territories of the Amurru, these could very well mean: "Yahweh is God." *Andri-yami* of Taanech, in the Amarna era, could also be a name compounded with Yahweh, just as, in the eighth century, *Yau-bi'di* of Hamath on the Orontes. Perhaps even the name Judah is to be interpreted as *Yah-uada* (Yahweh leads), in which *Ya-hû* ("Ya — he") would appear to represent an elementary form of exclamation with which the believer pointed to heaven with his finger in order to assert the existence of the great God. Albright strenuously rejects such an interpretation. [16] Finally, Littmann suggests a connection between Yahweh and the Arian Dyaus, in view of the fact that it is generally acknowledged today that the ruling classes among the Hyksos were Arians who brought their Indian gods with them into the east. The initial *d* was eventually lost, just as it was in the Latin form of the name Jupiter. [17]

JBL 70 (1951), 199-209. Possibly Yahweh could also be an abbreviated form of a longer name, in the same form as the name of the God Shagan, whose full name is Ama-shagan-gub ("He who helps mothers at birth"). Yahweh's full name would be *Yahweh asher jihweh*, "He calls into being whatever comes into being." Albright, ZATW 49, 242. / J. Brinktrine, *Der Gottesname AJA bei Theodoret von Cyprus*, Bibl 30 (1940), 520-523.

---

14. Beer-Galling, *Ex., Exkurus über den Namen Jahve*, S. 29ff. / N. Walker, *The Tetregrammaton, Its Origin, Meaning and Interpretation* (1948), 32ff. (Cf. JZBG 2, 1953/54, 106).

15. Procksch, *Theol. des AT* (1950), 76ff. / J. A. Montgomery, *The Hebrew Divine Name and the Personal Pronoun Hū*, JBL 63 (1944), 161-163.

d) *The most common derivation* is proposed by the so-called Kenite hypothesis. This explanation supposes that Moses, on the occasion of his flight to Midian, took over the Yahweh cult from the Kenites and introduced it into Israel. Procksch takes a very strong position against the arbitrary character of this solution.[18] Cain, the ancestor of the Kenites, is regarded by the Jahwist (Gn 4, 1-16) as accursed before the face of Yahweh by reason of his murder of Abel, and could thus hardly be a worshipper of Yahweh; his genealogy does not exhibit a single name formed with the name Yahweh and there is not a single shred of evidence to substantiate the assertion that Yahweh is a Kenite god.

Such philological investigations are indeed necessary; but their yield is slight. Moses' experience of his vocation cannot be derived in terms of the history of religion. "The Enlightenment mentality might well be in a position to demonstrate the natural basis of the Biblical narratives — but eventually even the rationalists must capitulate and recognize the fact that, as in the founders of the other great religions, so too in the case of Moses, some indescribably great influence had left a profound impression upon his life and work." [19]

In this great intervention from without we recognize the one God of revelation who, in the course of the Old Testament, breaks through the narrow boundaries of time in a series of new and important revelations, choosing men to be his mouthpiece and his herald. The experience of this vocation, in the case of Moses, deserves to be put on a par with the prophetic inspiration. Whenever God calls upon a man, he also equips him for this vocation. Moses is the greatest of Israel's prophets. It was he who made Israel the people of Yahweh and Yahweh the God of Israel. In terms of purely secular interpretation and experience, this is quite beyond explanation. In the last analysis, we are faced with the unfathomable mystery of a God who reveals himself, a God who determines the course of human history, intervening with his personal direction at the appropriate hour.

---

16. Albright, *op. cit.,* 259.
17. E. Littmann, *Afo 1* (1936), 162.

---

18. Procksch, *Theol. des AT* (1950), 76. — Desgleichen G. Lambert, *Que signifie le nom divin YHWH?* NouvRevTheol. 84 (1952), 897-915.
19. Beer, *op. cit.,* 35.

C) THE WORK OF LIBERATION
(Ex 5 — 15)

The liberation of Israel from Egypt is prepared for by a series of plagues sent by God, natural catastrophes such as are frequent enough in the history of Egypt. To modern rationalist thinking there is less and less willingness to interpret natural catastrophes as a judgment from God. Antiquity, however, always saw the catastrophe as the expression of some god's anger, requiring expiation. When, accordingly, Moses threatens the Pharaoh in the name of "the God of the Hebrews" (Ex 5, 3) with plagues upon his land, if the Pharaoh refuses to let Israel go, he could count upon a ready audience; nobody in ancient Egypt could have doubted that the gods can in fact send plagues. The fact that the plagues which came were actually produced by the God Yahweh Moses explains each time by his prophetic words. The staff as a sign of prophetic office should not be primarily compared to the magician's staff. Moses has little in common with the blind magic of the professional magician or sorcerer who hopes to force the world of nature to serve him through his conjuring. Moses is fighting for ethical and religious goals, the liberation of his enslaved people, in the name of the God of his fathers. It is really God who is at work here, and not Moses. The staff, accordingly, does not possess any miraculous power in itself; it only serves as a sign of the fact that God's miraculous power is at work.

In order to understand the plagues of Egypt, there must be some foundation in faith. The plagues can be explained in terms of profane history; but it is only the prophetic word of Moses that shows the punitive hand of God at work. Just as Christ can be grasped only in faith, so too the earlier stages of salvation history. The plagues are both typically Egyptian and at the same time "divine."

√From all purely external appearances, the Israelite revolt in Egypt has much in common with a workers' revolution which gains in strength over the course of many years and finally, in conjunction with the same catastrophe, reaches a decisive point. On the subject of the origins, organization, and fate of the working class in ancient Egypt we are reasonably well informed, thanks to the ancient texts, particularly for the Ramessid era (1350 — 1100 B.C.). At the head of each individual work corps, into which the working men are organized, there stand head-workers, who are, in their turn, subject to overseers, managers, etc. Again and again, we find records of strikes and demonstrations directed against poor management. The strikers carry their complaints to the officials and are prepared to go all the way to the Pharaoh himself. The administration tries to ferret out revolutionary plans. From time to time it makes concessions and the workers are satisfied. But soon the revolt is taken up once again, in a process which contributes considerably to the eventual downfall of the Egyptian state.[20]

The "revolt of Moses" thus fits in perfectly with the Ramessid era. It has, however, not merely a social, but also an eminently religious tone. The Pharaoh is unwilling to part with his most valuable labor force; he resists as long as he can. No sooner has the plague in which he recognizes the judgment of God passed him by than he once again hardens his heart, only to be softened again by a further plague.

The numbering of the ten plagues is a popular stylized formula, as we have already discussed in our treatment of number symbolism. The ten plagues can be grouped on an ascending scale as follows:

1. Water into blood	6. Boils
2. Frogs	7. Hail
3. Gnats	8. Locusts
4. Flies	9. Darkness
5. Cattle	10. Death of First-born

The plagues apparently strike not all of Egypt, but only the territory of Tanis, in which Yahweh performed his signs and wonders. The west wind which carries away the locusts, casts them into the Red Sea. In Upper Egypt, it would have carried them out into the desert. The red coloration of the

20. Beer-Galling, op. cit., 41. / Kees, Ägypten, 168.

Nile is presented in connection with the inundation; the swarms of flies appear in myriads particularly during the fall months. The fly is, as a matter of fact, the symbol for Egypt (Is 7, 18; 18, 1). The dying of the fish, the pestilence upon the cattle, the boils, and the hail-storms regularly plague Egypt from time to time. The great darkness can be explained as a fearful sandstorm. Finally, Egypt is one of the most typical countries of antiquity for pestilence. In the tenth plague, the important element is the death of the first-born. There is, finally, not a single plague which could not be given a natural explanation. But it is impossible to escape the Bible's clear statement that the plagues were expressly sent by God himself as a divine punishment (in order to make the Pharaoh willing to let Israel go), without doing violence to the text. Any attempt to relegate the plagues into the realm of fairy tales or popular saga [21] is an unwarranted attempt to escape the hard evidence of the ancient sources, all of which insist that the plagues are to be explained as genuine catastrophes produced by God himself. Albright[22] makes short work of this hyper-critical position with respect to the prehistory of Israel when he says that we must rest content with the assurance that the hyper-critical position now in vogue has absolutely no justification when applied to the early historical traditions of Israel. The prehistory of Israel is not a drama which is enacted in the twilight of Ancient Near Eastern antiquity; its hour is far advanced in time, a pulsebeat which we can better gauge today thanks to the advances of archaeology.

The last plague to be foretold, the death of the first-born, is to be decisive in breaking the Pharaoh's obstinacy. As a protection for the Israelite first-born, Moses arranges for each family community to slaughter a lamb and mark the doorposts with its blood; Yahweh would then pass by their house unharmed, when he made his way through the city in order to strike the Egyptians (Ex 12, 23). It is from this "passing by of Yahweh" that the festival receives the name *pasch* (Hebrew *Pesah*).

---

21. Beer-Galling, *op. cit.*, 36.
22. Albright, *op. cit.*, 255.

Whether this Mosaic *pasch* had a predecessor in an annual spring festival celebrated by the shepherds on the occasion of which sheep were slaughtered, or whether it had already existed as a surrogate sacrifice designed to redeem the first-born from Yahweh we cannot determine; it is at all events possible.[23] For just as Abraham did not invent the ritual of circumcision but simply filled an older ritual with new meaning, Moses, too, may well have seized upon a popular practice in this hour of historical decision and filled it with new and deeper significance. From now on it loses the character of an indistinct nomadic festival and becomes instead the festival to mark the liberation and redemption of God's own people. Through the annual renewal of the Easter festival Yahweh's one-time historical act of liberation becomes alive for all generations. The paschal meal which is celebrated in the individual families has the character of a sacrificial and memorial banquet. When Christ, on the eve of the Easter celebration, institutes his own memorial banquet, he is thereby surpassing and fulfilling the Old Testament memorial banquet.

In that very same night in which Yahweh struck the first-born of Egypt, Pharaoh sent for Moses and said: "Rise up, go forth from among my people, both you and the people of Israel; and go, serve the lord as you have said" (Ex 12, 31). The Exodus of Israel has a religious motivation.

The Israelites departed from the city of Ramses and made their way towards Succoth in the Wadi Tumilat. There they must have been joined by many of their countrymen and many non-Israelites, who hoped to share their new freedom (Ex 12, 37). The given number (600,000 men, without counting women and children) is surely not to be taken as the truth: it would give a total number of more than 3 million people. The best

---

23. Procksch, *op. cit.*, 57 and 544ff. In geographic names the "passing by" usually refers to a ford across a river, e.g., Tapsacus (*Tiphsah*) on the Euphrates. B. Crouoyer, *L'origins égyptienne du mot "Pâque,"* RB 72 (1955), 481-496, proposes a derivation from the Egyptian, with the element *sh* meaning "Wounding, blow," and with the article, *pa-sh*, meaning the "blow of Yahweh," Yahweh's striking the first-born of the Egyptians.

explanation, in keeping with the historical possibilities of the situation, is the proposal that the word *'eleph* does not have the meaning of thousand, but rather "family, kin." This would mean that, under Moses' leadership, 600 families left Egypt, and the total number of the people would then run in the neighborhood of 10,000.[24]

From Succoth Moses did not take the direct route into Canaan, the so-called "Philistine Highway." It may have been that this route was too strongly guarded and a direct attack from the south would have been a risky venture. That is why he chose the way that leads through the wilderness to the Red Sea (Ex 13, 17ff.). The Egyptians, already in the Middle Kingdom, had operated extensive copper mines on the Sinai Peninsula, and had considerably enlarged the traffic in that region: accordingly, the expression "the way of the wilderness towards the Red Sea" would be easily understood by everyone. The text does not mean to imply that Moses, in advance, foresaw the necessity of a miraculous crossing of this water. Accordingly, they broke camp from Succoth, modern Tell-el-Mashuta, and made their way towards Etham on the edge of the wilderness (Ex 13, 20). The word corresponds to the Egyptian *hetem* (fortress) and refers to a military outpost on the eastern frontier of Egypt. In Numbers 33, 8, the wilderness of Etham is mentioned, while the same territory, in Genesis 25, 18; Exodus 15, 22, is referred to as "the wilderness of Zur," that is, the wilderness land directly bordering on the Egyptian frontier on the Sinai Peninsula. Was it perhaps the Israelites' inability to break through here that prompted Moses, upon God's command, to give the order for a change in course? At all events, they turned around and pitched camp before Pi-hahirot between Migdol and the sea at Baal-zephon.

There are four possible ford sites to be considered. All of them, how-

---

24. It is not impossible that the high number of 600,000 has arisen from a mystical evaluation of the Hebrew letters as their corresponding numerical values. (Cf. *Westminster Historical Atlas to the Bible,* 1947, 37.) Israel is here computed at 2-6000.

ever, are no longer to be found in the present-day "Red Sea." Hence the expression "passage through the Red Sea" is to be taken with some reserve. The text speaks simply of a "sea of reeds." On the stretch of land leading to the Mediterranean there are several seas, the seas of Timshah, Balah, and the Bitter Lakes. Between these bodies of water there were fords which could be negotiated from time to time. The first location to be considered is: 1. between the sea of Timshah and the Bitter Lakes, on the so-called bar of Serapaeum, or 2. between the northern and southern Bitter Lakes, or 3. south of the Bitter Lakes or, finally, 4. still further south on the el-šalûf.[25]

The greatest probability would seem to favor the second proposal. The argument is strengthened primarily by the identification of the place names Pi-hahirot and Baal-zephon. After the Israelites, in the neighborhood of the bar of Serapaeum, were not able to effect a passage, Moses felt that he would be able to get his people across to the other shore at the main ford which served the highway at Suez. Accordingly, he led his people in a southerly direction along the western side of the Bitter Lakes. This uncertain change of course was announced to the Pharaoh. He sent a detachment of armed chariots after the fugitives, and overtook them at their campsite before Pi-hahirot between Migdol and the sea, before Baal-zephon. He thus made it impossible for them to continue their trek further towards the ford at Suez. Israel was placed in a most desperate situation.

An Egyptian papyrus records that along the route to Suez between the highway and the Bitter Lakes there are dangerous marsh districts, which go by the name of *Henit ta-Khert;* similar marshes are also reported in the Delta territory. *Pi-hahirot* would accordingly be the Hebrew form of an Egyptian name meaning "marsh of destruction."

When Moses stood in his camp on the level ground, and turned his face towards the east, the Bitter Lakes were in front of him, the marshy districts of Pi-hahirot were on his left, and to his rear, on the gradually rising hills of Gebel Geneffe and Gebel Saluf the citadel of Migdol already fortified under Seti I (1317 – 1301), which, on the basis of a papyrus, was called Migdol Baal-zephon. A Semitic place name such as this is not too surprising in this time and territory since, with the spread of the Egyptian kingdom into the Semitic north, the worship

---

25. C. Bourdon, RB (1932), 542. / M. Noth, *Der Schauplatz des Meereswunders,* Fs. Eissfeldt (1947), 181-190. / Albright, *Exploring Sinai with University of California African Expedition.* The coast of the Red Sea was, within historical times, one to two meters higher in elevation. The thesis that the northern end of the Red Sea was further to the north in antiquity is thus countered. H. Cazelles, *Les Localisations de l'Exode et la critique littéraire, RB* 62 (1955), 321-364.

of the northern Baal (Baal-zephon) enjoyed an increasingly greater popularity.[26]

Montet [27] describes Israel's situation in the following terms: "Moses saw that the route to Suez was blocked from him; he had learned, however — perhaps through reconnaissance — of a ford across the Bitter Lakes. But he placed greater confidence in Yahweh's saving grace than in his own clever strategy. This strong faith, a mixture of human cunning and subjection to the will of God — and this is everywhere characteristic of Moses — gradually led to the development of his plan, which was to cross the ford under cover of night, and thus take advantage of the one remaining chance he had to reach the eastern shore. A powerful east wind blows the water back, making the ford more accessible. When, at the first light of day, the Egyptians became aware of the flight of the Israelites, they began to pursue them; but since the favorable conditions no longer prevailed, they all perished in the waves."

Even though this proposed solution hardly goes beyond the character of a more or less readily assailable hypothesis, still it does put us in a position to appreciate the human prerequisites for the passage through the Red Sea. Once again God's free intervention is based upon the natural possibilities. Even though Israel's flight forms only a fleeting episode in the history of Egypt, this tiny band of enslaved fugitives is marked out by the freely bestowed presence of Yahweh himself, who is present to his people during the day in the form of a pillar of cloud and by night in a pillar of fire. From this central position he directs their history and their route. "This presentation makes a mockery of every naturalistic explanation. We are to think neither of the smoke that may have arisen from the volcano of Sinai (for Sinai is not a volcano) nor of the fire which, in antiquity, and in present-day Arabia, was sometimes carried before the army or the caravan; this was not

---

26. Principal cult site of the "North-Baal" was in the vicinity of Ugarit on Mount Casius. He was worshipped as a mountain god, but also as a sea god with a boat. This was the most popular form of worship in harbor towns. O. Eissfeldt, *Baal-Zaphon, Zeus Casius und der Durchzug der Israeliten durchs Meer,* Bibl 33 (1952), 417.

27. P. Montet, *op. cit.,* 152ff.

done to point the way, but rather to honor some distinguished personage." [28]

After the crossing of the Red Sea, the era of Egyptian slavery had definitively ended. This tiny ethnic group had finally achieved its way to freedom, but not on the basis of Moses' particular talents as a leader, nor the solution he was able to discover in the most desperate situation; but rather through the miraculous power of God who intervenes with his divine direction in what appears to be "natural catastrophes." And thus the narrative of the Exodus closes with the simple statement: "And Israel saw the great work which the Lord did against the Egyptians and the people feared the Lord; and they believed in the Lord and in his servant Moses" (Ex 14, 31). The Egyptians saw the Israelites as rebellious and fugitive laborers; but the believer recognizes God at work.

The Pharaoh of the Exodus: the question as to who was Pharaoh during the time of the Exodus would seem, today, thanks to archaeological discoveries and excavations in Palestine, to have approached a definitive answer. After all the tentative hypotheses of the last decades, we can be relatively certain in our determination of the Pharaoh of the Exodus.[29]

a) *The Biblical chronology* proceeds from the date of the building of the Temple under Solomon. According to 1 Kings 6, 1, the building of the Temple was begun 480 years after the Exodus. The Exodus must, accordingly, have taken place in the year (969 + 480 = 1449 B.C.).

b) *This would mean that Thutmose III* (1502-1448) was Pharaoh during the time of the oppression and Amenhotep II (1448 – 1422) was the Pharaoh of the Exodus. The former was famous for his lengthy reign (Ex 2, 23), a particularly vigorous ruler within whose reign and policies the deliberate subjection of Israel to the position of forced laborers in the building of his cities would certainly be quite in keeping, while his main wars in Asia Minor would certainly appear to justify the preparation of the store-cities in the Delta. The Amarna letters, which recount the penetration of the Habiru in Palestine, would be the best

---

28. P. Heinisch, *op. cit.*, 116ff.
29. 18th and 19th dynasties; 18th dynasty – Thutmose I & II (1524-1502);
    Queen Hatshepsut (1502-1480) initial coregency of Thutmose III

evidence for the Israelite possession of the land.

But all these identifications are contradicted by the historical and archaeological material. The oppression of Israel presupposes the capital city of the Pharaohs being located in the Delta territory; under Thutmose the residence of the kingdom was at Thebes. The store-cities, which the Israelites were forced to build, Pithom and Ramses, clearly belong · to the era of the Ramessids. The earlier identification can, accordingly, no longer be supported.

c) *Ramses II* (1301 − 1234), *Pharaoh of the oppression, and Merneptah* (1234-1220), *Pharaoh of the Exodus*: according to the story of Moses, three are two Pharaohs to be distinguished. It is during the reign of the first that we date the youth of Moses and his flight into Midian where he marries and has children. "In the course of those many days the king of Egypt died" (Ex 2, 23). A change in ruler was, for Moses, an opportunity to return. He was at that time, according to Exodus 7, 7, 80 years old. This would presuppose a very long reign for the Pharaoh of the oppression. In the list of the Pharaohs, however, only two exhibit a suitably long reign, that is, more than 50 years: Thutmose III and Ramses II. But since the relatively high number of 40 has no chronological bearing as we have already pointed out, it cannot be appealed to for evidence in this question. Such a solution, moreover, would create insoluble difficulties in the face of the archaeological evidence.

d) *Seti I* (1317 − 1301), *Pharaoh of the oppression, and Ramses II* (1301 − 1234) *Pharaoh of the Exodus*: The oppression of Israel is intimately bound up with a profound change in the political course of Egypt's history. The descendants of Thutmose, building upon the remains of the Hyksos, established an Egyptian-Asiatic world empire centered in Thebes, an empire which collapsed in the Amarna era. The rulers of the 19th dynasty commit their entire resources to the recovery of their lost positions in Asia Minor. In order to support their expeditions into Syria and Palestine, they move the administrative center into the Delta territory, where a feverish building activity quickly follows. This change in policy was effected by Seti I.[30] It was he who undertook the reconstruction of the ancient Hyksos city of Tanis-Avaris, the imperial

---

(1502-1448); Amenhotep II (1448-1422); Thutmose IV (1422-1413); Amenhotep III (1413-1377); Amenhotep IV (Ikhnaton) (1377-1358); Tutankhamen (1358-1349); Eje (1349-1345). 19th dynasty − Haremhab (1345-1318); Ramses I (1318-1317); Seti I (1317-1301); Ramses II (1301-1234); Merneptah (234-c. 1220); confusion from the end of the dynasty to 1200.

---

30. H. H. Rowley, *op. cit.*, 132.

capital, but it was only under Ramses II that the building was completed. The reduction of Israel to a position of forced laborers must, accordingly, be dated at the beginning of the building activity, that is, under the reign of Seti I.

Ramses II pushed the preparations for war further: he was faced by an imminent decision with the growing power of the new Hittite empire in Asia Minor. Ramses-city and Pithom were primarily store-cities for this military drive. The actual confrontation took place in the battle of Kadesh on the Orontes in the year 1296, a battle which, for the Egyptians, was a Pyrrhic victory. They maintained their superiority in battle, but without effecting any political change in the power structure of Asia Minor. The Egyptian frontier, even after the successful battle, continued to run along the Nahr-el-Kelb, somewhat north of Beirut.[31]

After the conclusion of peace with the Hittites, in the year 1280, Ramses II devotes himself exclusively to his gigantic building projects. It is this era that may well have witnessed the decisive confrontation with Israel.

This dating, furthermore, is supported by archaeology. The most recent excavations in Palestine have shown that in the 2nd half of the thirteenth century there was a significant breach in the cultural development. This is true particularly of Jericho, whose destruction is generally dated at 1250 — 1200 B.C.[32] It was particularly in Tell-ed-Duwer (Lachish) that we note a considerable development dating from the restoration of Egyptian sovereignty after the expulsion of the Hyksos, and lasting until the middle of the thirteenth century, then immediately followed by a sudden catastrophe, which, in its turn, gives way to a new settlement which can be clearly recognized as Israelite.[33] Around 1231, in Lachish, in the ruins of the Canaanite city, we have a hieratic inscription, and immediately below it the Israelite stratum.

If, accordingly, around the year 1230, Israel is already involved in establishing itself, then the Exodus from Egypt must have taken place approximately one generation earlier, between 1270 — 1260, that is, in the first half of the reign of Ramses II.[34]

---

31. A. Scharff, *Geschichte Ägyptens* (1950), 157ff.

32. On the Jericho question, cf. the section "Conquest of Jericho."

33. L. H. Vincent, *Les fouilles de Tell-ed-Duwêr-Lachis,* Revue Bibl 48 (1939), 250-277; 406-433; 563-583; H. T. D. / Sparks, *Lachish and the date of the Exodus,* Journal of Theol. Studies, 42 (1941), 178.

34. R. de Vaux dates the Exodus in the second half of the reign of Ramses II: in DBS (1948), 737 Albright dates the Exodus in 1290, since he postulates a generation for the conquest of Transjordania. *From the Stone Age to Christianity,* p. 256. Today the Exodus is generally dated in the 13th century. Cf. P. Heinisch, *op. cit.,* 72ff.

What significance, accordingly, are we to attach to the mention of Israel on the stele of Merneptah? This Pharaoh had won a mighty victory over the Libyans and records it in a victory inscription. At the conclusion of this inscription, together with other conquered Canaanite cities, we find the mention of Israel: "Israel is desolated, Israel has no more seed." Israel here is not the indication of a foreign land, but only of a foreign people. This means that Israel, already around 1230, was still engaged in establishing its position in the promised land, and had not yet definitively established itself. The "Israel-stele" is thus not a reference to the crossing of the Red Sea; it records an incident in Israel's invasion of the promised land.[35]

Our dating would be proven false by a text from Ugarit, which achieved its greatest development around the year 1350, since around this same time the tribes of Zebulon and Asher had already settled in northern Palestine. But the references to these tribes prove to be an error in interpretation. The supposed tribe of Asher is really a verb, "they marched," and the word *zebulun* conceals the common word *zebul*, "high place." [36] The Ugarit text is thus deprived of whatever evidential value it may have had.

After successfully passing through the Red Sea, Moses and his sister Miriam sing a victory song. The sentiments expressed certainly fit the contemporary picture of the Exodus, in its expression of powerful poetic exuberance (Ex 15, 1-22): "I will sing to the Lord, for he has triumphed gloriously; the horse and the rider he has thrown into the sea." Yahweh has proven himself to be the saving God of miracle, the God who has set Israel free from its servile existence in Egypt and will now transform them into his chosen people at Sinai. The Exodus from Egypt thus represents a new religious and national beginning, a beginning made possible only by the spontaneous and gratuitous intervention of Yahweh and the miracles he works.

---

35. Texts in Galling, *Textbuch zur Geschichte Israels* (1950), 34. / Beer-Galling, *op. cit.*, 79 sees this as the Egyptian military record of the catastrophe at the Sea of Reeds, a defeat which, as frequently happens in Egyptian records, was turned into a victory in the recording, since Israel fled across the water. The argument is answered in the above text.

36. Albright, *Archaeology and the religion of Israel* (1946), 61.

CHAPTER VII

THE COVENANT WITH GOD AT SINAI

LITERATURE

The Westminster Historical Atlas to the Bible, 1947, 38: "The route of the Exodus" (good maps). / P. Heinisch, *Geschichte des AT,* 1949, 81ff: "Gesetzgebung am Sinai" (good bibliography). / M. Noth, *Geschichte Israels,* 1950, 110-121: "Bund vom Sinai" (dissolves the Moses-Sinai relationship — hypercritical). / H. Cazelles, *Loi israelite,* DBS (vol. V), fasc. XXV, 1952, 497ff. (development of Israelite legislation). / P. Heinisch, *Theologie des AT,* 1940, 141: "Der Sinaibund und sein Gessetz." / O. Procksch, *Theologie des AT,* 1950, 82ff: "Sinaibund; 503ff: "Theologische Bedeutung des Bundes." / W. Eichrodt, *Theologie des AT,* 1948, Part I: constructs his entire theology on the concept of Covenant; Covenant relationship between God and people; Law of Covenant; essence of the Covenant with God; organs of the Covenant; Book of the Covenant; completion of the Covenant. / A. Jepsen, *Die "Hebräer" und ihr Recht,* Afo (1945 — 51), 54-68.

A) FROM RED SEA TO SINAI
(Ex 15 — 19)

After the miraculous passage through the Red Sea Moses' next mission was to lead his people, now set free from Egyptian slavery, to the mountain of God, the mountain of revelation (Ex 3, 12). The stations along this trek through the wilderness are accurately enough described in Exodus 15, 22ff. and in

Numbers 33, 8-15, but they cannot be geographically located with anything approaching this same precision. After crossing the sea, they first made their way for three days through the wilderness of Shur, without finding water (Ex 15, 22). This steppe country which spreads out along the Egyptian frontier apparently takes its name from the defense wall (*shur* = wall), which the Pharaohs had built as a protection against Beduin inroads. Insofar as we can reconstruct their route today, their path did not lead them through an uncharted wilderness. Rather, Moses followed the ancient caravan route along the shore of the Red Sea, in a southerly direction. The rest stations along this route are dictated by nature herself, since only few springs are available. The first station at Marah might well have been 'Ain Hawar, some 60 miles from Suez, where Moses made the bitter water drinkable by throwing wood into it.[1] From there they came to the next oasis, Elim, which might well correspond with the Wadi Gharandel, with its twelve springs and seventy palm trees (Ex 15, 22). Along their further course they sometimes kept parallel to the coast, and sometimes deviated into the interior, into the wilderness of Zin (Ex 16, 1), to Dopkah (Nb 33, 10-12). The derivation of this name[2] would appear to point to the district of the copper mines of *Serabit-el-Khadim.* The Egyptians maintained a flourishing mining operation here during the Middle Kingdom. The land was particularly rich in copper and turquoise which was highly valued in those days. There are numerous Egyptian inscriptions from this era as well as records in the most ancient Semitic alphabet form.[3] On the Sinai Peninsula there dwelt also the "smith tribe" of the Kenites (*qain*-Cain-smith), who probably got its name from the copper works (Nb 10, 29; Jg 4, 11). The wilderness Zin would thus

---

1. Identification of Marah as '*Ain Musa,* three hours' journey from Suez, is impossible because it is too close: Ex 15, 22 presupposes a three days' march.
2. *Dophkah* could be derived from *daphak,* "to knock," perhaps "to hammer." Cf. the "iron hammers" in the Alps where the bronze was worked after mining.
3. Chester C. McCown, *The Ladder of Progress in Palestine* (1943): "The Alphabetic Inscriptions of Serabit el-Khadim," S. 107ff.

be the plateau of *Debbet el-Ramleh* in the southern part of the pennisula, from which many valleys lead up to the Sinai massif proper.[4] At Rephidim the Amalekites tried to bar Israel's route, by blocking their access to the upper pasture lands which they had heretofore been using. The struggle was decided by the power of Moses' prayers (Ex 17, 1ff.).

In the wilderness of Zin Moses received the visit of his father-in-law Jethro or Reguel, upon whose advice he established a new system of justice. Prior to this time, he alone had been the one to decide contested issues by his "word from God." But Jethro saw that Moses would soon collapse under this heavy pressure and that the people would have no one to help them. Accordingly, he made the proposal that the administration of justice be divided among judges who would be set up over groups of 1000, 100, 50, and 10 (Ex 18, 1ff.).

The territories through which Israel passed are called, in Scripture, "wilderness" (*midbar*), not in the sense that they were totally without vegetation, but that they served better as pasture land than farm country. Such steppes afforded sufficient pasture for the flocks during the rainy season. But even though the flocks supplied milk, butter, cheese, and meat for food, this was not sufficient to last during the dry periods. Hunger and thirst are, even today, the greatest natural enemies of men who dwell in the steppe country. That is why, in these days of want, Egypt with its fleshpots became the object of great longing for the Israelites, and they began to murmur against Moses. But just as Yahweh had led them from the land of bondage with signs and wonders, so even now the power of his providence was not inactive in the wilderness. He provides for the people's drink with water from the rock (Ex 17, 6), and feeds them with meat from the great flocks of quail (Ex 16, 8), and gives them manna for their daily bread (Ex 16, 14).

Excepting in the case of the miraculous spring, the other two wonders do not exceed the realm of natural phenomena.

---

4. *The Westminster Hist. Atlas* (1947), 38ff: "The Route of the Exodus."

On their course from south to north, the quail annually cross over the Sinai Peninsula in great flocks. But it was God's own doing that they landed at precisely the proper time and in such abundance at the very place where Israel was camped.

/ So far as we can determine today, the miracle of the manna is also based upon a natural phenomenon. The question of the Israelites *man hu* is to be translated: "Is that *man?*" They had probably heard, either in Egypt or on their route to the wilderness of Zin, of the tamarisk manna. Moses certainly was familiar with it, but the people themselves were uncertain (Ex 16, 15). Moses pointed out God's goodness to them: "This is the bread that Yahweh gives you to eat."

/ The manna of the Sinai Peninsula is produced by two species of beetle who produce tiny drops on one species of tamarisk tree, varying in size from the head of a pin to a pea; in color they are either milky white or bright yellow brown or even dark brown. Under the influence of the sun the manna drops from the trees and hardens during the night. It is particularly the months of June and July that produce this phenomenon. The manna is sweet in taste, somewhat like crystallized honey; it can be eaten either in its original state or mixed with flour (Ex 16, 23).

The narrative does not say that, during their trek through the wilderness, the Israelites lived exclusively on manna. They also had their flocks which provided them with milk and meat. They offered sacrifices in connection with which, if they were peace sacrifices, there was always a sacrificial meal. They slaughtered the paschal lamb and ate the prescribed unleavened bread; according to Deuteronomy 2, 6 they wanted to secure provisions from the Edomites, and in Joshua 1, 11 they were preparing provisions for their entry into western Jordan. The whole narrative would thus suggest the conclusion that they used manna only on particular occasions and in particular places (where there were tamarisk trees).

There are, of course, some indications of the miraculous. It is impossible to suppose that, given a purely normal production, there would be sufficient manna in a comparatively small territory to supply several thousands of people for a week at a time, even providing that the manna constituted only a part of their necessary diet. God gives the Israelites much more manna than could be expected under the situations of normal productivity. Furthermore, it was miraculous that the manna began to appear on precisely the day that Moses had foretold; perhaps it began earlier than normal. What is more, the manna does not spoil; according to Exodus 16, 20, however, Yahweh allowed that the manna that the Israelites had gathered for the next day, against his explicit orders, to spoil. But one certainly miraculous element is the fact that the manna did not appear on the seventh day.[5]

/Thus, granted that there is some miraculous element about the blessing of the manna, God has once again, as he regularly does, adapted himself to the natural situation and accomplished this miracle simply by improving upon nature. Just as the miracles in Egypt had a clear reference to the natural phenomena of that country, so here too, the miracle narratives of the wilderness are intimately bound up with certain natural properties of the wilderness between Palestine and Egypt./

The location of Sinai: 1. The traditional location which we are following in our presentation places the mountain of divine revelation on the southern tip of the peninsula, at modern Gebel Musa (that is, the mountain of Moses). The Sinai Peninsula resembles a triangle, relatively flat towards the north, along the Mediterranean, but rising to a powerful mountain range in the south, with several massive peaks. This situation is witnessed to already by the pilgrimage of Silvia. Emperor Justinian left some impressive buildings there. The Biblical text itself (Dt 1, 2) suggests this location, since it requires 11 days travel from the mountain of God to Kadesh. This information would also fit the location of Serbal, somewhat west of the mountain of Moses, or the rock plateau of Serabit-el-Khadem as the mountain of revelation. One of these gigantic mountains on the Sinai Peninsula is also to be identified with Horeb, the mountain to which Elijah makes his pilgrimage (I K 19).

All this only strengthens the claim that the mountain of God is to be located on the Sinai Peninsula rather than somewhere else. Sinai and Horeb could in fact refer to the same mountain, an identification suggested by their interchangeable use (Ex 3, 1; 16, 1; 19, 11; Dt 1, 2).

2. The identification of the mountain of God with a site across the Gulf of Aqabah is occasioned by the fact that the phenomena described in Exodus 19, 16 aré interpreted as referring to a volcano. Since there are no volcanos on the Sinai Peninsula, scholars have sought a nearby volcanic area as the location of the phenomena described in the Bible. Such a territory is indeed to be found across the gulf, but it has been demonstrated that the volcanoes there were no longer active within historical times.[6]

---

5. P. Heinisch, op. cit., 83ff.
6. W. F. Albright, op. cit., 262ff, says that there is neither an active nor an extinct volcano in the entire territory of Sinai. In the neighboring districts of Hauran and Arabia there are many volcanoes which must have been active within the last millennia. If some natural "volcanic" activity is necessarily to be assumed as the substratum

3. Equally questionable is the location of the mountain of God in the vicinity of the oasis of Kadesh, an identification favored by the religious-history school which attempts to explain the narrative of the trek through the wilderness as the product of poetic imagination. This involves a contradiction with the clear statements of the Bible whose reliability is more and more established by recent investigation.[7]

The greatest probability would thus favor the Gebel Musa as the mountain of the law. The people had ample opportunity here to enjoy a relatively long period of rest, since there are springs and pasture land in the approximately three square miles of open plain that form a semi-circle around the base of the mountain which itself rises abruptly some 2,000 feet, visible from every side, a most solemn stage provided by nature itself for the great revelation that is about to take place.

B) THE COVENANT IN BLOOD
(Ex 19 − 24)

After three months the Israelite refugees from Egypt arrived at Sinai. Here, in the midst of the grandiose mountain landscape, far from all the cultural centers of the Ancient Near East, was the site determined by God for his most decisive intervention into human history. This mountain of revelation had been the deliberate goal set by Yahweh for the first part of his people's trek through the wilderness. At Sinai it is not human activity which comes to the fore; religion is not the work of any human agent, but the free and gratuitous gift of God himself.[8]

Since it is primarily God who acts, the human agent must first be made capable to meet with God by an interior purification. Moses proclaims the necessary rites to purify the people. The people needs to sanctify itself, to wash its clothing, and to abstain from intercourse with the women (Ex 19, 10). The mountain itself is surrounded with boundaries which are not to be crossed under penalty of death. But still more important than this external preparation was the interior expression of

---

for this episode, then it might still be the embellishment added to the narrative by a later editor who had witnessed volcanic activity elsewhere. But is such a complicated process really necessary?

---

7. P. Heinisch, *op. cit.*, 82ff. / Beer-Galling, *op. cit.*, 98.
8. Beer-Galling, *op. cit.*, 98.

assent to the great plan that God is about to announce. For God never forces his will upon man. If man deliberately closes his mind to the free call of God, even the all-power of God himself is impotent. God's plan is clear. He means to make Israel into "a kingdom of priests and a holy people" (Ex 19, 6). But first Yahweh must demand the full agreement of his people Israel. Moses thus convenes the leaders of the people, the elders, and explains God's plan to them. In this foundation of a new order all profane elements of people and kingdom are to be elevated into the order of the holy. What Sinai established is not primarily a new national community, but rather a new religious community. The people declare themselves ready for this divine venture: "Everything that Yahweh commands we will do" (Ex 19, 8).

After the people had decided in favor of Yahweh's initiative, the way was open for God's intervention. On the third day God came down upon Mount Sinai in all his glory (Ex 19, 16ff.). In terms of external appearances, this theophany is best understood from the point of view of the Israelite people, as the manifestation of a powerful storm on Mount Sinai, with thunder and lightning and all its glory and awe. It is precisely under this figure of a powerful storm moving northwards from the desert of Sinai that Yahweh appears at the beginning of many songs both ancient and more recent (Dt 33, 2ff.; Jg 5, 4ff.; Hab 3, 2) and the splendid storm psalm (Ps 29) is certainly full of the very presence of Yahweh. The ancient interpretations thought of a volcanic eruption and, as a matter of fact, some elements in the description of the theophany do suggest a volcanic activity, such as the sulfurous smoke which settled over the entire mountain and the earthquake of the entire countryside (Ex 19, 16, 18); but there never have been any volcanos on the Sinai Peninsula.[9] Even though the apparition of God has many similarities with a thunderstorm or a volcanic eruption, this was only the external vesture of his apparition, which veiled his theophanic glory (*kebôd yahweh*), and thus, in the last analysis, is not subject to purely rational explanation, just like all of

---

9. Procksch, *op. cit.*, 82.

God's other interventions into the world of time. The awe-inspiring externals served only to help the people appreciate the *tremendum mysterium,* the awe-inspiring mystery of God's revelation, and to function as a guarantee of God's actual presence and activity. The natural powers thus unleashed proclaim the all-power of Yahweh over the world of nature and creation. No thing and nobody can possibly resist him. Everything that is, is bound up in his protection. The all-powerful Yahweh is the covenant-partner of Israel and, as such, requires unqualified obedience to his commandments.[10]

The mediator between Yahweh and his people is Moses. He is so completely the herald of the divine commandments that his person completely disappears behind the words of God. When we read in Exodus 20, 1, that "God himself spoke the ten commandments," this is only an abbreviated form of expression, and it is designed to lend particular stress to the primary agent by eliminating all reference to the intermediary. The proclamation of the ten commandments is not to be understood in the sense that suddenly a voice and message echoed down from the mountain; the voice of God, before which the people were struck with awe, is the thunder and lightning (Ex 20, 19). The people beg that Yahweh no longer speak to them in thunder and lightning, but rather through the intermediary, Moses.

Moses, in answer to God's call, made his way into the cloud, where he received the law which he wrote upon stone tables and proclaimed to the people. The entire people answered with a single voice: "All the words which the Lord has spoken we will do" (Ex 24, 3). Moses then proceeded to conclude the covenant. At the foot of the mountain he erected an altar in the midst of twelve memorial stones, and sacrificed peace offerings and holocausts; half of the blood was poured out upon the altar. After Moses had read the law before the entire people and they had once again declared their willingness and promised their obedience (for the 3rd time Ex 19, 8; 24, 3; 24, 7), Moses took the other half of the blood and sprinkled the book

10. Beer-Galling, *op. cit.,* 98.

and people with these words: "Behold the blood of the covenant which the Lord has made with you in accordance with all
these words (*debarîm*)." Moses, together with the elders, then
went back up the mountain and witnessed himself the glory
of Yahweh. The conclusion of the covenant was a sacrificial
banquet before the face of Yahweh (Ex 24, 11).

The ceremonial surrounding the conclusion of the covenant
at Sinai was not something simply invented by Moses. Since
God himself is the best guarantee of fidelity to a covenant,
it was customary to conclude peace treaties by means of sacrifice.
The description of the peace treaty between Laban and Jacob
contains many similarities with the covenant on Sinai. Memorial
stones were erected, sacrificial victims slaughtered, a sacrificial
banquet was held, and the God of judgment was invoked as
witness to the treaty (Gn 31, 43ff.). The particular difference
in the Sinai covenant lies in the fact that in this case the second
partner to the treaty is not a human agent, but Yahweh himself.
The ritual is, accordingly, typically Ancient Near Eastern, but
the content represents a quite singular act of divine revelation
on the part of God himself. Thus begins a new chapter in
both the national and religious history of Israel.

With respect to its tribal organization, Israel also followed
the customs of the world around it. It holds inexorably to the
number 12 in determining the tribes, even though, with the
adoption of the two sons of Joseph, there were 13. Genesis
itself refers to other instances of the number 12. In Genesis
22, 20-24 there is an enumeration of 12 tribes of Arameans, in
Genesis 25, 13-16, 12 Ishmaelites, and in Genesis 36, 10-14, 12
Edomite tribes, while in Genesis 36, 20-28 there is a list of 6
Horite tribes. The Israelite system of 12 tribes is thus not a
special or particularly different phenomenon. This use of the
number 12 is neither arbitrary nor accidental; it draws its
origin from the necessity of social and religious life. If we
recall, further, that similar alliances of 12 tribes were known in
ancient Greece and Italy, and, for that matter, always existed
in connection with a ritual to be observed at a common sanctuary, perhaps in the form that each of the 12 tribes was charged
with the ritual observance for one month, or for two months in

the case of an alliance of 6 tribes, then the alliance of 12 tribes in Israel not only loses nothing of its historical credibility, but, on the contrary, gains considerably by being further exemplified in the full light of Ancient Near Eastern history. For we thus recognize the fact that Moses did not establish his religious conception of 12 tribes arbitrarily as a sort of "sacred experiment," but, rather, that he was acting on the basis of actual precedent. The 12 tribe alliance of Israel was not, in terms of its organization, particularly different from the tribal organization of the Ishmaelites, the Edomites, or the Arameans. Seen in the eyes of profane history, Israel appears in the form of a religious federation of 12 tribes united around their God Yahweh. The very fact, however, that this Sinai covenant outlived the other alliances of 12 tribes and developed an unheard of religious dynamism either is destined to remain an historical riddle or it must be attributed to the actual intervention and revelation of God.

Just as the Old Testament is a type of the New, so is the covenant concluded on Sinai a type of the covenant concluded in Christ. Both covenants have many points in common:

a) Both covenants are concluded by sacrifice; the Old Testament involves the sacrifice of animals, while the New is characterized by the sacrifice of Christ on the cross. Both sacrifices, particularly the blood of both sacrifices, are related to each other as type and antitype, a point made very forcefully by the Epistle to the Hebrews (9, 15ff.): "Therefore Christ is the mediator of the new covenant, so that those who are called may receive the promised eternal inheritance, since a death has occurred which redeems them from the transgressions under the first covenant .... Hence even the first covenant was not ratified without blood." In order to demonstrate this interior relationship more clearly, Christ made direct reference to the Sinai covenant in his establishment of the new covenant, by taking up the words of Moses: "This is the blood of the new covenant" (Mt 26, 28). Christ opposes the new covenant, in the 12 apostles, to the old covenant of 12 tribes. Just as the people of God of old, so also the new people of God is brought into being by sacrifice. There can be no other way, since sacrifice is the one prerequisite for encounter with God.

b) The symbolism of the Epistle to the Hebrews goes further into the interpretation of the blood of the sacrifice. Part of the blood was poured upon the altar, while the rest of it was sprinkled upon the people. Even so, Christ shed his blood upon the altar of the cross, and sprinkled mankind with that same blood: "You have come to Jesus, the mediator of a new covenant, and to the sprinkled blood that speaks more graciously than the blood of Abel" (Heb 12, 24). The only remaining question is the manner in which the new people of God are sprinkled by blood. Christ did indeed die once and for all, and has thus instituted an eternally valid covenant, but the individual man is called upon to incorporate himself into this divine covenant by faith and by the sacraments. The sacrifice of the Mass is nothing more than the continuing renewal of the covenant for all times, and it is in strength of this renewed covenant that the new people of God comes into existence and continues to be.

The conclusion of the covenant on Sinai was marked by awe-inspiring signs, so that ever afterward the Old Covenant was considered to be a covenant of fear, of awe, and of bondage. "You did not receive the spirit of slavery to fall back into fear" (Rm 8, 15). St. Augustine contrasts the two testaments by the characteristic words *Timor et amor,* fear and love." The words of St. Paul were spoken in protest against the pharisaical piety which had forced the breadth of the Old Testament faith into a narrower bounds of purely formal obedience to the demands of the Law. St. Paul's most fundamental objective is, however, to lay bare the fundamental power of the Old Testament revelation of God, which is after all the basis of the new Christian faith. St. Paul, properly understood and interpreted, cannot thus be advanced as an argument against the power of the Old Testament.

The revelation of Sinai is, in the last analysis, to be interpreted as God's revelation of love. For Yahweh binds himself with the people of the 12 tribes in a freely determined covenant, in order to work his plan of salvation for the entire world. It is true that the manner of revelation is different on Sinai than in the new covenant. "Moses' belief in Yahweh is loaded with dynamite, with the internal power to break all resistance and the liberating power to overcome the bonds of slavery. It is the impetus of the divine majesty which reveals itself on Sinai before which the human person both trembles and is raised up, which is the first and primordial phenomenon of religion." [11] Christ has come, not to take away this primordial element, but to lead it to its final fulfillment (Mt 5, 17).

C) DANGER TO THE COVENANT

The conclusion of the covenant at Sinai was a great religious venture. The fact that this magnificent plan succeeded can be

---

11. Procksch, *op. cit.,* 84.

ascribed to the powerful personality of Moses. The people still had a long way to go before they could appreciate the ideas of Moses, and they frequently opposed them. On the day the covenant was struck the reaction was silent, overcome by the unfamiliar natural phenomena which accompanied the solemn act. But when Moses, after the solemn day, went back up the mountain and remained for 40 days (that is, a very long time), the opposition began to assert itself. They persuaded Aaron, the brother of Moses, "to have the statue of a bull (the golden calf) made for the community as a religious symbol. Aaron, accordingly, had the gold and jewelry collected and did the bidding of the people. Aaron then made a proclamation: 'Tomorrow it shall be a feast to Yahweh.' And they rose up early on the morrow, and offered burnt offerings and brought peace offerings; and the people sat down to eat and drink, and rose up to play" (Ex 32, 1ff.).

What were the forces at work behind this "revolt?" Was it really a defection from Yahweh? According to the actual wording of the text, it was not. For the festival that Aaron proclaimed was in honor of Yahweh (32, 5); why then should the whole proceedings have so infuriated Moses that he shattered the tables of the law he had brought down from the mountain and proceeded to root out this cult of the bull with fire and sword, and with bloody inexorability?

The cult of the bull [12] is hardly Egyptian in origin. The Egyptians worshipped living bulls such as Apis in Memphis and Mnewis in Heliopolis. In the case of the golden calf it is rather a cult image in the form of a young bull (*'egel*).[13] This practice is to be found in various Semitic tribes. Among the Akkadians and Arameans, it is primarily the thunder god Hadad together with the moon god, and among the Canaanites it is Baal, and among the southern Arabians it is the moon god Shahar who are honored in connection with the bull cult. This proves that

12. Based on H. Junker, *Traditionsgeschichtliche Untersuchungen über die Erzählung von der Anbetung des goldenen Kalbes,* Trierer Theol. Zt. 60, 222-242.

13. Albright, *op. cit.,* 298.

the image is originally bound up not with one definite divinity, but is meant to serve as a religious symbol of general significance.[14] The bull is the incorporation of strength and power, as well as sexual fertility, and it was Baal who was worshipped as the source of all these gifts. We must certainly suppose that this common Semitic symbol for the divinity had made its entry into Egypt in the popular forms of worship introduced by the Israelite tribes who sojourned there. Thus the bull is not meant as the image of the divinity in the proper sense of the word, but only the symbolic indication of the deity's presence. Pictorial representations of this image are frequently encountered among the Babylonians, Arameans, Hittites, and Canaanites, all of them meant to represent the divinity in terms of a specific animal sacred to that god. The Israelite religion had no image of Yahweh; the adoption of the bull as the symbolic bearer of divinity would have left the position of the divine image quite empty, considering the image of the bull, very much like the ark of Yahweh, as an empty throne for the divinity which was meant to suggest the presence of Yahweh, worshipped without any image.

But since such an animal symbol would naturally suggest, in terms of its own individual characteristics, the nature and essence of the divinity itself, Moses could not tolerate this in the worship of Yahweh. For his reform was aimed primarily at cleansing Israel's concept of the divinity from every animal and naturalistic element. This explains his particularly rigorous interventions. He made his way through the gate of the camp and called upon the people for a decision: "Who is on the Lord's side? Come to me." With the help of his own tribe, the Levites, he singled out and killed everyone from among the people who obstinately continued to cling to the worship of the golden calf. By this bloody purgation, in which the Levites took the initiative, they acquired the perpetual priest-

---

14. Gressmann, AOB (1927), Nrs. 252, 257, 270-272, 276, 307, 331, 335, 338, 345, 354-356. E. Borowski, *Siegel der Sammlung Layard*: Nr. 12 portrays the storm god Hadad with a bundle of lightning bolts in his hand and standing upon a bull. Or 21 (1952), 179.

hood in Israel (Ex 32, 26ff.; Nb 25, 10ff.). From that time forward, like the Cherethites and Pelethites in the case of King David, they formed a bodyguard for Moses. They are his powerful assistants in the work of teaching Israel the commandments of the Yahweh.

In the erection of the golden calf [15] we see the emergence of an elementary religious reaction, supported by a considerable number of the people, who are as yet not sufficiently mature to accept the concept of a cult of Yahweh without images. But the equally elementary initiative taken by Moses saves the concept of the divinity from its essential dependence upon the power of earth and nature. The God who had called him from the burning bush, the God who had revealed himself already in the fathers, is not to be reduced to any image. The symbol of the bull would have reduced him to the chaos of the Ancient Near Eastern deities, but the refusal to portray him by any image makes him stand out solitary and alone, without comparison, high above the whole cosmos. "Moses can, accordingly, be considered as the great founder of a *theologia negationis et supereminentiae*, who, in mute reverence, worships a God whose grandeur cannot be comprehended by any human representation." [16]

In the antithesis between Moses and Aaron we also note the distinction between true and false leadership. Aaron follows the instincts of the masses without any initiative of his own, and cooperates in making the image. Moses' reaction is quite different. Animated by great love for his fellow-countrymen, and prepared to face death for them, this leader opposes them, when it is a question of honor, justice, and truth, bowing only

---

15. The golden image of the bull might also have been in the form of a standard, or a military banner. For the people demanded of Aaron that he make them "a god to go on before them" (Ex 32, 1). Similar standards are familiar from the Ancient Near East. In the Mari excavations (1933/34) we find the representation of a triumphal procession which is led by a man carrying a standard with a small image of a bull upon it. H. Junker, *op. cit.*, 232-242.

16. H. Junker, *op. cit.*, 242.

to the will of a higher being. Only in this way can Moses become an instrument worthy of his great God Yahweh and only in this way is it he and not Aaron who is the true leader of the people.[17] By the worship of the golden calf the newly developed monotheism might have died aborning, and the great new foundation established by God himself through the miracle of the Exodus might have come to nought. But the fact that, despite this peril, the work begun at Sinai proves to be a lasting and eternally valid foundation (the Old Testament) and the fact that, from Sinai, monotheism proceeds to conquer the entire world, is, second only to God's own work of grace, owing to the bold leadership and foresight of Moses who proves himself to be, in the truest sense of the word, a great religious founder.[18]

D) THE LAW OF MOSES

Can we even consider the possibility of a Mosaic Law without involving ourselves in insoluble historical difficulties? M. Noth, in his *History of Israel*, promotes the earlier critical hypothesis that Moses has nothing to do with the historical events described at Sinai. It is thus historically impossible to characterize him as the organizer and legislator of Israel. It would, accordingly, be quite misleading and not at all in keeping with the later more developed Mosaic tradition to characterize him as the "great religious founder" or even to speak of "a Mosaic religion." [19]

As opposed to this complete lack of faith in the historical credibility of the Biblical tradition, many other voices have been raised to substantiate the historical reality of this great personality, on the basis of the history of Ancient Near Eastern law. The laws handed down in the tradition of the Pentateuch

---

17. Beer-Galling, *op. cit.*, 156.
18. H. H. Rowley, *The Antiquity of Israelite Monotheism Exposition LXI* (1949/50), 333-338.
19. M. Noth, *op. cit.*, 118.

may well have experienced a period of interior development and further formation,[20] as we shall discuss more fully in the section devoted to Pentateuchal criticism; but it would be most arbitrary to deny that the first legislative impulse came from Moses. His activity is not confined to the purely profane legislation; it has universal direction and touches upon the establishment of a new world order under the command and in the direct mission of God. In the service of this command he enlists the entire wealth of his natural gifts and thus becomes the herald of the divine will in the social, political, and religious life of his people. Only with the great religious personalities such as Zarathustra and Mohammed, in whose careers the political and national activity was intimately bound up with their religious reforms, can we attempt to set up any kind of a comparison. But this very analogy should warn us in advance that we must never consider Moses as a servant of God or a holy man at work within the narrower circle of a particular moment.

One thing is immediately clear: this organizer without any proper political power, this popular leader without military force, this founder of the divine service without any priestly ordination, this agent of the new awareness of God without the legitimization of any gift of prophecy, this doer of wonders who stands far above the realm of mere magic makes clear to us from the very beginning the fact that the Israelite religion is not the fruit of a tradition which has been carefully preserved and developed by historical traditions, and further that it does not rest upon any particularly clever or successfully thought out office, but rather that it is the creation of the spirit who blows wherever he wills, and, in open mockery of the rules we make for him, draws upon the great wealth of his miraculously equipped personalities in order to weld together what appeared to be disparate or even contradictory elements into a powerful and life-bearing work. This means that at the beginning of the Israelite religion we find charisma, the particular and

---

20. H. Cazelles, *Loi israelite,* in DBS (1952), fasc. XXV, 497ff. (For a clear treatment of the development that takes place in the Israelite Law.)

individual endowment of one person. It is this personality upon which the entire foundation rests, so completely that it would be unthinkable without him.[21]

The existence of the nation rests solely upon the divine will. The newly developed order of state and world is, accordingly, essentially a theocracy, a rule by God (Josephus Flavius, *Contra App.* II, 16). This explains the particular nature of the Mosaic legislation. Since the appearance of A. Alt's monograph on the origins of Israelite law (1934), scholars have distinguished two principal types of legislation in the Pentateuch: apodictic law and casuistic law. The former, to which the Ten Commandments all belong, has a categorical and divinely imperative character; there is no casuistry here, no ifs or buts, only simple obedience to the word of God. This apodictic form of law has no parallels anywhere within the Ancient Near Eastern law; the character of the divine revelation is most clearly evident here. It can be historically explained only by presuming its time of origin to be contemporary with Moses himself.[22]

Whereas the apodictic form of law is clearly characterized by its divine immediacy, the typical legislation of the Ancient Near East is more in evidence in the casuistic law, which has undergone its peculiarly Israelite formation in the Book of the Covenant (Ex 20, 22 − 23, 33). Moses has, for the greater part, simply given a new formulation to the common Semitic customary law already developed before his time, just as the other great Ancient Near Eastern legislators, such as Hammurabi and Bilalama of Eshnuna also relied on the tradition of earlier

---

21. W. Eichrodt, *op. cit.*, 143.
22. Albright, *op. cit.*, 267. / H. Schmökel, *Biblische "Du-Sollst"* − *Gebote und ihr historischer Ort. Zs. der Savignystiftung für Rechtsgeschichte* 67 (1950), 365-390. In connection with the Decalogue and the Execration Text of Shechem, presents several other corpora of texts, one of them containing 50 "Thou shalt" laws and 15 "Ye shall" texts. They belong to the "confessional discipline" of the sanctuaries, like the *leges sacrae* of the Greco-Roman temples, and function as an answer from a consecrated hand. In genre, they are referred to as "temple catechism." (No matter how questionable this thesis might be, it does at least stress the extreme age of the commandments.)

material in their legislation; their codes thus represent a new formulation and a reform of the ancient law. Even before the Sinai legislation there must have been a law in Israel, in order to decide the relative merits of disputed cases; in fact, upon the advice of Jethro, Moses himself has reorganized the administration of magisterial justice shortly after the Exodus from Egypt (Ex 18, 13ff.). At Sinai, on the basis of the new divine revelation, this law was reformulated and reformed. Even critical examination suggests that the Book of the Covenant, with its pastoral milieu, actually dates back to the time of Sinai.[23]

It would thus be primarily the Ten Commandments in the Book of the Covenant which form the basis for the "words" (*debarîm*) of the Sinai covenant.

1) THE TEN COMMANDMENTS: Exodus 34, 28 explicitly states that there are ten commandments: "And he wrote upon the table the words of the covenant, the Ten Commandments (*'aseret had-debârim*)"; it is a matter of general tradition that the words of the covenant were grouped into two parts. There is less universal agreement on the subject of the division between these two parts; Philo presumed that there were two groups of five. To this end, he divided what is normally taken as the first commandment into two (faith in the one God and rejection of the image cult), and thus counted the commandment to honor one's parents as the fifth commandment in the first half; on the other hand, he took the two commandments against coveting as a single commandment. His direction was followed in the early Christian era, by Origen, by the Greek Catholics, and, more recently, by the reformed churches. The division familiar to the Latin Catholics and the Lutherans, into three commandments referring to one's relations to God and seven to one's fellow man, goes back to St. Augustine. But more important than these formal divisions is the content of the commandments, which represents a new climax in the history of religion.

a) The first part is concerned with the sacral law (*fas*): at the beginning stands Yahweh's formal introduction: "I, Yahweh, am your God." He refers to himself not as the Lord and Creator of the whole world, but rather as the God of revelation and election, who has set

---

23. H. Cazelles, DBS (1952), *op. cit.*, S. 503, dates the codification of the "Book of the Covenant" only from the Transjordania era, RB 52 (1945), 173-191.

Israel free from the bondage of Egypt. It is he who has chosen Israel, and not conversely. Before Yahweh makes a demand, he gives a gift. The greatest gift, however, is the revelation of his unicity. Beside him there are no other gods. In order to emphasize this unicity, the cult of images is formally prohibited; for the great and only God can be distinguished from the other gods who are represented in statues and images in no more arresting manner than by the very fact that he has no images. The grandeur of Yahweh also makes it unthinkable to "take his name in vain," literally, to misuse it for "nothingness, useless things," (*šaw'*), a prohibition by which we are to understand the rejection of necromancy, conjuring, witchcraft, false oaths, etc. Yahweh dwells in the bright light of day and has no need of dark magic and superstition.

To keep this faith in God from becoming something merely common-place, mankind is commanded to keep the sabbath day free for God. Since the paschal festival has, from most ancient times, coincided with the full moon, and since, moreover, the division of the calendar in terms of weeks is closely connected with the phases of the moon, one might easily get the impression that the sabbath of the decalogue is meant to stand as a memorial to the day of redemption from Egypt. The sabbath is thus essentially a day of commemoration (Ex 20, 8: *zakor* — remember). Carrying this idea one step further, the Christian Sunday observance is also a day on which redemption is commemorated. A Mosaic date for the sabbath commandment can thus not be denied on the basis of any cogent argumentation, even though the nature of the memorial has developed and transformed in the course of time.

Piety towards God is necessarily balanced by piety towards one's parents. In the world of the Ancient Near East, it is certainly remarkable that the mother is named as deserving the same reverence that is normally reserved for the father. What is at question here is not the kinship, tribe, or ethnic community; the commandment is primarily concerned with protecting the basic cell of family life.

b) The second half of the Ten Commandments deals with profane law (*ius*), and expresses the basic moral obligations towards one's neighbor. Murder,[24] adultery, theft, false witness, and covetousness are apodicti-cally forbidden. It is certainly remarkable to note how these five words protect and guarantee the morality of the whole people. The negative form of the commandments only serves to place sharper emphasis upon their positive content.

---

24. The fifth commandment does not forbid all taking of human life, as is evident from the clear stipulations regarding the death penalty (Ex 21, 16ff); *'al tirsah* means rather, "you shall not murder," that is, put someone to death unjustly. J. Gabriel, *Die Todesstrafe im AT*, Fs. Innitzer (1952), 69-81.

These ten short "words" are not meant to set up a purely external juristic statute; their point of reference to the human individual is his innermost responsibility, his conscience. What is concerned is not purely external, visible conduct, but rather that final interior purity of heart which can serve to check even the rise of human passions and emotions. The Ten Commandments are, accordingly, not so much a statement of positive law as they are a norm for human morality.

"The decalogue is valid for the people of God at all places and times, in the wilderness and in the Promised Land, in town and city, in the heights and the depths of the populace. And since Yahweh is more than the God of an individual nation, his law goes far beyond the national boundaries and asserts itself throughout the whole moral world. All this is certainly remarkable to the highest degree; for there is, in the whole literature of the world, no such moral law of equivalent grandeur. But the man who can recognize Yahweh as the one true God, the God who has chosen his people for his sole possession upon earth, such a man will also look to the prophet of Yahweh to lay the foundation for such a law on the basis of his awareness of God. The significance of the decalogue for the conclusion of the covenant (Ex 4, 27; 20, 1-17; 24, 11) clearly justifies its dating in the era in which the people of God first came to be." [25]

2) THE BOOK OF THE COVENANT (Ex 20, 22 − 23, 19): at the conclusion of the covenant at Sinai, Moses takes the "Book of the Covenant" (*sepher habberît*) and reads its stipulations before the entire people; together with the Ten Commandments, the other essential contents are the stipulations mentioned in Exodus 20, 22 − 23, 3. The Book of the Covenant prescribes the social relationships of a not yet fully organized ethnic community, still characterized primarily by the shepherd's life and outlook. Agriculture plays only a very secondary role.[26]

It is this that distinguishes it primarily from the Code of Hammurabi, which presupposes a well established social community already divided into clearly defined classes. The far-reaching similarities between the Book of the Covenant and the Code of Hammurabi are to be explained on the basis of a common Semitic body of law which, both in Babylonia and in Israel, in keeping with the respective differences in the individual situation, has retained a very definite and recognizable stamp.[27]

---

25. O. Procksch, *op. cit.*, 84-90: *Der Dekalog.* / H. H. Rowley, *Moses and the Decalogue*, BJohnRylLibr. 34 (1951), 81-118.
26. H. Cazelles, *op. cit.*, 503.
27. Alfred Jepsen, *Die "Hebräer" und ihr Recht*, in Afo XV (1945-51), 54-68, explains the similarity between the Code of Hammurabi and the Book of the Covenant on the basis of their common ethnic origins from the Amurru who are establishing an empire in the east under

The Book of the Covenant is introduced by the very ancient-sounding series of regulations regarding the sacrificial liturgy. It is followed by the corpus of law proper, with its prescriptions about slave law (Ex 21, 2-11: protection of freedom), the penal law (21, 12-32: protection of life) and the property law (21, 33 — 22, 16: protection of property). The regulations for legal suits and the establishment of the festival dates (23, 1-9 and 23, 10-19) form the conclusion. Exodus 23, 20 departs from the legislative form in favor of an oracle from God which proclaims the concretely historical mandate to conquer the land of Canaan under the leadership of the angel of Yahweh.

In terms of its form, the Book of the Covenant is mostly casuistic law, recognizable as such from the introductory formula: if this or that happens, then such and such must be the decision. This form of legislation goes back to the ancient Sumerian era.[28]

Despite the common content of the Book of the Covenant and the Babylonian law, the law of the Bible exhibits a peculiar element all its own, characterized primarily by a gentle humanism. The Babylonian law is extraordinarily strict in its provisions. It represents almost exclusively the point of view of the land-owner and master: all its attempts to secure real justice are focused primarily upon preserving the rights of the free-born and land-owner, and only rarely does it exhibit any real understanding for the position of the oppressed and impoverished. The author of the Book of the Covenant, on the other hand, wherever possible, attempts to focus the same emphasis upon the condition of the poor and persecuted citizen who most needs protection and help. He reduces the penalties to the measure of the possible and shows particular concern for the slave and the alien. The Israelite is to be particularly considerate towards the alien, since he himself sojourned as an alien in Egypt. The laws, in the form in which we have them today, express the sensitiveness of a people who have themselves lived in misery and oppression, a factor which must be evaluated as some guarantee of the extreme age of these stipulations.[29]

Hammurabi and in the west under the Hyksos and codifying their laws. According to Jepsen the Book of the Covenant is a remnant of the "Hyksos Code." Whatever the position taken with respect to this thesis, one thing is clear: in the Book of the Covenant we are dealing with very ancient material.

28. W. F. Albright, op. cit., 267.
29. B. Bonkamp, Die Bibel im Lichte der Keilschriftforschung (1939), 221-224. — J. K. Mikliszanki, The Law of Retaliation and the Penta-teuch, JBL 66 (1947), 295-303: The fundamental principle of "an eye for an eye, etc." cannot possibly mean that such justice was ever literally dispensed. It is rather a popular expression of the absolute

3) THE CULT LAW: Moses is not only the reorganizer of the social order; the Bible also insists upon representing him — and no amount of criticism can completely obliterate this claim — as the founder of the Yahweh cult. Granted that many stipulations regarding the official cult may be later additions,[30] still the recent discoveries from the Ancient Near East force us to take a position of greater trust in these texts which clearly contain a most ancient tradition.[31]

The external impetus for the cult reform was the defection of the people to the service of the golden calf (Ex 32, 1ff.). Here too, as in the social legislation, Moses did not go to work without a precedent; he gave a new form to cult practices that were already in existence. Animal sacrifice and food offerings were practiced by all the surrounding Semitic peoples. The divine cult of Israel was not, in this respect, in any way distinguished from the pagan cults. But Moses succeeded in filling these forms with the soul of the Yahweh faith, and thus giving them a quite particular form and meaning. It is this accomplishment which marks him out as a prophet working entirely under the divine impulse.

On Mount Sinai he received the mandate to construct a new tabernacle, according to some specific instructions (Ex 25 — 27). Bound up with this is the institution of the Aaronitic priesthood and the prescriptions on the subject of the priestly vestments and consecration (chs. 28 and 29). When, after Moses' return from the mountain, the people's defection which had expressed itself in the worship of the golden calf had been violently suppressed, Moses proceeded to the introduction of the new cult law. The tabernacle was built and furnished, the priestly vestments were prepared (chs. 35 — 40), the priestly consecration took place after the promulgation of the sacrificial laws (Lv 8). The greater portion of the ceremonial law is contained in the Book of Leviticus, especially the sacrificial law (1 — 7), the dietary laws and the prescriptions for legal purification (11 — 15): one compact body is formed by the laws in chapters 17 — 26 regarding ritual holiness. The epilogue (26), with its promulgation of blessing and curse, gives the laws of the Book of Leviticus the nature of a compact collection which stands as an appendix to the prescriptions regarding vows and tithes (Lv 27).

The Book of Numbers records the special selection of the Levites, their formal investiture in office, their consecration, and the provisions

---

equality of each man before the law: the punishment must fit the crime. The *lex talionis* is already an ancient custom in Biblical times.

30. H. Cazelles, *op. cit.*, 504ff.
31. W. F. Albright, *Archaeology and Religion of Israel* (1946), 36ff. — *From Stone Age to Christianity*, 266. The archaeologist finds it not at all difficult to demonstrate the extreme age of many individual elements in the Priestly Code.

for the income of both priests and Levites (Nb 1; 4; 8; 18), the confirmation of the Aaronitic priesthood (16; 17), and a series of pre-scriptions regarding individual points of ceremonial law.

Though there is obviously some historical evolution at work here, the whole law is still animated by the original source which first comes to light at Sinai, under divine impulse, and then, in the course of time, takes on a more developed form in keeping with the historical situation. The form may have changed in non-essential points, but the spirit that animates it remains the same, the faith in Yahweh who is "a jealous God" (Ex 20, 5) watching over his chosen people, and tolerating no other gods beside himself.

4) ANCIENT NEAR EASTERN LEGISLATION: recent excavations put us in a position to compare the Mosaic Law with various other legal codes of the Ancient Near East. This comparison further emphasizes the unique character of the Law. Excavations at Babylonia, Assyria, and in Asia Minor have yielded specifically legal texts and collections.

a) *In Babylonian law,* until very recently, the Code of Hammurabi [32] was considered the most ancient source for ancient law still extant. More recently, it has surrendered this position, and is now in third place. Hammurabi, at the beginning of the 2nd year of his reign (c. 1726 B.C.), had already begun the work of restoring peace and order to his country by a new legislation. The approximately 300 legal statements, arranged in 51 columns, are engraved on a round, columnar, black diorite block. The laws stood for 155 years in the Temple of Esagila in Babylon, before being carried off by Shutruk-Nahhunte (1207 – 1171 B.C.), among the booty that he brought to Susa. It was discovered there in the French excavations in the year 1901. The text consists of three sections, a prologue, the corpus of the laws, and a hymn-like epilogue. On the front there is a representation of the god Shamash, giving the laws to King Hammurabi. The corpus of law proper considers questions of litigation, property law, personal law (soldiers, marriage, etc.).

b) *About a century and a half older* than the Code of Hammurabi is the Code of King Lipit-Istar of Isin. It is preserved only fragmentarily on seven clay tablets, which were discovered in the excavations at Nippur. The laws are composed in the Sumerian language. The code exhibits

---

32. The best edition of the Code of Hammurabi, A. Deimel, *Codex Ham-murabi: transcriptio et traditio latina,* Rome (1930); W. Eilers, *Die Gesetzesstele Chammurabis* (1933), VD 31, 3-4. — Translation by H. Gressmann, AOT (1926), 380ff; J. B. Pritchard, ANET (1950), 163ff. — Relationship to Bible: B. Bonkamp, *Die Bibel im Lichte der Keilschriftforschung* (1939), 185ff.

the same construction as the Code of Hammurabi and can well have served as a model for the later work. It is dated in the first half of the nineteenth century.[33]

c) *In the time between* Lipit-Ishtar and Hammurabi we must date the law code recently discovered in Tell-Harmal near Baghdad. It is the work of King Bililama of Eshnunna. It is written in Semitic.[34]

The Middle-Assyrian laws [35] are also preserved only fragmentarily; they are distinguished from among the other Ancient Near Eastern laws by their extremely strict penal provisions. They were discovered at the German excavations in ancient Asshur (*Qal'at šergat*) in the years 1903 – 1914, and the corpus was enlarged by subsequent partial discoveries.

The Hittite laws[36] of Asia Minor have been known only since 1922. They are extant in several recensions, exhibiting a progressively milder form of punishment, apparently promoted by the desire to weld the people closer to the dynasty in the midst of uncertain times. In terms of style, the texts are mostly casuistic law.

It is surprising to note that, as opposed to the Sumerians, Semites, and Hittites, the Egyptians have left no great code of law behind them. When Moses, on Sinai, gives a new codification to the law of the Israelite people and breathes the spirit of the new faith of Yahweh into the ancient ethnic customs, his reform work is to be evaluated primarily against the background of the earlier Semitic laws.

---

33. Critical edition by Francis R. Steele in AJA, LII (1948), 425-450.
34. Published by A. Götze in der Zeitschrift "Sumer," Juliheft (1948). — English in ANET (1950), 161.
35. Translations in AOT 412ff. and ANET 180ff.
36. Translations in AOT 423ff. and ANET 188ff.

CHAPTER VIII

THE SACRED TABERNACLE
AND THE ARK OF THE COVENANT

LITERATURE

Fr. Nötscher, *Biblische Altertumskunde*, 1940, 270-279: "Zeit und Lade."
/ P. Heinisch, *Das Buch Exodus* 1934, 197ff.: "Die Vorschriften über
die Einrichtung des Kultes." / W. Eichrodt, *Theologie des AT* I, 1948,
44-47: "Die heiligen Gegenstände." / O. Procksch, *Theologie des AT*,
1950, 94-99: "Der Kultus." / G. Beer and K. Galling, *Exodus*, 1939, 128ff.:
"Die Anordnungen für den Kultus."

THE cult with its definite provisions and utensils for divine
service, is not only designed to accompany the phenomenon
of religion, but also to serve as its most intimate expression,
since it means to permeate the totality of human life, by making
not only its spiritual and personal side, but also its physical
nature, the bearer and intermediary of its workings.[1] It is precisely from the cult form that the essence of a religion can best
be concluded: "Every form of religion presses for some physical
manifestation."[2] In the case of ancient man, the external form
takes on a much greater evidential significance than in our
modern western cultures. The relationship with God is main-

---

1. W. Eichrodt, *Theologie des AT*, 1 (1948), 39ff.
2. W. Stählin, *Vom Shinn des Leibes* (1930), 105.

tained not only on the personal level of interior spirit, but also by the process of physical gesture, kneeling and prostration at prayer, in the sacred dance and in responsorial song, in the setting off of the sacred precinct, in the vestment of the priests, in the preparation of the sacrifice, in the solemn stillness which accompanies the actual offering of the sacred gifts to God, in the rising of the incense smoke before the altar. All these visible elements are filled with evidential character, and thus represent, not an indifferent or secondary, but rather a very necessary and essential consequence of the religious experience.[3]

If the external forms of the cult are, from the human side, meant to be the witness of man's interior dispositions in the face of God, they are transformed by God into the bearers and instruments of the divine blessing and grace. "In the external cult activities the divine power and blessing is shared with the concretely existing form of humanity: the sacred action becomes a sacrament," the occasion for the infusion of God's grace.[4] In prefixing these remarks, we are not misapplying a New Testament way of thinking to the Old Testament. An ancient religion without a cult is absolutely unthinkable. This is even more true of the cult of the Old Testament, which clearly refers back to "a divine impulse" and a prophetic institution, thereby becoming the one legitimate occasion for encounter with God within the whole range of Ancient Near Eastern religion. The position of Israel among the Ancient Near Eastern peoples explains many of the similarities in the cult form. These external common properties must not, however, mislead us as to the existence of some essential interior differences; on the one hand there is the cult of the various gods, as opposed to the worship of the one true God who has revealed himself to Israel as Yahweh.

Recent investigations[5] have established the fact that Israel's

---

3. W. Eichrodt, *op. cit.*, S. 40.
4. *Ibid.*, S. 40.
5. P. Heinisch, *Das Buch Exodus* (1934), 199. — Albright, *Archaeology and Religion of Israel* (1946).

cult has undergone a long history, gradually growing in splendor. The cult forms characteristic of the wilderness must have been much simpler than after Israel's entry into the land. The investigations of literary criticism have actually made it clear that, in the Pentateuch, we have a whole series of precepts that represent later additions, and in many other cases, where the influence of the later hand is not so clearly recognizable, scholars might still conclude, with greater or lesser degree of probability, to the existence of some later addition whenever there are sufficient internal grounds to suggest this conclusion. In many passages, such a suspicion is hard to avoid.[6] These few critical remarks must necessarily precede any overall presentation of the cult of Israel.[7]

Just as Moses had given a new form to the ancient faith of the fathers through the new revelation of Yahweh, even so this new faith, by a sort of inner necessity, progressed towards new forms of expression. After the conclusion of the covenant, while Moses was still on Sinai, Yahweh gave him the mandate to build a new sanctuary with various liturgical vessels. Israel has long possessed a "sacred tabernacle" with the "testimony" as the focal point of her religious life; in Exodus 16, 33ff., it is referred to as the "tabernacle of the assembly" ('ohel mo'êd). This tabernacle had been desecrated by the sin of Israel's rebellion, and Moses had taken the tabernacle outside the camp (Ex 33, 7-11). This was only one step towards the rejection of the older tabernacle, which was to be completed by the inauguration of the new. What happened to it is nowhere mentioned in the Pentateuch.[8]

In order to collect the necessary material for the building of the new sanctuary, Moses had a voluntary collection taken. The

---

6. P. Heinisch, op. cit., 199.
7. In the following presentation of the cult of Israel, we are following Emilian Schopfer, Geschichte des AT (1923), pp. 232-274, in the organization of the material, but we have attempted to enlarge upon the surface description by offering some depth of background in the form of historical developments that have led to the formation of the cultic laws which, in the Pentateuch, are presented more as a compact and self-contained unit.
8. Hummelauer, Das vormosaische Priestertum in Israel (1899), 1ff.

people supplied him with gold and silver and other valuables in great abundance. The execution of the plans were entrusted to the two artists *Besal'el* and *'Oholi 'ab*. In keeping with Israel's nomadic existence, the sanctuary too was movable and portable. It consisted of the tabernacle proper and an outer court.

The tabernacle itself was 30 cubits long [9] and 10 cubits in

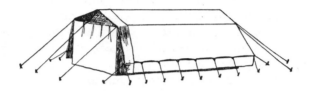

Figure 1: The tabernacle of the covenant

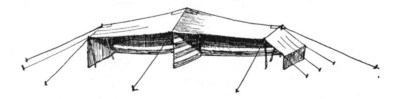

Figure 2: Present-day Beduin tent

From P. Heinisch: *Das Buch Exodus* (*Anhang*), Bonner Kommentar, 1934.

---

9. In Babylonia, and in Israel as well, the common cubit was 49.5 cm and the "royal" cubit was 55 cm. Both were in use side by side, while the Egyptians assigned the two measures a value of 45 cm and 52.8 cm respectively. (Heinisch, *op. cit.*, 201). / U. Cassuto, *The Palace of Baal*, JBL 61 (1942), 51 maintains that the erection of the Tabernacle has a polemic character, being directed against the Baal cult. The earthly tent of Yahweh develops from the heavenly palace.

both height and breadth; it was made of a wooden frame covered with boards of acacia wood that had been overlaid with gold, and it rested upon silver feet; it was covered by four curtains. The description, despite an abundance of individual detail, is not completely clear in every point. The real meaning of many technical expressions is uncertain. Attempts at reconstruction have always been more or less approximate. The lower hanging was made of "fine twined linen," with representations of cherubim in the four sacred colors: apparently this hung on the interior side of the plank walls. The second hanging of goats' hair, which is used even today as a protective cover for Beduin tents, formed the actual shape of the tabernacle, hanging outside the plank structure, fastened by lines which were secured to pegs driven into the earth. The third hanging of rams' skin and the fourth made from the tanned skins of walrus were stretched over the other hangings in the event of bad weather.

The space thus marked out was closed towards the east by a curtain, which hung from an architrave supported by five columns. The interior itself was further divided by another curtain into the Holy (20 cubits long) and the Holy of Holies (10 cubits long). The outer court was a rectangle 100 cubits long and 50 cubits wide. The outer precinct was formed by 50 columns of accacia wood plated with silver; their tops supported a beam from which a curtain hung. The entrance, 20 cubits wide, lay on the smaller eastern side, while the tabernacle itself stood somewhat back in the western half of the outer court, so that, in the outer court, the Israelites prayed towards the west.

In this sacred precinct, whose form was dictated by the conditions of Beduin life, which required a tabernacle that could be easily put up and easily taken down and transported, the vessels and utensils for the cult were set up.

Entering into the outer court, one would first see the altar of holocaust, along a straight line leading to the tabernacle. It was five cubits in length and in breadth, and three cubits in height, and was made of acacia boards covered with copper. There were horns on all four corners, as symbols of the power and fullness of Yahweh's blessing. The hollow interior was filled with earth and stones, which thus formed the actual altar itself, while the wooden structure served as a framework. It was upon this altar that the sacrifice of the "outer court" was offered, and for this purpose, a perpetual fire was maintained there. Behind this altar stood the copper laver in which the priest, before entering the altar or the tabernacle, was to wash his hands and feet. In the Holy Place, directly in front of the curtain leading to the Holy of Holies, stood the altar of incense. It was two cubits high and one cubit in length and in breadth, made of wood and overlaid with gold, with horns on the four corners, beneath which there were golden rings with poles for carrying it. Upon this altar, every morning and every evening, glowing coals from the "sacred fire" were laid, upon which was put the incense composed of four sweet-smelling ingredients. On the northern side of the Holy Place stood the table for the showbreads (loaves of proposition), made of wood and overlaid with gold, two cubits long, two cubits wide, and one and one half cubits high. Upon this table, from Sabbath to Sabbath, were laid twelve unleavened loaves made of the finest flour. Across from this was the seven-branched lampstand of beaten gold, with seven lamps that were filled with oil and lighted every evening.[10]

In the Holy of Holies stood the ark of the covenant, the greatest sanctuary of Israel. 'Arôn means simply "chest," "trunk," and thus also refers to the "casket" in which the remains of Joseph were brought back into Palestine (Gn 50, 26). It is important to clearly distinguish between the two component elements, the ark proper and the kapporet. The ark itself was made of wood, overlaid inside and out with gold; it was a box open on the top, two and one half cubits long, one and one half cubits in height and in breadth, bordered by a gold wreath and equipped with four golden rings from which the poles used to

---

10. Animal sacrifice, incense offering, and the custom of the gift table are common both to the Mosaic cult and the Ancient Near Eastern religions in general. Elijah offers animal sacrifice just as the Baal priests do. Moreover, the external forms are, to a great degree, identical. The religion of Moses is distinguished only by its monotheistic faith. For an Assyrian gift table, with showbreads, cf. E. Borowski, *Siegel der Sammlung Layard*, Or 21 (1952), 177, Nr. 8 u. 9.

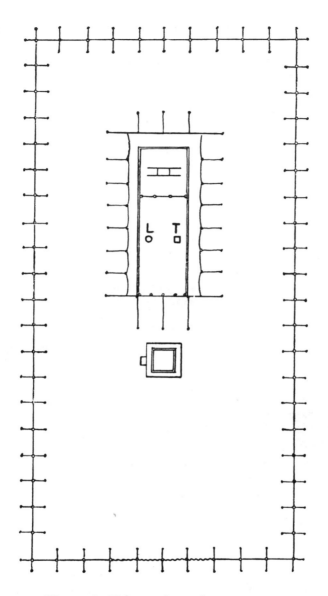

Figure 3: Tabernacle and outer court

L — lampstand   T — table of the showbreads

P. Heinisch

carry it were never withdrawn. In the ark were the two stone tablets of the law, upon which the decalogue as well as the statement of the covenant with the "words of the covenant" (*dibre habberît*) were written (Ex 34, 28; 25, 16; 32, 28; Dt 9, 9; 11, 15). According to Hebrews 9, 4, there was also a golden urn with manna and the staff of Aaron which had blossomed. The *kapporet* which covered the open ark was a golden plate, equal in length and breadth to the dimensions of the ark itself.

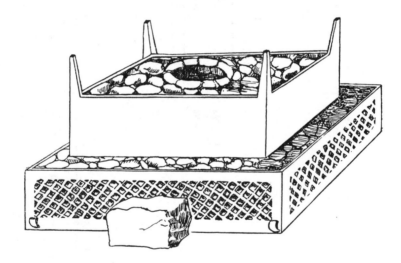

Figure 4: The altar of holocaust

P. Heinisch

Along the two narrow sides there were images of cherubim. Similar to the tutelary deities in Babel which, in those ancient times, were represented in human form, while the mixed be- ings make their appearance only later, these cherubim on the ark of the covenant are to be pictured in a much simpler manner than those of Ezekiel, that is, as human figures. The picture generally presented is two erect or kneeling figures, hollow on the inside. But the covering plate could hardly have been carried through the desert in such a form as this. More probably they were relief figures, worked onto the surface of the cover itself.

What is the meaning of the ark of the covenant? It is more than simply a repository for the tablets of the law. Since Yahweh revealed himself over the cherubim on the covering plate, it came to be the symbol of God's presence among his people (Nb 10, 34ff.; Dt 1, 30, 42). Hence the divine title of "Yahweh who makes his throne above the cherubim" (1 S 4, 4; 2 S 6, 2; 2 K 19, 14; 1 Chr 13, 6). The ark of the covenant must thus be considered as the throne of Yahweh (Jer 3, 16ff.), just as, among the Beduins, a chest is offered to the guest as a seat; or we might also think of it as his footstool (Ps 132, 7; 1 Chr 28, 2). The fact that the tables of the law were kept in the ark while Yahweh manifested himself over the "cherubim plate, making his throne above the cherubim," has many parallels in the customs of the Ancient Near East. In Egypt, as well as in Babylonia and in the Hittite empire, important documents were deposited in the sanctuary, "at the feet of the divinity." [11] The divinity is the best guarantee of fidelity to the covenant.

The tabernacle and the ark of the covenant have been the object of various symbolic interpretations. In the New Testament it is primarily the Epistle to the Hebrews (8, 1ff.) which stresses the typal character of the Old Testament cult, in order to lay greater emphasis upon the eternal validity of the new covenant by contrasting it against the transitory background of the old. Further, there is the description in the Book

---

11. Cf. P. Heinisch, *op. cit.,* 200ff. for the Tabernacle and its furnishings. The representation of a god throning upon the cherubim is a further tie between Israel and the Ancient Near Eastern world that surrounds it. E. Borowski, *op. cit.,* 181, Nr. 15a, shows a griffin (cherub) bearing the throne upon which the deity sits.

of Revelations (21, 3), which refers to the beginning of God's revelation at Sinai: "Behold the tabernacle of God among men, and he dwells with them." The fact that God himself, from Sinai, establishes his throne among his people in person, is one of the greatest scandals of the Old Testament, but it is at the same time its greatest mark of distinction. This self-contradictory living reality of God, who is always present in the darkness of the Holy of Holies, determines and controls the further progress of the fate of this people of God.

CHAPTER IX

THE PERSONNEL OF THE CULT

LITERATURE

Grimme, *Der südarabische Levitismus und sein Verhältnis zum Levitismus in Israel*, Muséon, 1924, 166-199. / A. Eberharter, *Der israelitische Levitismus in vorexilischer Zeit*, ZkTh, 1928, 492, 518. / J. Gabriel, *Untersuchungen über das alttestamentliche Hohepriestertum mit besonderer Berücksichtigung des hohepriesterlichen Ornates*, Theol. Stud. der öst. Leogesellschaft Nr. 33, 1933. / K. Möhlenbrink, *Die Levitische Überlieferung des AT*, ZATW, 1934, 184-230. Fr. Nötscher, *Biblische Altertumskunde*, 1940, 313-316: Die Leviten. / W. Eichrodt, *Theologie des AT*, 1948, I; *Die Organe des Bundes; Priestertum in der Geschichte Israels; Die religiose Struktur des Priestertums*, 197-219. / F. Stummer, *Gedanken über die Stellung des Hohenpriesters in der alttestamentlichen Gemeinde* in "Episkopus," Fs. f. Kard. Faulhaber, 1949, 19-49. / M. Greenberg, *A New Approach to the History of the Israelite Priesthood*, JAOS 70, 41-47. / A. Kuschke, *Die Lagervorstellung der priesterlichen Erzählung*, ZATW 63, 1951, 74-105. / H. Cazelles, *La dîme israelite et les textes de Ras Samra*, VT 1, 1951, 131-134. / A. Lefèvre, *Lévitique (organisation)*, DBS V, 1952, 389-397. (Discusses the current state of the question.) For the older scholarship, cf. Hoonacker in DBS IV, 1949, 134ff. / W. Kornfeld, *Das Heiligkeitsgesetz*, 1952.

It can hardly be doubted that, with his new organization of the Yahweh cult, Moses also gave a new form to the organization of the cult personnel.[1] Cult and ritual, especially in the case of sacrifice, had been in practice long before the time of Moses. One might well raise the question as to who were the legitimate personnel in charge of the cult in the time before Moses, especially since, according to St. Paul (Heb 5, 4), at least an indirect call from God is required for the essence of the priestly office: "One does not take the honor upon himself, but he is called by God, just as Aaron was." The Jewish tradition, which is followed by many of the Fathers and by the more recent theologians, has always maintained that it is the first-born who also function as priests, especially empowered to offer sacrifice. There is nothing in Scripture to support this opinion; in fact, Scripture regularly recounts the offering of sacrifice by people other than the first-born (Abel, Abraham, Jacob, etc.).

The sanctification of the first-born, which is adduced as proof of a sort of priestly consecration, has nothing to do with the question. The positive law on the subject of the first-born was first proclaimed immediately before the Exodus of Israel from Egypt (Ex 13, 2), in fact it would even seem that it came into full power only after the time of Israel's entry into the land, when the Aaronitic priesthood was already functioning. The consecration of the first-born is indeed a consecration made to God, but not in the sense that it empowers anyone to perform ritual acts; it is, rather, an acknowledgment of God as sovereign lord over all life, by the free surrender of the first (and best). God is the supreme arbiter over people and land. By the killing of the first-born of the Egyptians and the sparing of the Israelites, he has also acquired a new claim and thus the practice of the consecration of the first-born,

---

1. Though we owe many valuable insights to M. Noth, *Geschichte Israels,* in other points, his presentation of the events at Sinai seems to be hyper-critical. It is not possible to consider the earliest beginnings of the people of Israel apart from Moses. His presentation is determined by a sort of religious-history flux from which new religious beginnings are crystallized. But why should we depart from the concrete existence of an historical person and take refuge in the incomprehensible semi-twilight of some unclear community or church conception? One wonders at the justification today, after the most recent discoveries in the Ancient Near East, of statements like this: "This would tend to demonstrate the fact that Moses has no historical connection with the events at Sinai. It is thus quite unhistorical to characterize Moses as the great organizer or law-giver of Israel. The events at Sinai are, moreover, very mysterious for us in that we do not find a single human agent at work in determining or interpreting the whole series of events." In the Notes we read: "It is quite erroneous and certainly not at all in keeping with the later, more developed form of the Mosaic tradition to see Moses as the great religious founder or even to speak of a 'Mosaic religion.' " (M. Noth, *op. cit.,* 118).

which goes back to early Beduin times, was promulgated as a law in Israel. When we said above that the Mosaic legislation is, in many points, a reform of ancient legal practices, this is true primarily with respect to the law of the first-born. Whether the first-born is further obligated to a special code of conduct with respect to God is nowhere mentioned in the law. The sanctification of the first-born seems rather to have been motivated by the concept of an obligation to serve in the sanctuary, that is, to assist the offering of sacrifice by the officially appointed personnel. In actual practice, they were freed of this obligation through a ritual redemption.

The priesthood was, accordingly, in the time before Moses, not the exclusive privilege of the first-born; at the beginning there was no special cult personnel, given legitimate office by any positive law. The priesthood was exercised by those who, in the broader or narrower sense of the word, represented the interests of the family. Just as it was from the fathers of the families, the tribal heads — and in certain cases the first-born — that people expected the decision which determined the conduct of the tribe or the family, so too these persons were primarily responsible for the community's relationships with God. It was thus their special prerogative to ask for the divine blessing before any undertaking, by offering the appropriate prayers and sacrifices, and to offer the appropriate sacrifices of thanksgiving and propitiation afterwards.

The unity of the religious priestly office and the profane office of leader is quite in keeping with the patriarchal system of life. Our historical knowledge cannot determine whether, during the time of the sojourn in Egypt where the patriarchal family grew to the proportions of a people, an official priesthood also developed. But if there had always been a priestly class in Israel, since the time of Egypt, the institution of a new priestly family necessarily implied the rejection of the earlier system. This process could not have taken place without creating some friction. Apart from the account of Kore, Dathan, and Abiron, and the revolution they engineered (Nb 16; 17), the Bible makes no further reference to the difficulties occasioned by this transition.

Through the Mosaic law the priesthood became the exclusive function of Aaron and the male posterity of his line (Ex 28, 1), while the other members of the Tribe of Levi were assigned to the priests as servants in the function of their sacred office, and, for this purpose, were given over to Yahweh as his "property." They had thus succeeded to the first-born and became Yahweh's "property" in the same manner as the first-born were by the very fact of their birth (Nb 3, 6ff.).

The entire cult personnel was thus chosen from the tribe

of Levi in keeping with the following system: 1. On the lowest rank were the non-priestly Levites or the Levites, in the stricter sense, as servants of the priests; 2. The Aaronites as the priests proper; 3. The highest position was occupied by Aaron and his first-born successors, acting as high-priest. This triple division corresponds to the three-fold division of the sanctuary itself, insofar as the Levites were restricted to the outer court, while the priest could enter the sanctuary, and the high priest alone could enter into the Holy of Holies.

A) THE LEVITES

Shortly before the rebellion of the people in the wilderness at Sinai, the Levites were solemnly consecrated and initiated into their service. This consecration, whose details are recorded in Numbers 8, 5-22, took place through a three-fold purification ritual (symbolic of the inner purification of the human person, who is to enter into the presence of God). The Levites were then directed to their sacred service, as the representatives of the people imposed their hands upon them, whereupon Aaron led them first to the entry of the tabernacle and then back to the altar of holocaust (symbolic of submission to Yahweh). The ritual concluded with a holocaust and an offering of propitiation. This ceremonial was valid for all generations to come, and did not need to be repeated.

The ritual functions of the Levites were either immediately connected with the divine service (service at God's house, 2 Ez 11, 22), such as the assistance of the priests at the sacrificial cult, the maintenance and protection of the tabernacle, the transport of the tabernacle during the trek through the desert, the preparation of the show-breads, etc., or they were external work, primarily the instruction of the people in the law (1 Chr 26, 29). The Levites, according to Numbers 4, 3ff., were obligated to the heavy service already from their thirtieth year, and, according to Numbers 8, 23, from their twenty-fifth year they were obligated to the lighter service; the later system established by David also includes the twenty-year-old Levites as obligated to service. The time of service was completed with the fiftieth year (Nb 4, 3ff.).

When the portions of the Promised Land were assigned by Lot, the tribe of Levi did not receive any special tribal territory as its possession; the Lord himself was to be their part and heritage (Nb 18, 20). Forty-eight cities (13 of them in the neighborhood of Jerusalem, for the priestly families) were assigned by Lot, throughout the entire country, for the Levites to dwell in (Nb 35, 1-8; Josh 21). God himself was responsible for their livelihood, by assigning to them the taxes which he, as the true Lord and possessor of the land, lawfully received from his people. The Levites received a tithe of all the natural produce of the land, but were themselves obligated to pay a further tithe of this produce to the priests (Lev 27, 30-33; Nb 18, 21-28). The Levites were also recommended to the generosity of the people (Dt 12, 19), and enjoyed freedom from military service and taxation.

Without going into the historical reconstruction presented by Well-hausen, we must still briefly examine the position maintained by the school of higher criticism regarding the origins of the Levites, especially as it is represented by its chief proponents today: G. Hölscher, S. Mo-winckel, W. Eichrodt, K. Möhlenbrink, H. Rowley.[2]

The "sons of Levi" are not so much a tribe as an official priestly community of Midianite origin. The word Levi, which has been dis-covered on inscriptions in El-Ela, where Midianite influence is clearly evident, means simply "priest," "interpreter of fate." The Levites would thus be simply the official priestly class functioning in Kadesh al-ready in the time of Moses, and Moses, in his religious service in the have won them over and appointed them for the divine service in the tabernacle. Together with the charismatic personality of the leader there is now an official position which is entrusted with the administration of the closely determined institutions of a sacrificial cult, no matter how simple, at the tabernacle of the covenant, the management of lots and oracles and all the cult activities at the tabernacle and in the ark. Thus, not only were the cult formulae for the new faith in God established with the authority of new norms, but there was also a certain guarantee for the fact that the covenant struck with Moses could not simply be

2. A. Lefèvre, DBS, fasc. XXV (1952), 394: "Prêtres et Lévites." / G. Hölscher, Artikel "Lewi" in Realencyklopädie. / Pauly-Wissowa, XII, 2155-2208. / W. Eichrodt, op. cit., 197ff: "Organe des Bundes." / K. Möhlenbrink, Die levitischen Überlieferungen des At, in ZATW (1934), 184-230. / G. von Rad, Das Geschichtsbild des chronistischen Werkes (1930), 80-119. / H. H. Rowley, The Re-Discovery of the OT (1945), 77-93.

abandoned, the continuity of its development being firmly established. The Levitical priesthood would thus be simply the appropriation and adaptation of a non-Israelite institution into the service of Yahweh.

Our presentation up to this point has already made it clear that revelation has the closest possible ties with the historical situations of the Ancient Near East. What is new are not the external forms, but the interior content of the faith. There is, in principle, no reason why the Midianite priestly organization could not have simply been taken over into the service of Yahweh. On the other hand, this possibility is supported by too little evidence to be taken simply as historical truth. The interpretation of the inscriptions of El-Ela leaves many questions unanswered.[3] Furthermore, Scripture dates the institution of this new cult at Sinai, and not after Kadesh. Just as the possibility that the name of Yahweh was taken over from the Midianites must remain a questionable hypothesis, even so the Levitical hypothesis, unless it is supported by additional inscription material, is a question that requires further clarification.

B)   THE   PRIESTS

The priests had to trace their lineage from Aaron, and be able to prove their descent (cf. Ex 28, 1; Nb 3, 10; Ezra 1, 62); unlawful usurpation of the priestly dignities and prerogatives was punishable by death. The priesthood was solemnly confirmed upon the family of Aaron by the sentence passed upon Core, Dathan, and Abiron, and their followers by the blossoming staff of Aaron which, as a commemoration of this event, had to be preserved in the ark of the covenant (Nb 16, 17). This genealogical requirement is so characteristic of the Old Testament that its abrogation through the priesthood of Christ, who is a descendant of the tribe of Judah, has to be coincident with the abrogation of the Law itself (Heb 7, 12). It is thus a hallmark of the messianic era that priests and Levites can be taken even from among the pagans (Is 66, 21).

In order to preserve the priestly dignity from any contempt, perfect physical constitution was obligatory; those who were afflicted with disfiguring physical characteristics were excluded from the exercise of the priestly service, although they

---

3. A. Lefèvre, DBS (1952), fasc. XXV, 394: "Lévitique." / Heinisch, *op. cit.*, 89, denies any connection between the Israelite priesthood and the South Arabian inscriptions.

were not excluded from their share in the income (Lev 21, 16-23).

The priests, moreover, were obligated to a high level of moral perfection, as demanded by the immediacy of God's presence in the divine service. They were obligated primarily to avoid all Levitical uncleanness, since this would exclude them from the exercise of the sacred service, and during their time of service in the sanctuary, they were obligated to complete abstinence from marital intercourse and intoxicating drink (Lev 21, 1-9; 9-11).

St. Paul (Heb 5, 1) sees the office of the priest realized in the position of mediator, the role which the priest plays between God and man. His privileged position is not a private mark of distinction, but rather a service to the people before God. It is his duty to present the concerns of the people before God and to bring back God's blessing and grace upon the people. The priest thus stands so close to God that he can be expressly called the property of God, chosen explicitly by God, from among the people, to perform his service (Joel 1, 9); since he thus enters into the very sphere of God himself, he has some share in that property of God which most especially characterizes the God of the Old Testament, his holiness. The priests were obligated to attend to the entire sacrificial service, as well as maintain a sacred fire. During the sacrifice, they could be helped by Levites, even by laymen; but the sacrificial activity proper must be attended to only by the priests. To this office was added the whole of the sanctuary service, maintaining the lamps, setting out the show-breads, etc., as well as the priestly blessing after the morning sacrifice. Their activities, however, extend far beyond the divine service proper; they are also charged with the instruction of the people in matters of the Law (Mal 2, 7), and the decision in particularly difficult legal cases (Dt 17, 8-12). The priests are, accordingly, not only the sacrificers, but also the teachers and jurists for the people. Religious and civil spheres of power are closely bound together.

The priest was allowed to approach the sacred service only in his proper official vesture. This official clothing consisted of linen breeches and an over-garment, also of linen, which reached to the ankles, held in at the waist by a long and brightly colored cincture; the head was covered with a sort of turban (mitre, tiara) (Ex 28, 40-43).

C) THE HIGH PRIEST

At the head of the priesthood stood the high priest, referred to in the more ancient texts simply as "the priest" (*hakkohên*), since it seems, in ancient Israel, that titles of honor were regularly avoided. But if several priests functioned at one large sanctuary, one of them must have had a position of higher rank. In the royal era the title "most high priest" (*hakkohên haggadôl*) or "priest, head" (*kohên hârôš*) is expressly attested (2 K 12, 11; 22, 4, 8; 23, 4; 25, 18). Any kind of organization could hardly have been managed without some very clear sense of structure. At the same time, we know from the inscriptions in Ugarit that the superior of the local priesthood was, already in the fourteenth century before Christ, referred to as *rabbu kâhinîna* "superior of the priests."[4] Since his head was anointed with oil on the occasion of his consecration, he was also called the "anointed priest." That these titles were not used in more ancient times is no proof of the fact that there was not at that time any high-priesthood. It is only to be expected that, in the course of time, the power and dignity and also the privileges of the high priest should have become more prominent, as well as the distinction between him and the ordinary priests; but, the greater the progress made by archaeological investigation, the less question there can be as to the Mosaic origins of this priesthood.[5]

The vesture of the high priest consisted of a dark blue outer garment, which reached to his knees, the ephod with its breast-plate (*hôšên*). The ephod appears as the priestly garment in 1 Samuel 2, 28; 22, 18; the young Samuel, during his time of

---

4. Albright, *op. cit.*, 281.
5. P. Heinisch, *op. cit.*, 213ff. / J. W. Bailey, *The Usage in the Post-Restoration Period of Terms Descriptive of the Priest and the High-Priest*. No fixed terminology for the high-priest before the Maccabean era, JBL 70 (1951), 217-225.

service in the sanctuary, also wears an ephod (1 S 2, 18). This garment was a "linen ephod" (*'ephôd bad*). This was different from the ephod which served as the medium for ascertaining the future or determining a particularly difficult legal question. This ephod is never called the "linen ephod," and, moreover, it was to be found, when needed, in the sanctuary. The high-priestly ephod was a garment which covered the upper body front and back, reaching as far down as the hips, and letting the shoulders free. It was gathered around the body by a sash, while two straps, woven with gold, supported it across the shoulders; it was adorned with precious gems and the names of the twelve tribes. When the high priest entered into the sanctuary, he appeared as intermediary between God and the people and bade Yahweh to be mindful of Israel in love and mercy. But the ephod takes on its true value and significance only in connection with the breastplate.

The breastplate represents something very much like our modern purse. On the outside it was adorned with 12 precious stones, and bound to the ephod by four rings and a golden chain and cords. The breastplate had a two-fold significance: the 12 precious stones were to commemorate the 12 tribes of Israel in the presence of Yahweh and especially to hold the Urim and Thummim. The etymological interpretation of these two words is uncertain. The Septuagint translates: "revelation and truth." At all events, it was through this medium, on the occasion of critical decisions, that Yahweh's judgment was secured, whence it was called also "the breastplate of judgment" or simply "judgment" (Ex 28, 30). The exploration of the divine will took place through the high priest's formulating the question in such a manner that the answer could be yes or no, for instance: "Shall I do this? Is he guilty? (cf. Josh 7, 16ff.; 1 S 14, 37ff.). Probably the Urim and Thummim were two stones of different color or two little batons with different marks (cf. the arrow oracle, Ezek 21, 26); the priest, after asking his question, reached into the purse (1 S 14, 19), and drew out one of the stones. Sometimes Yahweh would give no answer at all; thus it is possible that there was a third stone in the purse, whose appearance was equivalent to a refusal to answer. Or

perhaps the purse was shaken until one of the stones fell out
(Ezek 21, 26). So far as we are in a position to determine today, the ephod and the oracle purse are not specifically Israelite;
there are Egyptian and Ancient Near Eastern parallels for
both. These objects take on their particular value and significance
only in connection with the Yahweh cult.[6]

On his head the high priest wore a head covering of linen,
with a gold plate fastened to it above the forehead by a cord,
containing the title "Yahweh is holy." This marked him out as
the particular property of Yahweh and thus elevated him above
the others as mediator between God and the people. As far
as the specifics of the official service are concerned, the high
priest could perform all the priestly functions if he so chose.
Exclusively his was the expiation of the entire people on the
great day of Atonement, as well as the request for the Urim
and Thummim in public questions of great importance. The
high priest had supreme control over the entire priesthood,
the divine service, and the temple treasury, and his was the
final decision in all religious matters.

Aaron and his sons, before the establishment of the tabernacle sanctuary, were initiated into their office by a special,
seven-day ritual of consecration. They were washed, clothed
in their official garments, and anointed with a specially prepared oil. The second part of the ceremony consisted of a series
of sacrifices. Moses took some of the blood of the sacrifice
and brushed it upon the earlobe, the right thumb, and the right

---

6. Heinisch, in his commentary on Exodus (p. 216ff), points to Egyptian
   parallels. From the Enuma Elish epic we are familiar with the Babylonian tablets of destiny which, after his victorious battle, the God
   Marduk takes for himself as the expression of his supreme power. In
   the Baal myth recently discovered in Ras-Shamra, the victor in the
   battle, Gepen Ugar, is supposed to receive, as his reward, the ephod
   and tablets of destiny. / Virolleaud, *La mort de Baal, poème de Ras-
   Shamra*, in Syria XV (1934), 305ff. / Cf. Bonkamp, *Die Bibel im
   Lichte der Keilschriftforschung*, (1939), 88. / On the priests' vestments,
   John Gabriel, *Untersuchungen über das alttestamentliche Hohepriesterlichen Ornates*, Theol. Stud. der öst. Leogesellsch. Nr. 33 (1933). / S.
   v. Gliazynski, *Verusuch einer Identifizierung der Edelsteine am Amtss-
   child des jüdischen Hehepriesters*, FF 21/23 (1947), 234.

big toe of the person to be consecrated, thereby consecrating the entire person for the sacred service. In order to symbolize the investiture with the sacrificial gifts, Moses laid part of the sacrifice in the hands of the priest and "wove" these parts as a "web" in the presence of Yahweh (by a horizontal motion directed towards the sacred tabernacle.). Then the persons to be consecrated were sprinkled with the oil of the anointing and the blood from the sacrifice, and the entire ritual was concluded with a sacrificial meal. This ceremony was repeated (perhaps only partially) every day for an entire week. What we have here are very ancient symbols of consecration. Sprinkling with blood signifies the dedication of a person to the divinity. By the solemn anointing, a person is set apart from other men and, through the investiture with the sacred garments, he is entrusted with the sacred service.

The priests received the tithe of the tithes received by the Levites, the price paid for the redemption of the first-born of humans and animals unfit for sacrifice, and from the animals prescribed for sacrifice they received only the flesh stipulated for the sacrificial banquet. They also received the first fruits of all the land's produce which had been offered to God, and certain parts of the sacrifices.

The institution of an official priesthood means that, together with the charismatic leader who, like Moses and the prophets, was expressly called by God to undertake a particular historical mission, there is also the office which, by its very nature, is a permanent institution. In terms of their structure, both elements represent a natural sort of tension which had to be arbitrated throughout the course of the Old Testament. It is precisely the prophets who become the most impassioned opponents of a cult which has grown too external.

CHAPTER X

THE SACRIFICIAL SERVICE

LITERATURE

R. Dussaud, *Les Origines canaanéenes du sacrifice israélite*, Paris 1921. / F. Heiler, *Das Gebet*, 1921, 71ff. / A. Wendel, *Das Opfer in der alttestamentlichen Religion*, 1927. / F. Blome, *Die Opfermaterie in Babylonien und Israel*, 1934. / F. X. Kortleitner, *Formae cultus mosaici cum ceteris religionibus orientis antiqui comparatae*, Innsbruck, 1933. / P. Heinisch, *Das Buch Leviticus*, (BB), 1935, 20ff. / *Theologie des AT*, 1940, 189ff. / Fr. Nötscher, *Biblische Altertumskunde*, (BB), 1940, 320ff. / D. M. L. Urie, *Sacrifice among the West Semites*, PEQ 81, 1949, 67-82. / H. H. Rowley, *The Meaning of Sacrifice in the OT*, BJohnRylLibr., 33, 74-110. / W. H. Stevenson, *Hebrew 'olah and zebach sacrifices*, Fs. Bertholet, 1950, 488-497.

A) CONCEPT AND DIVISIONS

"In the concept of sacrifice we are confronted with the primordial phenomenon of all religions, a phenomenon which has a significant role to play in the Old Testament, as it is visible in Christianity. It is important to have a proper concept of this phenomenon and to examine its roots and origins."[1] In this respect, unfortunately, the first admission we must make is that we cannot possibly expect theoretical discussion on the subject

---

1. Procksch, *op. cit.*, 551.

of the origin and nature of sacrifice in the Old Testament. It is an ancient practice which corresponds to the divine will and rests on divine instruction. The Pentateuch legislation prescribes the kind and the performance of the sacrifices, but it is not an entirely unified body of precepts since, in the course of time, many changes proved to be necessary. We thus have more ancient precepts side by side with more recent ones, enlarging, altering, or entirely abrogating the older law, without leaving a clear picture of the line of development in individual details. Considerable influence from the neighboring districts is not to be excluded, but the very nature of the subject dictates that the ritual forms of sacrifice exhibit a more or less common form all over the world.[2] Still, it is wrong to attempt to explain the Old Testament sacrificial cult simply on the basis of the general history of religion, without examining any of the peculiarities of the Old Testament concept of God which, despite what appears to be a similarity in external forms, has been totally transformed within, since it is now the soul of the Yahweh faith which inspires the cult forms of sacrifice.[3]

If we wish to develop a phenomenological appreciation of the essence of Old Testament sacrifice, the best point of departure will be the concept of a gift to the divinity. Taxes and tribute, and partially also the first fruits and the tithes, are surrendered to the sanctuary or to its servants without any particular ritual, and do not make their way to the altar. The person who makes this gift needs only to guarantee that the gifts are presented in the prescribed quantity and quality (Dt 26, 12). But if such a gift is given as the sole property of the divinity accompanied by a definite ritual (perhaps by a priest), then, through this ritual, it becomes a sacrifice, whether, since it now belongs exclusively to the divinity, it is burned in its entirety upon the altar, or whether part of it is set apart for the services of the priest or the man offering sacrifice. The essential element is the ritual and the personal devotion. At

---

2. Nötscher, *Biblische Altertumskunde* (1940), 321.
3. Eichrodt, *op. cit.*, I, 61.

all events, the sacrifice is a gift, and a gift of the very best and most valuable things that man possesses.[4]

Since the gift is an external symbol, the meaning of the symbol is dependent upon the sentiment of the giver. Sacrifice can thus be the expression of adoration, thanksgiving, petition, guilt, or expiation. At all events, the sacrifice becomes an occasion for encounter with God, a moment in which the mighty chasm between the holy God and the unholy human is bridged over and communion is made possible between God and man. Through sacrifice, man enters into the sphere of God's holiness (*hitqaddeš*).[5]

With respect to the material of the sacrifice, the Old Testament sacrifices are divided into bloody and unbloody sacrifices. The material for the unbloody sacrifices was grain and wheat, together with oil, incense, and salt. The bloody sacrifices consisted of large and small animals, oxen, sheep, and goats; in some cases the sex of the sacrificial animals was not determined; in other cases, for particular sacrifices, we find one or the other sex prescribed. Sacrificial animals taken from the flocks must be at least eight days old, although, for individual sacrifices, a higher age, in the case of sheep and goats at least one year, was demanded. In general, the sacrificial animal could not, either by reason of its tender age or its advanced years, suggest the character of weakness or imperfection; it must be sacrificed at the time of its full vital powers. As a gift made to the supreme Lord, the animal chosen for sacrifice must be without blemish. Damaged or blemished gifts are an insult rather than an act of devotion to God.

The significance of the prescribed sacrificial material is bound up with the fact that man is to sacrifice only the means of life, and from among these, only the product of his own normal work and occupation (flocks or agriculture). The material for the sacrifice is thus intimately bound up with human life, and thereby becomes symbolic of the human person himself, who

---

4. Nötscher, *op. cit.*, 320.
5. Procksch, *op. cit.*, 551.

offers himself to God in his gifts. The sacrificial gift is thus bound up with the culture of the sacrificial community. Cult and culture, especially in the Old Testament, proved to be so indissolubly united that, even etymologically, they derive from the same root. Sacrifice cannot be offered with just any gift, but only with the produce of one's own culture. The Hebrew sacrificial prescripts make it abundantly clear that only domesticated animals and cultivated plants are fit materials for sacrifice; of the domestic animals, the ox, sheep, goat, and dove; of the cultivated plants, the fruits of the field or the orchard.[6]

The sacrificial prescripts (Lev 1 — 7) distinguish five kinds of sacrifice: holocaust (*'olah*), peace sacrifice or sacrificial meal (*zebah šelamîm*), sacrifices in acknowledgment of sin (*hattât*) and guilt (*'âšam*) (generally there is not a precise distinction between these last two), and food sacrifices (*minhah*).

B) THE SACRIFICIAL RITUAL

The common ritual for bloody sacrifices comprises the following essential elements:

a) The sacrificial animal was brought into the outer court, "in the presence of Yahweh" (*liphne yahweh*), by the sacrificer himself, where it was taken by the priest and examined. The outer court of the tabernacle of the covenant (and later the Temple) was the one legitimate place for sacrifice. Actually, there were a number of exceptions, in which we can clearly follow the development of the sacrificial cult. For example, sacrifices were offered on Ebel (Josh 8, 30, 31), on Bochim (Jg 2, 5), at Beth-shemesh (1 S 6, 15). Samuel offered sacrifice in many places upon his journeys (9, 12), and built an altar in his home country of Ramathaim (7, 17); in the Northern Kingdom there were sacrificial altars at various places, as we can see from the objections lodged by Elijah: "The sons of Israel have destroyed their altars" (1 K 19, 10, 14).

---

6. *Ibid.*, 552.

b) The next element, in most of the sacrifices, was the imposition of hands. This did not have the same meaning in all cases. It could signify blessing (Gn 48, 14), investiture with office (Nb 27, 18; Dt 34, 9), the handing over of power (2 K 13, 16). The laying on of hands is an expression of the passing on of personal guilt only in one case, the scapegoat, who, on the Day of Atonement, is driven out into the wilderness, but this is not really a sacrifice (Lev 16, 21). In general, the laying on of hands, which is a ceremony that always takes place on the occasion of holocaust, peace offerings and sacrifices of expiation (excepting for the sacrifice of birds), cannot possibly signify the passing on of guilt or representation of guilt; otherwise the sacrificial flesh could not possibly be holy and could not possibly be consumed by the priests: it would have to be annihilated as being laden with curse and guilt, and therefore ritually unclean. Hence, the laying on of hands can serve only to signify the intention to make a gift and to hand over the rights of ownership. The human agent gives up his claim to the gift and surrenders it entirely to God.[7]

c) The slaughter of the sacrificial animal is accomplished by the sacrificer himself, while the priest catches the blood, which he uses for the expiatory ritual of sprinkling. It is a matter of very ancient belief that, in both man (Gn 4, 10; Job 16, 18) and in beast alike (Lev 17, 11, 14; Dt 12, 23), the soul lives in the blood, and gushes forth together with the blood, so that the blood may never be consumed, but must be offered to God alone as the supreme Lord of life. The classical passage for this belief is to be found in Leviticus 17, 11: "For the life of the flesh is in the blood; and I have given it for you upon the altar to make atonement for your souls (*lekapper 'al naphšekem*); for it is the blood that makes atonement, by reason of the life." Not as if the blood were some special substance which, by some magic ritual, could exercise this peculiar effect, but simply because it is the seat of the living soul, the blood has the power to achieve expiation.[8] The fact that the blood is

---

7. Nötscher, *op. cit.*, 327.

thus removed from all profane usage through the Levitical legislation — not even the flesh in which the blood is can be eaten — is perhaps to be explained as a precaution against animistic rituals and practices, according to which the consumption of blood was believed to confer magical powers.[9] In the Israelitic sacrificial cult, blood takes on the further preeminent meaning of expiation and reconciliation. This is a power it enjoys not of its own natural essence; even this blood cult is without meaning unless the sacrificer displays the proper interior attitudes. The zeal of the prophets is a powerful argument against a misinterpretation of the myth of blood: "Do I eat the flesh of bulls or drink the blood of goats? — Every beast of the forest is mine, the cattle on a thousand hills" (Ps 50, 12, 10).

d) The final act of the sacrificial ritual was the burning of the flesh. Only by destroying the flesh was the sacrificial gift removed once and for all from any profane usage. Either the entire animal was burned, or only the fat parts and the choice portions. In the last case, the rest of the flesh was used for the sacrificial banquet.

C) THE INDIVIDUAL SACRIFICES

1) *The holocaust* (*'olâh*). This sacrifice is called a holocaust (*holocaustum*) and derives its name from the fact that the entire animal (a male ox, sheep, or goat, and eventually also young doves or turtle-doves) is completely burned as an expression of supreme adoration of God, — excepting for the hide, and, in the case of birds, the maw and the feathers. This sacrifice could never be interrupted, so that it was also referred to as *tamid* (*iuge sacrificium*), perpetual sacrifice. Every day, both in the morning and in the evening, a lamb was slaughtered, and made to burn throughout the entire day and the entire night (Lev 6, 9-13).

---

8. Procksch, *op. cit.*, 560.

9. Nötscher, *op. cit.*, 326.

2) *The sin offering* (*hattat*). As the very name implies, this sacrifice is offered as an expiation for sin (*sacrificium pro peccato*). This is not a sin "committed with a high hand" (Nb 15, 30, 31), sins which could be expiated for only by death, but rather transgressions which proceeded from rashness, or in order to remove the sacrificial incompetence which derived from levitical uncleanliness. Since it is the element of expiation which stands in the foreground in this sacrifice, the ritual is also characterized by the ceremonies involving the blood. For the sacrifice in behalf of an individual person, the blood was smeared on the horns of the altar of holocaust; for a sacrifice of the entire community or the priests, the blood was brought into the sanctuary and sprinkled seven times against the great veil of the Holy of Holies, and then smeared on the horns of the altar of incense; on the great Day of Atonement, however, it was carried into the Holy of Holies itself, where it was sprinkled seven times on the floor before the plate over the ark of the covenant, and then sprinkled upon the plate of expiation itself. Of the sacrificial flesh itself, the fat parts and the choice selections were burned on the altar. Of those sacrifices whose blood was carried into the Holy Place, all the rest of the flesh — outside the limits of the camp at first, and later outside the city itself — was burnt; the flesh of the other sacrifices fell to the possession of the male priests and, as "very sacred" (*sancta sanctorum*) could be consumed only in the outer court (Lev 4; 6, 25 to 30; 16).

In addition to the sacrifice of expiation, there was also the sacrifice of guilt (*'āšam, sacrificium pro delicto*), with a very simple ritual. The blood was sprinkled upon the altar, the fat portions burned, and the rest of the flesh fell to the possession of the priests. For this sacrifice only smaller animals were used, usually rams. The priest had to make an estimate of the value of the animal, but no substitute sacrifice could be allowed. This is in keeping with the significance of the guilt sacrifice. From the individual cases in which it was prescribed it is clear that it must be sacrificed for those sins which involve misappropriation, or some other violation of property or justice. Thus, since it involves a recompense for a material damage, it was always bound up with some form of indemnification, as well as the imposition of a penalty, consisting of one fifth of the value (Lev 5, 14ff.; 7, 1-7).

3) *The peace sacrifice* (*zebah šelamîm*) (*victima pacifica, hostia pacificorum*). The characteristic element of this sacrifice was the sacrificial meal. After burning the fat portions, the brisket was dedicated to the Lord through the ceremonial of "weaving" (horizontal motion towards the sanctuary and back), and the right hind leg was taken out, and both were offered to the priests. The remaining flesh was used by the sacrificers for a banquet, in which the whole family, including the slaves and the poorer Levites, were permitted to share (Lev 3; 7, 11-21). The significance of the peace sacrifice is explained already by its name.[10] It is, accordingly, a sacrifice in which the sacrificer shows himself as God's friend, and attempts to manifest and strengthen the relationship of peace (*šalôm*) and friendship with Yahweh. This idea is expressed primarily in the sacrificial banquet. On this occasion God is the host, the sacrificer is God's guest, and the banquet itself is pledge and symbol of their mutual friendship. This sacrificial banquet is a type of the meal frequently mentioned in Scripture, which Yahweh is preparing for mankind in the messianic kingdom. In ancient times, the peace offering had a great role to play as a sacrifice of joy; there was danger that it would be secularized and misused, a prospect against which the prophets take a most intransigent position.

As particular forms of the peace sacrifice we must mention the sacrifice of the oath (*neder*) and the sacrifice of praise and thanksgiving (*zebah hattôdâh*). Here too the element of joy is clearly recognizable, an element which, even in the age of the psalms, was so popular that it could not even disappear. This might be the very grounds of encounter where the cult song, the psalm, joins in intimately with the sacrificial activity, as the spiritual expression of a joyous religion.

---

10. According to Procksch, Theol. A. T. 556 not to be derived from *šalôm* "peace," but rather from *šelem* "perfection," since the meal also included fruits and wine, and was thus a complete, or perfect meal. Most probable is the derivation from *šallem*, "to fill"; hence, instead of "peace sacrifice," we should read "fulfillment sacrifice," by which vows were satisfied.

4) *The food offering*: the unbloody sacrifices are generally called *minhah* (gift, *oblatio, munus*); frequently, however, only the part of the sacrifice which consists in a grain offering is called by this name, as contrasted with the libation or sacrifice of wine connected with it. The grain was never offered in its raw state, but either ground into coarse meal, or as fine flour, or even in the form of unleavened cakes. In all the unbloody sacrifices there were the additional gifts of oil, which was either poured over the sacrificial gifts or mixed with them, as well as salt and incense. In the case of most of these sacrifices, only a small portion was burned on the altar together with incense (as an *'azkârâh* — "portion of remembrance," since it was designed to make Yahweh mindful of the sacrificer), while the rest fell to the lot of the priests; the wine was poured out on the altar. The food sacrifices which the priests offered were burnt in their entirety, and this is true primarily of the daily *minhah* of the high priest. The unbloody sacrifices were partly additional gifts meant to accompany the holocausts and peace sacrifices, and partly independent sacrifices. They were offered either in the outer court or in the Holy Place. Among them we might count the daily incense offering, the showbreads (loaves of proposition), the offering of wine, and the light of the golden lampstand. Of these various sacrifices offered in the outer court, particular importance accrues to the daily sacrifice which the high priest himself was obliged to offer both for himself and for the whole priesthood, and also the sacrifice of expiation for the poor who did not possess sufficient means for a bloody sacrifice (Lev 2; 4, 11-13).

The primitive idea of feeding the gods may well have survived in popular circles, but it is completely at variance with the ancient Israelite faith in Yahweh. Yahweh is the great Lord of the universe, and he does not need to be fed by his human creatures. The sacrifices offered to him are, on the contrary, designed to recognize Yahweh and worship him as the giver of all good gifts.

Ancient Israel thus created a sacrificial cult which was able to bring the full breadth of the religious soul into play (sin, guilt and expiation, thanksgiving for help, adoration, and worship), a cult which, in its external rituals, exhibits many similarities with the formulae and expressions of the Ancient Near Eastern religions, and which, for precisely this reason, was always subject to the danger of defection to the pagan deities, but, within, is characterized by the faith in Yahweh which gives new meaning and bearing to all the external form.

The faith in Yahweh also implies a confession of mankind's hopeless and lost position. Since Paradise, there has been a great chasm between God and man. The wrath of God remains upon humanity, despite his choice of Israel. The curse of death and guilt is constantly to be brought to the awareness of the people in his uninterrupted sacrificial offering to God. That is why, fundamentally, only a bloody sacrifice, a sacrifice accompanied by the surrender of the life which is in the blood, can achieve this expiation. Just like the individual human life, so the life of the people too, is, in all its generations, subject to guilt; in the sacrifice of expiation the necessity of expiation is to be held before the eyes of all generations, with the annual days of atonement, and, every day, in the morning and evening sacrifice of the *tamid*, and still the expiation is not ended. The sacrificial cult thus becomes a violent plea for redemption. As the Old Testament religion becomes a more and more interior involvement, the emptiness of this cult based on the blood of animals is more and more recognized. In the Songs of the Servant of God (Is 53), we see the first dawning of the redemptive thought that only a guiltless human sacrifice offered as a substitute (*âšam*) for the guilty people, could create a people fundamentally reconciled with their God.[11]

If we mean to properly understand the Old Testament sacrificial cult, we must take all these important elements into consideration. The cult is not a mechanically guaranteed ritual. It loses all its meaning if the interior dispositions are lacking. In the final decades of the Old Testament the external cult in many circles becomes an end in itself and thereby loses all

---

11. Procksch, *op. cit.*, 561.

justification. This is the moment in which Jesus appears with his whip of cords to chase the merchants and the buyers from the Temple, and to restore the ancient and proper attitudes of the Old Testament sacrificial service: reconciliation with God by submission and faith.

CHAPTER XI

THE LAWS OF CLEANLINESS

LITERATURE

J. Döller, *Die Reinheits-und Speisegesetze in religionsgeschichtlicher Be-deungtung*, Münster 1917. / P. Heinisch, *Über die Reinheitsvorschriften im "Buch Leviticus"* 1935, 52ff. / Fr. Nötscher, *Biblische Altertumskunde*, Bonn 1940, 334ff. / W. Eichrodt, *Das Heiligkeitsgesetz*, 1952.

"THROUGHOUT the whole of the Old Testament there is no form of law which has had such manifold effects and been so generally perceptible in the whole life of the people as the precepts regarding cleanness and uncleanness and the distinctions between clean, permitted, and unclean, not permitted foods. It was these precepts that brought the law home; it held the faithful under tight control in his eating and drinking, in his every activity, and made him responsible even as he slept" (Haneberg). With precepts such as this, the Old Testament is not an isolated exception to the religions of the Ancient Near East. The history of religion provides an overpowering abundance of material to compare with these precepts on legal cleanness and uncleanness, and the ritual for restoring the legal cleanness that had been lost.[1] A primitive tabu may partially

---

1. The material is collected in Döller, *Die Reinheits-und Speisegesetze im AT in religionsgeschichtlicher Beleuchtung* (1917).

explain this practice. But once again we must be very cautious about the prospect of concluding to formal identity on the basis of externals alone. The final objective of the comparative study of religion must once again be determined, precisely what the Yahweh faith has made of the material adapted from the ancient faith and ritual.[2]

A) CULTIC CLEANNESS

The concepts of clean and unclean are first formed and developed with reference to the cult. Everything that is unclean can have no place in the cult. This is true equally for persons and things. A sharp distinction is drawn between sacred and profane, and persons and things are divided into two groups: clean and unclean, those which can perform a sacrificial activity and those which are excluded from this exercise. The uncleanness (incapacity to offer sacrifice) has various degrees. The least degree consists in the practice of excluding a man from entrance into the outer court until the evening of the day involved. This uncleanness could be removed simply by washing the body or even the clothing. Cultic uncleanness could, however, last for as long as one or two weeks, or even more. If it lasted at least seven days, then the ritual for removing it necessarily involved a sacrifice.

The law distinguished three categories of cultic uncleanness:

a) The uncleanness of a human corpse or an animal carcass. The corpse made a house in which it lay unclean, as well as the people who lived in the house, the furnishings of the house, and all open vessels, as well as clothing that came into contact with it — all this for a period of seven days. The purification ritual consisted, not of a normal washing, but in sprinkling with the "water from the ashes of the red cow."[3] A

---

2. Eichrodt, *op. cit.,* I, 57ff.
3. During the sojourn in the wilderness, a red-brown cow which had not yet borne the yoke was slaughtered as an expiatory victim, ac-

carcass made the person who touched it unclean only until that evening.

b) *The uncleanness of leprosy*: The man afflicted with leprosy was unclean as long as the disease lasted; he had to dress in robes of mourning, and make his home far from human society, outside the camp or the city, and warn everyone who approached him by calling "unclean." If he were healed of this disease, and the priests alone were competent to judge this case, he must still undergo a complicated purification ritual (Lev 13ff.).

The law also makes provision for a form of uncleanness which is caused by a sort of "leprosy" found on buildings (a species of decay) and on clothing (perhaps mildew).

c) *In the area of sex* (Lev 12; 15) it was primarily pathological, but also many natural conditions and processes which could cause, in either a man or a woman, a legal uncleanness which lasted for an entire day and was communicated to everything which the person touched. Cleanness could be restored seven days after the cessation of the original condition, by bathing and washing as well as by a holocaust or sin offering (a dove). Hygienic and moral grounds are only very indirectly involved in these precepts, since also involuntary nocturnal emission and normal marital intercourse can produce uncleanness for a day (Lev 15, 16; Dt 23, 11), the menstrual period makes a woman unclean for a period of seven days (Lev 15, 19-24), during which time she is to have no intercourse with her husband. The uncleanness of a woman after childbirth lasted for 40 days in the case of a boy, for 80 in the case of a girl; it was ended only by a holocaust and a sin offering: a lamb and a dove, or, in the case of the poor, two doves (Lev 12; cf. Lk 2, 22).

These precepts cannot possibly be regarded as any contempt

---

cording to a special ritual, and completely burned, cedar wood, hyssop, and wool being thrown into the fire. The ashes were preserved and used to mingle with the water for the sprinkling ritual that was prescribed for the cleansing of levitical uncleanness.

for marriage or birth, since a large family was regarded as the supreme blessing, while childlessness was a great disgrace and punishment from heaven.[4]

The meaning and purpose of these precepts: the levitical uncleanness cannot be simply identified with moral uncleanness or sin. It can also be incurred independently of human volition. The consequence of this uncleanness is not to interrupt the interior communion with God, but only to produce an external prohibition from cultic acts. In the study of theology, however, it is impossible entirely to avoid the suspicion that death, leprosy, and sexual activity produce uncleanness simply because "the reek of sin" is upon them. They could very easily come to be regarded as a consequence of the original sin, as a punishment for which death and all its consequences, and the bearing of children in pain and travail made their way into the world. The man who dared to approach Yahweh must be free of all these consequences and effects of sin. Through the precepts for cleanliness the service of Yahweh is lifted above the profane and sinful sphere and carried into the light of inaccessible holiness. The concepts and rituals of legal cleanliness thus have for their purpose the creation of a holy people for Yahweh. Ritual cleanliness is familiar to the Ancient Near East; but the application of these precepts to the cult of Yahweh endows them, in ancient Israel, with a specific meaning which is different from that of the world around them.[5]

B) THE DIETARY LAWS

The dietary laws, just like the laws on ritual cleanness do not represent anything unique to Israel. They were in practice among the other peoples of the Ancient Near East in very much the same form. We know of ancient Egypt that, even apart from pork, the consumption of fish or bones (which according to the Old Testament was not a matter of religious scruple at all) was considered undesirable and could also make one ritually unclean. In much the same manner, it was unlawful to eat cows, by reason of the connection between this animal and the goddess Isis with her cow's horns.[6]

The distinction between clean and unclean animals in the Old Testament is purely external. Of the quadrupeds, for ex-

---

4. Nötscher, *op. cit.*, 327-328.
5. Eichrodt, *op. cit.*, I, 59.
6. Herodot, II, 37; Erman, *Die ägyptische Religion*, 337.

ample, those which ruminate and also have a cloven hoof are clean; of the water animals those are clean which have fins and scales. Among the unclean animals are counted primarily the camel, the ass, the pig, the badger, and the hare. In the Pentateuch there is no particular emphasis on the prohibition against the eating of pork, although in a later era this commandment becomes the shibboleth of unfaithfulness to the Mosaic Law and is seen as equivalent to defection from the Israelite religion (Is 65, 4; 66, 3, 17; 2 M 6, 18ff.; Dn 1, 8, 12; Tb 1, 11; Jdt 10, 5; 12, 12; cf. Acts 10, 12). The reason for this strange evaluation of many animals can only be surmised. Some scholars have argued that it is occasioned by the possible connection with pagan sacrificial cults, by the voracity of many of the animals, or by their revolting appearance. But the reasons cannot, in the last analysis, be rationally interpreted. It is probably true that the Israelite law incorporates ancient popular practices, which it freely adapted to its own needs, at the same time enlarging upon them and giving them a new significance but, at all events, giving them a sound religious foundation and thus creating a sort of ascetical although quite external educational medium. Since the origins of these practices are not to be found in one unified source, the manifold character of their differences is easily explained.[7]

These dietary laws, which, in the last pre-Christian centuries, turned into a long and involved series of casuistry, at all events, did achieve one great accomplishment: it was through these precepts that God's people of the old covenant was clearly and sharply distinguished from all the pagan nations. They so embodied the need for confession of God's prerogatives and so embraced the entire ethnic unity of the people that, even after the loss of political autonomy, after the destruction of the Temple, this people could continue to exist in its national and religious individuality. When the early church abrogated the dietary laws (Acts 10, 11), this means that the national framework had fallen away and the kingdom of God had entered upon a supranational and world-wide mission.

---

7. Nötscher, *op. cit.*, 339.

CHAPTER XII

THE SACRED SEASONS

LITERATURE

Fr. Nötscher, "Sabbat und Feste," *Biblische Altertumskunde*, 1940, 350ff. / H. J. Elhorst, *Die deuteronomischen Jahresfeste*, in ZATW 42, 1236ff. / J. Hehn, *Siebenzahl und Sabbat bei den Babyloniern und im AT*, Leipzig 1907. / P. Heinisch, *Theol. des AT*, Bonn 1940, "die Feste," 199ff., bibliography. / W. Eichrodt, *Theol. AT*, 1948, I, 51ff. / O. Procksch, *Theologie des AT*, 1950, 543ff. / G. W. Anderson, *Hebrew Religion, OT and Modern Study*, 1951, 283-310.

EVERY cult requires not only a sacred site, but also a sacred time. This time is dependent upon the natural course of the sun and the moon; the sun forms the seasons for the life cycle of nature, while the moon is the ancient measure of time, dividing the year in twelve more or less equal parts.[1] This natural rhythm finds its expression primarily in the great nature festivals. The birth and growth and maturation of the fruits largely determines the content of the annual festival cycle: the offering of the first-fruits in the spring and, seven weeks later, at the conclusion of the grain harvest, the Festival of Weeks (the two festivals were later identified with Easter and Pentecost), the living in the tents on the occasion of the fall

---

1. O. Procksch, *op. cit.*, 543.

fruit and wine harvest. It was through this festival rhythm that the simple peasant life of Israel took on a religious orientation. Similar natural festivals were observed also by the Canaanites. But in Israel we note the decisive further element of a powerful connection between the phenomena of nature and the great events in salvation history: the Israelite festivals are thus elevated above the simple rhythm of nature. In the festival calendar of Israel we can distinguish primarily three classes: a. the Sabbath festival, b. the three great feasts of joy: Easter, Pentecost, and Tabernacles, c. the Day of Atonement. This festival cycle is determined largely by the sacred number seven: the seventh day of the week is the sabbath, the seventh month is the sabbath month, the seventh year is the sabbath year, the seven-times-seventh year is the year of jubilee. The Festival of Tabernacles and the Day of Atonement fall in the seventh month, while Pentecost is celebrated on the seven-times-seventh day after Easter. The two principal festivals of Easter and Tabernacles each last for seven days.

The calendar of the Old Testament has, in the course of its history, undergone certain transformations. The following stages can be determined with greater or lesser probability:

1) THE SOLAR CALENDAR: the apocryphal books of Jubilees and Henoch count in terms of a lunar year of 364 days, which is divided into 4 quarters of 13 weeks or 91 days each. Each month counted 30 days, and after every third month an intercalary day was introduced. The year thus had 12 months and 4 intercalary days. The months were numbered simply from 1 to 12. Seven years formed a week of years, and 7 weeks of years formed a jubilee. Accordingly, the Book of Jubilees divides the world history from the creation to the institution of the Pasch into a series of jubilees. In terms of this manner of reckoning time, the year counts 52 years. New Year's Day always falls on the same day of the week, Wednesday.

The Book of Jubilees claims that this calendar was created by God himself. Actually, its origins lie in the deluge narrative and the story of the Exodus from Egypt.

2) THE LUNAR CALENDAR: when, around the year 200 B.C., Palestine came under the domination of the Syrian Seleucids, among the other Hellenistic reforms that were introduced was the Greek lunar calendar. Daniel 7, 35 records the fact that Antiochus Epiphanes "changed the

times." Since the lunar month counts only 29 or 30 days, it was necessary to introduce an intercalary month after every second or third year, in order to bring the lunar year back into harmony with the solar year. This lunar calendar was the official calendar of the later Jewish religion, and has continued to be so to the present day. Among the more pious circles, the ancient solar calendar was also preserved, so that at the time of Jesus there were actually two calendars in use, the official calendar according to which the Pharisees and high priests celebrated Easter, and the popular calendar according to which Jesus celebrated the festival (Mt 26, 17; Mk 14, 12; Lk 22, 7; Jn 18, 28).

3) THE PEASANTS' CALENDAR: a further system of reckoning time dates back to the era of the Amorite migrations; it was in use in ancient Assyria and Babylonia, as well as in Syria and Palestine. According to the rhythm of peasant and agricultural life, the year was divided into seven units of fifty, that is, 7 x 7 = 49 + 1 = 50. Each period thus consisted of 7 weeks and one additional day which was celebrated as a festival. The year thus began, for example, with the offering of the fruits. Seven weeks later, on the 50th day, came the Feast of Tabernacles at the conclusion of the grain harvest. Every period of 50 days thus had its own particular character. In order to bring this system of units of 50 into proper harmony with the lunar year, another 15 additional days were added to the 350 days of this calendar year. This ancient calendar has left its trace in the calendar of Israelite festivals. It was constructed upon the rhythm of the peasant life. But the harvests all began at a different time in the different areas of the country. This is probably what motivated Solomon to introduce the unified new solar calendar which corresponded to the growing needs of a great unified kingdom.[2]

A) THE SABBATH FESTIVAL

a) The Sabbath was one of the most important of all festival days, the seventh day of the week. Since the Hebrews reckoned the day from evening to evening, the Sabbath began on Friday evening. It was celebrated by complete rest. Every form of work was prohibited under penalty of stoning to death; the manna, for example, could not be gathered, nor could fire be kindled and foods prepared; such necessary works had to be done on Friday, which was, accordingly, called the "day

---

2. E. Vogt, *Antiquum Kalendarium Sacerdotale*, Bibl 36 (1955), 403-413. / J. Morgenstern, *The Calendar of the Book of Jubilees, its Origin and its Character*, VT 5 (1955), 34-73.

of preparation." This precept was binding also on the pagan slaves; moreover, the draft animals could not be used for work. Probably to be distinguished from this Sabbath rest is the quite different rest from work which consisted in the avoidance of civil or professional work on the normal new-moon festivals (excepting for Tishri 1). In the post-Exilic era this precept of Sabbath rest was given a much more stringent formulation, so that it was no longer felt as a benefit but rather an un-welcome yoke, an abuse with which Jesus, in word and in deed, took the sharpest possible exception. The celebration of the festivals consisted in doubling the daily holocaust, in set-ting out new show-breads, and in a sacred festival assembly.

Concerning the origins of the Sabbath [3] there is considerable diver-gence of scholarly opinion. In Israel it was regarded as a very ancient institution. The Old Testament presupposes the Sabbath as such, but says nothing about its institution; it only intensifies its observance (Ex 20, 8; Dt 5, 12) and gives it a religious and social foundation. The seven-day rhythm is probably connected with the phases of the moon, but still the derivation of the Israelite Sabbath from the Babylonian day of the full moon is more questionable, since the distinctions are too great. General official days of rest are not known in ancient Babylon (or in Egypt), much less a consecutive numbering of seven-day weeks. The counting by periods of seven begins anew with each lunar month. In Israel, however, the weeks are counted continuously independently of the lunar phases, throughout the entire year. Furthermore, the Baby-lonian lunar days (new moon — warhum, and full moon — šabbattu) are unlucky days, days on which a person was advised to avoid certain business, since on these days power was given to the demons. These moon-days had, as it seems, a purely religious significance, and little civil importance. But it is very questionable whether these periods of seven, in Babylonia and Assyria, ever determined the civil life of the citizens in the sense that it was affected by the Israelite Sabbath. At all events, there was also a five-day week (one-sixth of a month), which seemed to form the basis for business life. The Israelite Sabbath is not Babylonian in origin; it represents a completely independent and new religious creation.[4]

---

3. Cf. also the section on "sabbath" in Volume I, p. 228ff.
4. On the Sabbath, cf. Nötscher, op. cit., 351ff. / Br. Meissner, Babylonien und Assyrien II (1925), 92ff. / B. Bonkamp, Die Bibel im Lichte der Keilschriftforschung (1939), 333ff. / O. Procksch, op. cit., 544.

b) *The new-moon festivals*: Just like the beginning of the week, so also the beginning of the month (*neomenia*) was celebrated by the offering of sacrifice (Nb 28, 11-15); even more solemn was the first day of the 7th month of Tishri (approximately September — October) (Lev 23, 23-25; Nb 29, 1-6), the ancient new year's festival which only under Assyrian influence was transferred into the spring.

c) *The sabbath year*: Corresponding to the weekly Sabbath, every seventh year was dedicated to rest. It was to be a year of rest for the entire land. Plowing of the fields, sowing the crops, and harvesting the fruit was all forbidden. Whatever grew of its own volition, whatever the vineyard and the olive bore without cultivation was to be the common property of all, and it was particularly the poor and aliens, in fact even the animals, who benefitted from being allowed to share this bounty (Lev 25, 4).

In this year the Israelite debtor could not be forced to repay a loan. Moreover, during the Festival of Tabernacles held during the Sabbath year the Law was to be read to the entire people assembled in the sanctuary (Ex 23, 10, 11; Lev 25, 2-7).

The religious meaning of these arrangements is immediately clear. It was supposed to be a recognition of Yahweh's proprietary rights to the land and its yield. But the law is so idealistic in its conception that it probably was never fully carried out. The only case recorded in the Old Testament in which an attempt was made to carry it out as prescribed does not attempt to minimize the serious difficulties bound up with it (1 M 6, 49, 53). The renunciation of an entire year's harvest was, for the impoverished classes, a well intentioned but hardly practicable stipulation.

d) *The Jubilee Year* (every 49th or 50th year): Apparently so called for the peal of the ram's horn (*yôbêl* — ram),[5] with

_____

5. This popular etymology is rejected by R. North, *Sociology of the Biblical Jubilee* (1954), 98ff. Neither does he favor the derivation from *ybl*, "to produce, bring forth." He decides, following LXX, in favor of the meaning "abundance, gift, exemption," and sees the cause of the Jubilee Year in the growing threat of the large estate owners. By the practice of restoring the properties to their original owners every 50 years the stability of the peasant land-holdings would

which it was heralded and introduced throughout the entire land on the Day of Atonement. Like the Sabbath year, it was a year of rest for the farmland (Lev 25, 2-7). It is also called a free year, because during the jubilee year all real estate reverted to its original owner without the refund of the price of purchase, even the houses of the Levites which had been put up for sale. This sale was, accordingly, only a lease arrangement: the purchase price was determined in terms of the time elapsing until the next jubilee year. In the jubilee year, furthermore, all Israelite slaves must be returned to freedom (remission of debt and emancipation). By the restoration of all properties, the original division of the land, which rested upon the very will of Yahweh himself, was to remain unchanged among the Israelites for all times to come. The same spirit animates the law of emancipation. In the people of God there should be no permanent slavery. These laws clearly betray the idealism of the era prior to the entry into the promised land; their actual execution quickly comes to grief against the hard facts of everyday life and the low ebb of the people's religious sensitivities.

B) THE GREAT ANNUAL FESTIVALS

Three times in the year every male Israelite was obligated to make a pilgrimage to the sanctuary at Jerusalem (for wives and children it was a free choice), in order to participate in the great religious festivals (Ex 23, 17; 34, 23). These are the eight-day *Pesah-Massot* (Easter) Festival, beginning on Nisan 14 (April), the Festival of Weeks, Harvest, or Pentecost, 50 days later, and the eight-day Feast of Tabernacles (*succoth*) on Tishri 15 − 21/22 (October). There is also the Day of Atonement on Tishri 10. Apart from this last, they are all joyous festivals which are meant to commemorate an historical

---

be assured. The Jubilee Year is thus to be compared to a bankruptcy proceedings, a year in which all the moneys owing on a mortgaged property became forfeit. For a thorough critique of this position, cf. H. Cazelles, in VT 5 (1955), 321-324.

event and at the same time express a relationship to the agrarian calendar.[6]

1) *The Easter festival* combines two orginally different festivals, the *pesach* (Aramaic *Pascha*) with the slaughter of the Easter lamb, which is, presumably, bound up with pre-Mosaic shepherd customs, and the festival of the *Massot* (unleavened bread), which has its predecessors in the ancient peasant religions. Even though the roots of these combined festivals go back to pre-Mosaic days, just like many other things in the Old Testament, they take on a new meaning in the Yahweh religion. Easter becomes a feast to commemorate the redemption of Israel from the slavery of Egypt. On the eve of the Pesach the historical event of the Exodus from Egypt was to be reenacted as accurately as possible (Ex 12ff.). The slaughter of the lamb, the painting of the doorposts, the eating of the meal in preparation for travel, etc. — all these ceremonies were designed to renew the miraculous redemption of the night of Exodus from Egypt.

The ritual of the Easter banquet [7] was, in later times, somewhat different than that of the Exodus. The lambs were slaughtered during the afternoon in the outer court of the Temple, while the blood was caught in bowls by the priests and sprinkled upon the altar, the fat being burned upon the altar. The lamb was roasted on a wooden spit; under penalty of flogging no one of his bones could be broken (Ex 12, 46; Jn 19, 36). Together with the lamb there were unleavened bread and bitter herbs; in later times the prescription stipulating that the meal was to be eaten in travelers' guise, in haste, was no longer observed (Dt 16, 1-18).

On Nisan 14th followed the festival week of the unleavened bread (*Massot*), an ancient peasant festival. Before the beginning of the new

---

6. Nötscher, *op. cit.*, 355, a thorough presentation of the history of the festival in the Mishnah. Beer, Giessen (1921), 1-109, to be read with caution.

7. Strack-Billerbeck, *Kommentar zum NT aus Talmud und Midraš* IV, 41-76.

harvest, the entire content of the last year's harvest had to be used up in order not to desecrate the new harvest by contact with the old. In Israel this peasant festival, because of its relationship with the Exodus from Egypt, takes on a salvation-history significance. It was celebrated a. by a daily festival sacrifice; b. by eating the unleavened bread; already on Nisan 14, before the Easter banquet, all yeast had to be removed from the houses (Ex 12, 15), and throughout the entire week only unleavened bread could be eaten; c. the first and last day were free of work and festival assemblies were celebrated (Ex 12, 16); on the second day (altero die sabbati, on the day after the festival day, Nisan 16) the community offered Yahweh a sheaf of grain as the first fruits (harvest festival, beginning of the harvest).

2) *The Festival of Pentecost*: From the second day of Easter week seven weeks were counted, and on the next day, that is, the 50th day, this festival of the "fifty" was celebrated (*Pentecoste*, Acts 2, 1), also called "festival of weeks" (*šabû'ôt*)[8] (Ex 34, 22). It was celebrated for only one day, and marked by a pause from work, a festival assembly, special festival sacrifices, many voluntary sacrifices, and joyous banqueting. It was a festival meant to celebrate the conclusion of the harvest with appropriate expressions of thanksgiving. That is why, on this day, two loaves of leavened bread made of the new flour were offered to Yahweh (Nb 28, 26). It was only in a later era that the idea of the harvest was connected with the commemoration of the giving of the Law upon Sinai.

3) *The Festival of Huts* (*skenopegia, hag hassukkôt*, Deuteronomy 16, 13; Lev 23, 34, 40) was celebrated in the fall (in the 7th month, Tishri, September/October), at the end of the fruit, olive, and grape harvests. It lasted for seven days, from Tishri 15 − 21. During the festival week the people were required to live in huts, or "tabernacles," which were erected from the branches of trees either in the open air or upon roofs, streets, or market places. The first day was characterized by

---

8. In keeping with ancient custom the weeks were counted, not beginning with Easter, but from the day of the offering of the first-fruits, a date that could vary in different years. It was only later that Easter achieved the position of a unified point of departure for the reckoning. (Lev 15ff).

rest from work and a festival assembly. In the Sabbath year, it was on this day that the Law was read to the people. This week was followed immediately by a 8th festival day, 'aseret, "conclusion," because it formally ended the Festival of the Tabernacles and the whole annual cycle of festivals. Rest from servile work and festival assemblies was prescribed (Lev 23, 36, 39; Nb 29, 35-38). The Festival of Tabernacles was a festival of thanksgiving especially for the recently completed olive and grape harvest and for the whole harvest in general; with respect to historical antecedents, the festival came to be joined with the commemoration of the sojourn in the wilderness, where the Israelites lived in tents or huts. This festival was, accordingly, an especially joyful festival, and is referred to simply as "the festival" (1 K 8, 2; 12, 32), while Philo calls it "the greatest of the festivals" (heortōn megistē), Josephus calls it "the holiest and greatest festival" (herotē hagiōtatē kai megistē).

In the post-Exilic era, the celebration of these festivals was further developed by two additional ceremonies. First came the libation of water with the invocation from Isaiah 12, 3: "You shall drink water in joy from the fountains of salvation." — On each morning of the seven days, about the time of the morning sacrifice, a priest would take water from the fountain of Siloe in a golden vessel, carry it to the altar of holocausts, and pour it out beside the wine of the drink offering into the ducts provided in the altar, to the accompaniment of music and festival song. It was probably this ceremony that Christ used as the basis for his image of the living waters to which he compared the mission of the Holy Spirit (Jn 7, 2, 37-39).

Recent scholarship [9] has connected the Festival of Tabernacles with the hypothesis of a specially developed festival in honor of Yahweh's accession to the throne. In terms of origin, the Festival of Tabernacles might well have been a new year's festival (beginning the year in fall). In the Babylonian cult the new year's day is also called the day of the enthronement of Marduk and the king. On the basis of Canaanite in-

9. Eichrodt, op. cit., I, 53ff. / P. Volz, Das Neujahrsfest Jahves (1912), 20ff. / H. Schmidt, Die Thronfahrt Jahves (1927). / H. Zimmern, Das babylonische Neujahrsfest (1926). / H. J. Kraus, Die Königsherrschaft Gottes im AT. Postulates a royal Zion festival on the first day of the Festival of Tabernacles. Beiträge z. hist. Theol. Tübingen 13 (1951). / Rejected by A. R. Johnson, Divine Kingship and the OT, Expos Tim LXI (1949/50), 36-42.

fluence, the kings of Israel (perhaps Solomon) may well have introduced a similar festival by reinterpreting the fall harvest festival. Some psalms speak expressly of Yahweh's kingship, especially Psalms 24, 47, 93, 96 (in the Hebrew counting). The argument would have it that, on this new year's festival, the coming of Yahweh to his people would have been represented as a sort of cultic drama: Yahweh's approach in solemn procession with the ark of the covenant, accompanied by king, priests, and people. Sacred dances, sacrifices, and prayers would also form an essential element of the liturgy for this festival. Yahweh is reenthroned as the king of Israel, and the earthly king of Israel is reconfirmed as "his son" in the kingship established by God's free gift. With the catastrophe of a kingly family living in Exile, this festival would then have disappeared from the Israelite calendar.

No matter how enticing this reconstruction might be, and no matter how many passages of Scripture would tend to confirm this hypothesis, still the available source material is, at present, insufficient to establish the definite existence of such an enthronement festival honoring the God Yahweh in Israel.

C) THE GREAT DAY OF ATONEMENT

The great Day of Atonement (*yôm hakkippûr*) was celebrated five days before the Festival of Tabernacles as a great festival involving a Sabbath rest and a day of penance and strict fasting (Lev 16; 23, 26-32). Its introduction was associated with the sudden death of the sons of Aaron because of improper administration of the sacrifice (Lev 16, 1), but the real question as to the age and development of this festival, with its very definite ritual of expiation and atonement, is particularly difficult to determine, especially since no definite historical evidence is to be found in the Old Testament. It is possible that the carrying out of the expiatory ritual had long been a purely priestly prerogative and only in the post-Exilic time had it come to be a general day of penance and fasting, the "Good Friday of the Old Testament" (Delitzsch). The ritual gives the impression of great antiquity and can hardly have been a very recent invention.[10]

The ritual of the expiatory solemnity: after the morning offering, at which the high priest still wore his solemn robes,

10. Nötscher, *op. cit.*, 361.

the atonement proper took place; the ritual is handed down in varying forms. According to Numbers 29, 8, it was required to offer the same sacrifices as on the new year's festival (Nb 29, 1): one bull, one ram, and seven lambs with the appropriate food offerings. According to Leviticus 16, the ritual is much richer. The essential element, however, is the sprinkling with blood together with the ceremony of the scapegoat and the confession of sin, in order to achieve the absolution of priest, people, and sanctuary. The exclusive liturgical functionary for this day is the high priest, who, in a simple, white priestly vestment, lays his hands upon the bull and confesses his own sins and those of the whole priesthood. Then, as representative of the people, he casts lots upon the two goats, one for Yahweh and the other for Azazel. The goat upon whom Yahweh's lot fell became the sacrificial victim for a sin offering; the other was placed before Yahweh in order to atone before him and to be driven out into the wilderness to Azazel. The high priest then entered into the Holy of Holies with a vessel of incense and glowing coals, so that the incense covered the plate of atonement over the ark of the covenant. He then went out and took some blood from the bull, returned it to the Holy of Holies, and sprinkled the lid of atonement once, while sprinkling the ground before it seven times. The atonement for the priesthood was thus completed. The further ritual concerned the atonement of the people.

The goat upon whom the lot of Yahweh had fallen was now slaughtered, whereupon the high priest entered once again into the Holy of Holies with the blood of this animal and completed the same ceremony of sprinkling as described above in the case of the blood of the bull. He then made his way into the outer Holy Place and performed the act of expiation at the altar of incense by smearing the horns of the altar with blood and apparently also sprinkling the blood seven times upon the ground; the same ceremony took place in the outer court at the altar of holocaust.

After the expiation of the people had thus been completed, the goat destined for Azazel was brought in, the high priest laid his hands upon the animal, calling down upon him all the sins and faults of Israel, and then drove him out, laden with the sins of the people, into the wilderness. Following this, the two expiatory victims (a bull and a second goat), with the exception of the fat parts, were offered as a burnt sacrifice outside the camp (or outside the city). The high priest, now once again attired in his festival vesture, next offered two holocausts, the fat parts of the expiatory sacrifices being burnt along with them. The ritual concluded with the sacrifice, a holocaust, of seven lambs.

These expiatory rituals certainly date back to the most ancient times, where they were celebrated in much simpler forms, and then, after the Exile, under the influence of the national catastrophe, they must have undergone a much richer development. We can see how, in the last years of the Old Testament, the concept of expiation comes more and more into the fore of the religious thinking. The entire people, from the high priest right down to the last layman, needed atonement before God, and this could be achieved only by sprinkling with blood and by sacrifice. The atonement thus achieved found a very significant expression in the remarkable ceremony of the scapegoat. As opposed to Yahweh, Azazel must have been conceived as an equally personal being, a demon, whose residence was located in the wilderness. When the scapegoat is driven out to him, this is meant to symbolize the complete removal of all sin from the people of God. This deeply theological concept was further developed, in the course of time, by popular practices. The goat, on his route out into the wilderness, was insulted and provoked, and chased to a considerable distance so that he could not possibly ever return. In later times, he was actually forced off a rocky cliff near Jerusalem, so that he could not possibly ever return. This festival is, according to St. Paul (Heb 9, 10), a type of that great Day of Atonement on which Christ offered satisfaction for the sins of the entire world, and, moreover, the Letter to the Hebrews, in calling attention to the mutual relationship between the two, also strongly emphasizes the tremendous difference between type and antitype.

The high priest, a weak prefiguration of Christ (8, 1) made his way into the earthly Holy of Holies with the blood of animals, whereas Jesus, with his own blood, has entered into the true Holy of Holies of God (9, 12). The Old Testament expiatory ritual was concerned with cleansing from sins that had been committed throughout that entire year. Christ, however, by his blood, has offered complete and perfect satisfaction for all the sins of all men of all times (9, 28). Since Christ, by his expiation, has cleansed our conscience from dead works, so has he also opened up to us the gates of heaven (10, 20). The high priest could not effect any remission of sins, because he offered only the blood of animals (9, 9, 10, 13; 10, 4); that is why the Holy of Holies remained closed for the entire people (9, 8). That is also why the ritual of expiation had to be renewed year after year (10, 1-3). Regarding Christ, on the other hand, St. Paul repeatedly and emphatically stresses the fact that, by his sacrifice on the cross, he needed to enter into the Holy of Holies of heaven only once (9, 12).

Looking back from the point of view of the New Testament, the Old Testament sacrificial cult might well appear weak and ineffectual. But such a point of view must not ever cause us to underevaluate the facts. Within the Ancient Near East, the Old Testament rituals represent a true climax of religious experience. The religious motivations they incorporate — adoration of Yahweh the one God who suffers no other Gods besides himself, Yahweh the Lord of history who freely chose this people for himself, thanksgiving for the gifts of nature that come from God, petition for further help and direction, and, finally, expiation and confession of guilt — these are very worthy precursors of the religion instituted by Christ, and they take on their true proportions only in the religion of revelation.

CHAPTER XIII

FROM SINAI TO JORDAN

LITERATURE

M. R. Savignac, *La région de 'Ain Qedeis*, RB 31, 1922, 55-81. / J. S. Griffiths, *The Exodus in the Light of Archaeology*, 1923. / P. Heinisch, *Das Buch Numeri*, (BB), 1936. — *The Westminster Historical Atlas to the Bible: The Route of the Exodus*, 1947, 38. / W. F. Albright, *The Oracles of Balaam*, JBL 63, 1944, 207-233. / A. S. Yasuda, *The Name of Balaam's Homeland*, JBL 64, 1945, 547-551. / J. Guillet, "Iter in Deserto," *Recherses de Science Religieuse* 36, 1949, 161-181. / H. Schneider, *Numeri* (EB), 1952.

A) THE SOJOURN IN THE WILDERNESS

The year's sojourn at Sinai was of fundamental significance for the religious and political formation of Israel as a people. But Moses' failure to wield the discordant elements into a permanent and lasting unity is clearly pointed up by the various rebellions which, in the course of the further wandering through the desert, made their appearance with increasing violence and finally led to an open breach and the rejection of Moses' leadership by one part of the people. All this clearly shows that the new covenant with Yahweh entered into upon Sinai did not rest upon force and coercion, but rather upon the principle of voluntary acceptance: "All that Yahweh has commanded we will do" (Ex 24, 7). The Biblical presentation is full of great internal tension; it is not simply an outline narrative of the events — this alone is a powerful guarantee for the genuinity of the historical tradition.

In the second year the Israelites departed from Sinai. The various stations along the trek through the wilderness are recounted in the Book of Numbers. What this book is concerned with are not really numbers (*Numeri*), but rather "countings and musterings." The events of the last weeks before leaving Sinai were meant primarily to serve as preparation for the future possession of the land. Since hostile resistance had to be reckoned with, there had to be a count of those capable of bearing arms, and some form of organization into military units had to be determined upon (Nb 1, 1-54). Furthermore, an established and unvariable order had to be observed upon making and breaking camp, in order to avoid the danger of mass confusion. The Levites were entrusted with the transport of the sanctuary (3, 1 — 4, 49).

With the departure from Sinai begins the heroic age of Israel, an age which, however, proved to be very unheroic. It is true that the order of the march was properly observed; it was also true that in Hobab, the son of Jethro the Midianite, the people found an experienced and capable guide, but in the very first difficulties that occurred — lack of water and food — the malcontent elements quickly made their presence felt, so that even Miriam and Aaron took a position against their brother Moses (12, 1-16). But Yahweh over and over again intervenes to save the situation and to punish the rebellion.

The route next led through the wilderness of Paran. Of the stations counted in Numbers 33, 16-35, we can definitely identify only Hazeroth in the Sinai territory and Ezion-geber along the Gulf of Elath. From here they headed towards the great oasis of Kadesh-barnea, determined to make their conquest of the land of Canaan from the south. To this end Moses sent spies into the country, but, their pessimistic reports about the ferocity of the inhabitants undermined the confidence of the people (Nb 13). This alone would prove that the necessary internal unity of the people had not yet been achieved. The whole community revolted against Moses, in loud and violent protest that lasted throughout the night. The people all said to each other: "Let us choose a new captain and go back to Egypt" (Nb 14, 1-4). Moses thereupon announced his decision to undertake the conquest of Palestine from the east. The rebellious element in the people was not satisfied with this proposal either; upon their own authority they undertook to attack the Canaanites and Amalekites at Horma, where they were decisively defeated (Nb 14, 20; 14, 39, 45). After this reversal, which has been immortalized on the Merneptah stele,[1] Moses was determined to remain in the vicinity of Kadesh until a new, more docile generation had grown up. The sojourn at Kadesh is given as 40 years (Nb 14, 33; Ex 16, 35; Dt 1, 3). Apart from a few particular laws, all that remains is the judgment passed on the party of Core, and the reestablishment of the Aaronitic priesthood (Nb 16; 17).

The oasis of Kadesh offers sufficient life support for semi-nomadic tribes, since there are enough springs to support a modest agriculture. The location is, furthermore, favorably situated for traffic and trade, offering good communications in all directions.[2]

The Kadesh problem: In the critique of Old Testament history, Israel's sojourn in Kadesh plays an important role. Rowley[3] describes the entire problem very succinctly. There are actually two questions that need to be answered:

a) *Were all twelve tribes of Israel at Kadesh?* The question is answered in the negative. For not all the tribes were in Egypt. The Israelite possession of Canaan took place in two completely independent waves; it occurs in connection with the Habiru battles of the Amarna era, which took place in the north and south of the country, but not in the middle.

---

1. J. S. Griffiths, *The Exodus in the Light of Archaeology*, London (1923). Attempts to relate the text of the Merneptah Stele to this catastrophe. The connection is possible, but not convincing, since the Bible makes no mention of Egypt: we would have to understand Egyptian sovereignty operating through the Canaanite masters.
2. M. R. Savignac, *La région de 'Ain Qedeis*, RevBibl 3 (1922), 55-81. — Westminster Atlas, 63ff.
3. H. H. Rowley, *op. cit.*, (extensive bibliography).

The first wave occurred around 1440 B.C., in which time various Israelite groups, like the tribes of Judah, Simeon, and Levi, which were not in Egypt, camped for 38 years in the vicinity of Kadesh, allied themselves with the Kenites who also worshipped Yahweh, and, around 1400, attempted to take Canaan from the south. The tribes of Simeon and Levi succeeded in forcing their way as far as the Shechem, but could not maintain their advance, so that, around 1360, they gradually made their way towards Egypt. Shortly before their arrival, under Pharaoh Ikhnaton, Egyptian Joseph had achieved a position of great influence. At the same time, around 1400 B.C., the tribes of Asher, Zebulon, and Dan were making their way into the Canaanite territory from the north.

The second wave of Israelite conquest, according to Rowley, was made up of a group out of Egypt. The Pharaoh of the oppression was Ramses II (c. 1300), and the Pharaoh of the Exodus (c. 1220) was Merneptah. The Egyptian sojourn thus lasted only 130 years and began long after the Hyksos era. The Exodus took place under Moses, who was born around 1290. From the Midianite father-in-law he takes over the form Yahweh as the divine name. This new connection with Yahweh is documented by the establishment of the covenant and the decalogue. The trek through the wilderness lasted, not 40 years, but only two years, and leads, under Joshua, across the Jordan River into Middle Palestine.

It was only during the royal era that this manifold picture of the early history of Israel was given a more unified form and what were originally two ancient traditions were fused into one.

b) *How long was Israel in the wilderness?* The march from Sinai occurred in the 2nd year after the Exodus (Nb 1, 1), and Aaron died upon Mount Hor in the 40th year after the Exodus (Nb 33, 38). The entire Biblical tradition speaks only of a single sojourn in the wilderness, by all twelve tribes, and lasting 40 years (Nb 14, 33; Ex 16, 35; Dt 1, 3). The number 40, since it is the general number for a generation, is not to be pressed. Further, it must be admitted that, in the Pentateuch, as we shall later see in detail, various historical sources have been fused into a single unit so that historical abbreviation and condensation is always to be reckoned with. Rowley's theory would seem to cast light primarily upon the questions bound up with the Amarna letters. On the other hand, it must face the heavy burden of being opposed to the entire Israelite tradition. At all events, it does not produce historical certitude. The mere substitution of one historical construction for another is not, in itself, a guarantee of reliability.

We are here faced with a situation in which the peculiar nature of Biblical history is most transparent. The concrete course of events seems to have disappeared in many points. It is obviously not the object of Biblical historical writing to describe the trek through the wilderness with the closest possible attention to all the human ramifications of the history. It is, rather, to be presented as an instruction for later times, pointing up the fact that supernatural and, in a certain sense, suprahistorical powers have been at work in determining the fate of Israel.[4]

B) THE ROAD TO CANAAN

A new section in the narrative begins with Moses' decision to make a long detour into eastern Transjordania in order to attack Palestine from the east (Nb 20, 21). He accordingly sent an embassy from Kadesh to the king of Edom, to effect a free passage through the Edomite territory along the Royal Road (Nb 20, 17). Edom, however, refused to allow him passage, and prepared for armed resistance. The Israelites were thus forced to circle the Edomite territory. The actual route of their travel can no longer be accurately determined, since the location of Mt. Hor, the mountain upon which Aaron died 40 years after the Exodus from Egypt, remains uncertain, despite local traditions (Nb 21, 22).

According to Deuteronomy 2, 1, Moses led the people from Kadesh into the Sink of the Arabah, where they made their way as far as Ezion-geber. From here, apparently because of the Edomite resistance, he did not take the "Royal Road," but was forced to once again descend into the Sink of the Arabah, passing by the mines of Punon and the springs of Obot, and making his way up the Brook of Zered which forms the boundary between Edom and Moab. In order to avoid all possible conflict, the Moabite territory is also bypassed to the east. The first great military encounter took place when the King of the Amorites, Sihon of Heshbon, refused to allow Moses passage, whereupon Israel took up its weapons, defeated the enemy, and carried out the ban upon them (Nb 21, 21ff.). In their further advance, they also won a victory over Og of Bashan (Nb 21, 33), thereby gaining control over the entire territory of Transjordania from the Arnon as far as Bashan. After this war, the entire military force of Israel assembled in the Fields

---

4. H. Schneider, *Numeri* (1952), 5.

of Moab, across from Jericho, prepared to attack Palestine.

Among the religious events which occurred during the trek from Kadesh to Jericho, particularly significant are the miracle of the waters, the occasion on which even Moses himself, because of the chronic dissatisfaction of his people, began to doubt the patience of God, and was punished by being refused entry into the Promised Land, and the erection of the brazen serpent (Nb 20, 6-12; 21, 4-10). The serpents are called "seraphim" (burning), perhaps because of their bright red color, or, more probably, because of the burning sensation caused by their bite. In Punon (modern Feinan), there were in ancient times copper mines and foundries. It is tempting to locate the casting of a bronze figure in this territory.[5] The casting of the image of the snake and its raising upon the standard seemed to effect a victory over the serpents and render them harmless. This symbolic victory over the serpent was supposed to rid the community of the pestilence caused by the serpents. Whoever looked upon the brazen serpent in faith and confidence was kept alive despite the bite of the serpents (Nb 21, 8). The possibility of ancient Canaanite religious conceptions cannot be excluded from this brazen serpent. In the cult of the goddess Kadesh, the serpent is the symbol of life. A brazen serpent has also been discovered in the excavations at Geser.[6] Even during the time of King Hezekiah the Israelites were still offering incense sacrifices to the brazen serpent that Moses had made (2 K 18, 4). For John 3, 14 the serpent becomes a prophetic type of Christ's salvation on the cross. In each case the erection of the sign preserved the life of those who trusted and believed in it.

C)   THE ORACLES OF BALAAM
(Nb 22 — 25)

---

5. N. Glueck, *The National Geographic Magazine LXXXV* (Feb. 1944), 166-171, gives an explicit account of his archaeological examination of the Wadi 'Araba, with finds of remnants from the ancient copper mines in many places. Early date.

6. Schneider, *op. cit.*, 55.

The territories of Edom, Moab, and even Ammon had been left untouched by Israel during the approach to Palestine, apparently because of distant tribal relationships. But now that Israel had won victories over the Amorites, its existence became more and more threatening for Moab. Balak, King of Moab, did not have to resort immediately to armed resistance; he attempted to break Israel's power by magic and curses and charms; he felt that there were supernatural powers at play. Accordingly he sent for Balaam, the famous prophet from Petor (Akkadian: Pitru) on the Euphrates, bidding him come and curse the camps of Israel with his most effective curses [7] (Nb 22, 2-4).

Balaam realized that the spirit of Yahweh was preventing him from cursing Israel; thus, despite the prospects of great gifts from the king, he refused to come to Moab. Only after the insistence of a second embassy was he prepared to come. But even though Balak, the King of Moab, was asking for a curse, what came from the lips of Balaam was simply a blessing oracle. In the territory in which Scripture locates these oracles there are megalith monuments.[8]

In the first oracle, at Bamoth-Baal (the high places of Baal) Balaam praised the election, the great numbers, and the justice of Israel. In the second, delivered on the field of the spy (Sophim) from the peak of Mt. Pisga, he rejected Balak's request to revoke the blessing with these words: "Must I not take heed to speak what the Lord puts in my mouth?" (Nb 23, 12); then he explains the basis for his blessing: "God brings them out of Egypt; they have as it were the horns of the wild ox" (Nb 23, 22). There is no enchantment against Jacob and no divination against Israel. Its rejection of idolatry and its faith in the

---

7. According to Nb 22, 5, Balaam belongs to the "Sons of Ammo," in whose territory lies the city of Petor. The cuneiform texts confirm the existence of a tribe of the 'amau on the Euphrates. Cf. Albright BASOR 118 (1950), 15. The German translations, incorrectly, have "countrymen" (Henne AT 1937, 310). Samaritanus, Vulgate, and Syriac translations read "sons of Ammon," which can be explained as an attempt to clarify the word 'amau which was by that time no longer intelligible. Albright, in his examination of the Balaam son oracles, concludes, on the basis of ancient orthography, that the songs were recorded in the writing in the 10th century, but must date back at least to the 13/12. JBL 63 (1944), 207-233.

one God Yahweh make Israel invincible, so that it is like a lion who devours his prey at peace.[9] Then King Balak led him to the peak of Mt. Peor,[10] so that he would finally be able to pronounce a curse. There, seized by the spirit of God, he once again praises the blessings and prosperity of these people, the majesty of its kingdom, and its fearful power, capable of trampling down all its foes. In yet a fourth oracle the prophecy reaches its climax with the reference to the star destined to come forth out of Jacob, and the king who will conquer and devastate the enemies of Israel.

"I see him, but not now;
    I behold him, but not nigh:
a star shall come forth out of Jacob,
    and a sceptre shall rise out of Israel;
It shall crush the forehead of Moab,
    and break down all the sons of Sheth." [11]

This prophecy was partially fulfilled in David; as the promised ruler of Israel, he conquered and subjugated the hostile nations all around. The perfect fulfillment, however, must wait for the coming of Christ, the second David, who erects his own eternal kingship on the ruins of the pagan world empires (Dn 2, 44; 7, 14, 27). The oracles of Balaam show that the prophetic spirit was at work outside Israel as well, and that, even outside of Israel, among the pagans, the great power of the Israelite people was recognized, a power which lay in their faith in Yahweh. The neighboring nations all realize that here there was some mysterious, supra-rational, divine power at work, compelling Israel, despite

---

8. Vincent, *Canaan d'après l'exploration récente,* 424.

---

9. The speaking ass of Balaam is simply a dramatic presentation of the interior feelings that the beast's strange behavior awakens in Balaam. He recognizes it as the direction of God's will. A. Clamer, *La Sainte Bible de Pirot,* II (1940), 386.

10. The three mountains chosen for delivering the curse, *Bâmôth-Ba'al, Pisga,* and *Pe'or,* are three peaks in a chain stretching from south to north, all of them affording a fine view of the plain country to the northern end of the Dead Sea. They were also sacred high places in honor of *Ba'al, Ba'alpe'or,* and *Nebo.* Abel, *Géographie,* I, 383, n. 2.

11. By the sons of Sheth we are to understand all those people who are opposed to God. In a scroll discovered in 1947 at the Dead Sea, in the text entitled "The Wars of the Sons of Light with the Sons of Darkness," Moab and Edom are branded for all times to come as types for the enemies of God. Schneider, *op. cit.,* 65.

all its weaknesses and all its enemies, towards the God-willed purpose of seizing and controlling the land of Canaan. It is no wonder that the powerful awe of Yahweh himself marched before them.

Balaam recognized the true source of Israel's strength in his prophetic vision. This people could be harmed only by attacking the roots of its faith in God. He thus advised the Moabites to lead the Israelites astray, into the service of Baal (Nb 31, 16), and in this they actually succeeded. Many of the people let themselves be carried away by the intoxication of the cult offered by Baal-Peor (Baal honored upon Mt. Peor). This defection occasioned an even more decisive reaction on the side of those faithful to Yahweh; among them Pinehas (Vulgate: Phinees), a grandson of Aaron, distinguished himself by his zeal (Nb 25, 6-9). In order to guarantee that there would be no such further influence, Moses began the holy war against the Midianites, a war which ended in a pitiless annihilation. Balaam himself fell a victim to this violence (Nb 31, 1-12).

D) MOSES' FINAL WORDS AND DEATH

The conquest of Transjordania had prepared all the prerequisites for an attack upon the west, in an effort to finally take possession of the land promised to the fathers. For Moses, however, the time was drawing to an end. From the last Scriptural references to Moses we can see how "here, in an unchanged soul, the power of leadership continues uninterrupted." [12] Moses was permitted only to look into the land of longing from the peak of Pisga,[13] but the actual entry into the land of Canaan was not to be his. Yet it is precisely in these final days, filled with the presentiment of death (Nb 27, 12), Moses still delivers

---

12. M. Buber, *Moses* (1948), 284.
13. The view from Nebo (Pisga) is one of the most beautiful in Palestine. In the evening one can see the lights of Bethlehem and Jerusalem. During the night a bright starry sky shines magnificently, unequalled, over the solitary landscape. At sunrise one sees the desert of Judah, the mountains of Samaria, and even the peaks of Galilee, remarkably close at hand. Scripture is correct when it states that from this point of vantage the entire Holy Land can be observed (Dt 34, 1ff), a fitting place to take leave of one's life. In July of 1951 I was privileged to spend a few days at the excavations of the Franciscan Fathers on Mt. Nebo, an experience from which I brought home some unforgettable memories.

the final political and religious impulses that are destined to determine the subsequent fate of his nation. They are preserved primarily in the Book of Deuteronomy, whose basic nucleus, as we shall see in the subsequent chapter of Pentateuchal criticism, cannot be denied to Mosaic authorship. Moses' final arrangements are concerned with the following important issues:

1) First, Moses makes many provisions regarding the division of the land. The tribes of Reuben, Gad, and Manasseh had, apparently, distinguished themselves in the conquest of the Amorite kingdom, and had thus come into possession of great flocks. Moses assigned the tribes of Reuben and Gad the territories between the Arnon and the Jabbok, which were particularly rich in pasture land. The territory bordered, in the east, on the possessions of the Ammonites. The section north of the Arnon was given to the half-tribe of Manasseh.

2) There were further provisions for the conquest of Canaan. First of all he pronounced the very strict command to invoke the *herem* (the ban) upon the pagan Canaanites, that is, to annihilate them completely, and thus to avoid once and for all the possible danger of defection to the gods of the country. Next the boundaries of the land were described in greater detail and the division of the territory was determined by lot. He also established six levitical cities, three on each side of the Jordan, as a free city and place of refuge for those who had involuntarily shed the blood of a fellow citizen (Nb 33, 50 — 35, 34).

3) Finally, Moses established a successor to himself, to lead his people into their new home. Yahweh had already determined upon Joshua, the son of Nun, and Moses formally passed on his office to him through the imposition of hands (Nb 27, 23).

4) These political arrangements were coupled with a final legislative activity. Even though all the laws recorded in the Book of Deuteronomy do not, in their present form, date back to Moses, still it is impossible to deny the Mosaic origin of these

laws as a whole. Such a position would involve insoluble historical difficulties.

Deuteronomy 27 — 32 is a prophetic compendium of the
history of Israel and the whole theology of history, and thus
it has the greatest significance for the later books of Holy
Scripture. The Biblical historian turned to this source for the
leit-motifs behind his presentation of history: the fate of the
people of God is determined by its relationship to the Law. History itself supplies ample illustrations of this principle. In this
motif we can hear the mighty language of the prophets, stirring
up the people with their oracles of threat and salvation.

Already during the trek through the wilderness, Moses, acting upon
Yahweh's command, had recorded revelations and historical events from
time to time. The "Law" too, which he had proclaimed to the people
in Transjordania, he put in writing (Dt 31, 24) and entrusted it to
the priests, to be deposited in the Holy of Holies beside the Ark of
the Covenant, there to serve as witness against the people. Before his
death — apparently as a leavetaking — Moses pronounced a blessing
upon the twelve tribes (Dt 33), similar to the blessing spoken by Jacob.
The form of this blessing is the work of a later poet, but certainly
forms a fitting conclusion to the unmistakably divine theology of history
which is recorded in the five books of Moses.

Moses had been unable to complete his life's work, which was to
lead Israel, as the people of God's covenant of the twelve tribes, into
the land of God. He died in Transjordania, without ever having set foot
in Canaan; he was permitted to see it only from the distance, from
the peak of Nebo (Dt 34). The tragic element of this important figure [14]
takes on its fullest expression here; all his life long he had known only
foreign territory; even his grave lies on alien soil.[15] The Bible records
that no one knows the place where he is laid, as if it meant to preclude,
well in advance, any possibility of a hero cult. The possibility of his
having been put to death by his own people is difficult to believe.[16] There
is not a single detail in the narrative to substantiate this interpretation.

---

14. Procksch, *op. cit.*, 103.
15. The text of Dt 34, 6 does not, as many ancient, especially Jewish
    exegetes have believed, presuppose a miraculous burial of Moses
    by Yahweh. The unknown members of the funeral cortege buried
    him at a site whose location was later lost to memory. H. Junker,
    op. cit., 103.
16. Cf. Sellin, *Mose* (1922).

Moses is famous as the founder of a nation from the twelve tribes; Moses is equally famous as a legislator who, like the other great Ancient Near Eastern legal reformers, determined the rhythm of his people's life for centuries to come; but Moses is still greater as the prophet who was privileged to speak to Yahweh as a friend, face to face, to receive from him the revelation of the name Yahweh, and, acting upon his mandate, to establish the covenant with God. Moses' true grandeur thus lies not in the political and national spheres, nor in the juristic and legislative sphere, but in the religious sphere. He thus stands out above the narrow limitations of ethnic history and enters into the realm of the holy, with a claim upon all peoples of every age. He marks one of the most decisive turning points in salvation history, and at the same time he is a great promise and expectation for the future: "The Lord your God will raise up for you a prophet like me from among you, from your brethren — him you shall heed"[17] (Dt 18, 15).

---

17. J. Guillet, *Iter in deserto. Der Exodus ist für die Liturgie des AT soviel wie die Evangelien für das NT*, RechSciencRel 36 (1949), 161.

CHAPTER XIV

PENTATEUCHAL CRITICISM

LITERATURE

1. For a comprehensive treatment of the Pentateuch question: J. Goetts-berger, *Einleitung in das AT*, 1928. / A. Bea, *Institutiones Biblicae*, II, 1, 1933. / A. Merk, *Introductionis in S. Scripturae libros Compendium*, 1940, 164-200. / H. Höpfl, *Introductio specialis*, in VT (5th edition by Miller and Metzinger, 1946). / Hudal-Ziegler-Sauer, *Kurze Einleitung in die hl. Bücher des AT*, 1948, 106-127. / Simon-Prado, *Praelectiones biblicae*, 1949. / A. Bentzen, *Introduction to the OT*, Copenhagen, 1948, II, 9-80. / A. Weiser, *Einleitung in das AT*, 1949, 58-106. / Sellin-Rost, *Einleitung in das AT*, 1950, 28-74. / O. Eissfeldt, *Einleitung in das Alte Testament*, 1955.
2. On individual problems: A. Sanda, *Moses und der Pentateuch. Alttesta-mentliche Abhandlungen* IX, 4, 1924. / W. Baumgartner, *Wellhausen und der heutige Stand der alttestamentlichen Wissenschaft*, ThR 2, 1930, 287; 8, 1936, 179. / W. Möller, *Die Einheit der fünf Bücher Mosis*, 1931. / R. H. Pfeiffer, *A non-Israelite Source of the Book of Genesis*, ZATW 7, 1930, 66. / P. Volz — W. Rudolph, *Der Elohist als Erzähler*, BZATW 63, 1933. / H. Höpfl, *Critique biblique*, DBS II, 1934, 175-240. / W. Cassuto, *La questione della Genesi*, 1934. / A. Bea, *Der heutige Stand der Pentateuchfrage*, Bibl 16, 1935, 175-200. / G. v. Rad, *Die Priesterschrift im Hexateuch*, 1934. — *Das formgeschichtliche Problem des Hexateuch*, 1939. — *Deuteronomium-studien*, 1947. / A. Robert, *Genre historique*, DBS IV, 1941, 7-23. / M. Lagrange, *L'Authenticité mosaique de la*

Genèse et la théorie des documents, RB 47, 1938, 163. / J. Coppens, *L'Histoire critique de l'Ancien Testament,* 1942 (English: *The OT and the Critic,* 1942). / M. Noth, *Überlieferungsgeschichtliche Studien* I (Schriften der Königsberger Gelehrten Gesellschaft, 1942). / Engnell, *Gamla testamentet, en traditionshistorisk inledning* I, 1945. / H. H. Rowley, *The Prophet Jeremiah and the Book of Deuteronomy,* StudOT-Proph, 1946, 157-174. / *The Growth of the OT,* 1949. / Simpson, *The Early Traditions of Israel;* a critical analysis of the predeuteronomic narrative of the Hexateuch, 1948. / W. F. Albright, *From Stone Age to Christianity,* 1949, 68ff. / K. Galling, *Das Gemeindegesetz in Deut 23,* Fs. Bertholet, 1950, 176-191. / F. Y. Winnet, *The Mosaic Tradition,* 1949, ZATW 62, 1949/50, 270. / H. Schmökel, *Zur Datierung der Pentateuchquelle J,* ZATW 62, 1949-50, 319-321. / O. Eissfeldt, *Die neuste Phase der Pentateuchkritik,* ThR. N. F. 18, 1950, 91-112; 179-215. / E. Robertson, *The Old Testament Problem,* Publications of the Univ. of Manchester, CCCVII, 1950. / C. R. North, *Pentateuchal Criticism,* OT and Modern Study, 1951, 48-83. / R. de Vaux, *La Genèse* (Jerusalem Bible, 1951, 7-31). / C. Kuhl, *Die "Wiederaufnahme," ein literarkritisches Prinzip?* ZATW 64, 1952, 1-11.

THE present state of Pentateuchal criticism can be generally characterized in the judgment of A. Weiser:[1] "Old Testament studies are presently in the stage of a new scrutiny of literary criticism coupled with a continued examination along the lines of the history of tradition, form and cult." Leonhard Rost formulates the situation more precisely when he says: "It is obvious that we are in an era of ferment and transition, and certainly the individual literary sources can no longer be said to represent such fast and tangible magnitudes as had been originally supposed."[2] We do not need to share the disputable view of W. Möller who thinks that we have "unmasked the theory of source criticism, from beginning to end, as a great scientifically unscientific hoax, as the pure product of imagination."[3] Reaction to the Pentateuchal problem has grown much calmer today and, unless we are completely deceived, we can note the advent of a new objectively oriented line of research which has as its one purpose to approach as closely as possible to the real

1. A. Weiser, *Einleitung in das AT* (1949), 66.
2. Sellin-Rost, *Einleitung in das AT* (1950), 34.
3. W. Möller, *Biblische Theologie des AT* (1934), 43.

truth behind the origins of the five books of Moses.

Since history is the best teacher, it would seem most logical to approach the problems discussed by Pentateuchal criticism on the basis of the historical development of the questions themselves. No book throughout the whole literature of the world is on a par with the Pentateuch, in significance and in effect; its influence has been considerable on the religion and culture of Jew, Christian, and Moslem alike. This explains why so many scholars, operating from such a variety of religious backgrounds, took up the problem with an almost impassioned zeal and, in the enthusiasm of their discovery or their polemics, advanced such a number of varied hypotheses, all of which have been repeated by succeeding generations.

A) THE EVIDENCE FROM THE PENTATEUCH ITSELF

1) MOSES AS AUTHOR: What does the Pentateuch have to say about its own author? There is not a single title or colophon which specifically mentions Moses as author. Reference is made to Moses primarily in the third person. Only some individual historical and legislative sections are expressly attributed to his authorship: the invocation of the ban upon Amalek (Ex 17, 14), the Book of the Covenant, apparently with the inclusion of the Ten Commandments (Ex 20 — 23), a collection of words spoken at Sinai (Ex 34, 27); there is also the catalogue of stations from the trek through the wilderness (Nb 33, 2), and the whole law as given in the Fields of Moab (Dt 1, 5; 4, 45; 31, 9, 22, 24), together with the song of Moses. Does this mean that the other sections of the Pentateuch do not have Moses for their author?

In the New Testament era Moses' authorship was never doubted (cf. Mt 19, 7ff.; Mk 12, 26; Jn 5, 46; Acts 15, 21; Rm 10, 5). The early Church took over these traditions and this conviction from the synagogue, which has left ample evidence behind it in the Talmud and the Midrashim.[4] Moreover, already in the

---

4. On the attitude of the Rabbinic literature, cf. the abundant material in Strack-Billerbeck, *Kommentar zum NT aus Talmud und Midras,* IV (1928), 439-443.

later literature of the Old Testament itself Moses is expressly referred to as the author of the Law (Mal 3, 22; 2 Ch 25, 4; 35, 12; Ezra 3, 2; 7, 6).

2) MOSES NOT AS AUTHOR: The first doubt with respect to the unity and genuinity of the Pentateuch is found in Origen, who recounts of the philosopher Celsus that, on the basis of theological considerations, he divided and distinguished among the works of Moses (Contra Celsum IV, 42). John Damascene records the same thing of the Gnostics of his era who, in order to support their system, took a very arbitrary view of the Biblical texts. But this sectarian tampering with the sacred text has nothing in common with the principles of literary criticism which began to assert themselves already in the era of the Reformation, among the Protestants in Karlstadt (1520), and on the Catholic side in A. Masius (1574), B. Pereira (c. 1600), J. Bonfrère (16-25). But the real precursors of the later criticism must be identified as Baruch Spinoza (1670), Thomas Hobbes (1651) and, even more important still, Richard Simon (1712).

The criticism of these scholars is based upon the self-evidence of the Pentateuch, which directly excludes the authorship of Moses. In many passages, the post-Mosaic origin of the text is perfectly clear: Genesis 12, 6; 13, 7, "In those days the Canaanites dwelt in the country," presupposes the conquest of Canaan, as does the reference to Canaan as "land of the Hebrews" (Gn 40, 15; Ex 15, 15; Lv 18, 24; Dt 2, 12). The author's distance from the era of Moses is clearly expressed in the frequently repeated formula "up to the present day" (Dt 3, 14; 34, 6) and in the remark: "There arose in Israel no prophet like unto Moses" (Dt 34, 10). The use of the name Dan in Genesis 14, 14; Deuteronomy 34, 1, which comes into use as the name of the territory at the foot of Hermon only in the era of the Judges (Jg 18, 29), cannot possibly date from Moses. In many passages the geographical point of view taken by the author is clearly no longer that of Moses, as, for example, when Transjordania is referred to as simply "across the Jordan" (Gn 50, 10; Nb 22, 1; Dt 1, 1, 5), unless perhaps *'eber hayyardên* means simply the land on both the right and left banks of the Jordan.

A further consideration is provided by the doublets, which could not possibly be the work of one single author. There are, for example, two creation narratives (Gn 1 and Gn 2, 4ff.), two deluge narratives; according to the one the flood lasts for 40 days, while, according to the other (Gn 7), it lasts for a year. Further examination uncovers considerable linguistic and stylistic differences in the construction of the narratives, which would once again seem to demand two or more authors. Among the linguistic evidence, the different usage of the name for God presents a particularly puzzling problem. The name Yahweh occurs in the Pentateuch 1782 times, Elohim 241 times, and Yahweh-Elohim 21 times. As the following tabulation makes clear, in the books of Exodus, Numbers, and Deuteronomy, Elohim is used very seldom, and not at all in Leviticus. Yahweh-Elohim is found almost exclusively in Genesis.

Within the Book of Genesis itself, we find a further peculiarity: in Genesis 10, 1 – 16, 26 the word Yahweh occurs 36 times, and Elohim not at all. On the other hand, in Genesis 40, 1 – 45, 28 Elohim occurs 18 times, while Yahweh is completely missing. It is also worth noting that in the case of doublets recounting the same event the name for God changes: Genesis 6, 5: "And Yahweh saw that the wickedness of man upon earth was great...." Verse 12: "And Elohim saw the earth and behold it was corrupt...."

The Pentateuch can be divided in terms of the name used for God according to the following table:[5]

	Gn	Ex	Lv	Nb	Dt	Pent.
Yahweh	145	393	310	387	547	1782
Elohim	165	56	—	10	10	241
Yahweh-Elohim	20	1	—	—	—	21

The self-testimony of the Pentateuch thus presents some contradictory impressions. On the one hand, the authorship

---

5. Simon-Prado, *Praelectiones Biblicae;* Vetus Test. (1949), I, 277. The double form of the divine name cannot today be assumed as the criterion for distinguishing the various sources, since the new Ugarit texts are full of such forms. Cf. Gordon, Or 21 (1952), 382. The name for God changes in terms of "instinctive method," appearing as Elohim in reference to foreign countries and as Yahweh in reference to the Covenant. J. S. Wright, *How Moses compiled Genesis?* The Churchman 67 (1946), 53-64.

of Moses is expressly declared and, on the other hand, there are many passages which could not possibly date back to Moses. The attempt to solve this riddle has occasioned the following chief hypotheses:

B) THE OLDER DOCUMENTARY HYPOTHESIS

Jean Astruc (1766), the physican of Louis XV of France, a Calvinist converted to Catholicism, argued that Genesis was made up of various threads of tradition coming from four principal sources, from which, as he claimed, Moses had drawn the material for his narratives.[6] He further claimed that Moses wrote his narrative in four columns, and that the text of Genesis as we know it was formed by the confusion of these columns after his death. Among these documents it was particularly easy to isolate and recognize the Elohistic, and the Jehovistic sources, which he so named by reason of the appearance of the divine name Elohim or Jehova[7]

This work of the Paris physician, which today is generally referred to as the older documentary hypothesis, found little attention among the Catholics, but it was enthusiastically received by the Protestants in Germany. Whereas Astruc still held fast to the concept of Mosaic authorshop, J. G. Eichhorn (1827) introduced the concept of a later editor, different from Moses, who combined the Elohistic and Jehovistic documents together with other ancient records in one single work. Among his successors we must name primarily R. D. Ilgen, who found no fewer than 17 documents in Genesis, 15 of which he assigned to two Elohistic sources (E^1, E^2), and two to the Jahwistic. The editor of this composite work resulting from three basic sources would be post-Mosaic.

---

6. J. Astruc, *Conjectures sur les mémoires, dont il paroit que Moyse s'est servi pour composer le livre de Genèse*, Paris (1753).

7. Jehovah is an incorrect pronunciation of the divine name, dating from around the year 1100 A.D. It was occasioned by the Biblical text of the Massoretes, who pointed the unvocalized sacred name *yhwh* (which they refused to pronounce aloud out of reverence) with the vowels of the word *'adonai* (lord), writing *e* for *a* in keeping with the Massoretic rules for vocalization, thus giving the final form *yehovah*. This form was pronounced by the Christians, never by the Jews, as Jehovah. Cf. Haag, BibLex 779. On the pronunciation *Yeya, Yaya,* cf. P. Katz, VT 4 (1954), 428.

C) THE FRAGMENT HYPOTHESIS

The English scholar A. Geddes (1802) first proposed the solution known as the fragment hypothesis,[8] which was further developed by J. S. Vater (1826) in Germany.[9] They divided the entire Pentateuch into nothing but small fragments, thereby completely destroying the unity of the book: 39 such fragments were, they concluded, collected in the time of the Exile by an editor and from them the "Mosaic work" was created, a work which has, however, nothing to do with Moses. The hypothesis was further developed by A. Hartmann (1826) and de Wette (1849).[10] Since this thesis fails to take into account the unity of the construction of the Pentateuch, which is unquestionable, it demands a further hypothesis in its turn.

D) THE SUPPLEMENTATION HYPOTHESIS

This hypothesis was first proposed by Heinrich Ewald who, as a 19-year-old scholar, wrote the inspiring book *Die Komposition der Genesis* (1823) and developed primarily the theme of a unified composition. In a further work, *Kritische Untersuchungen über die Genesis* (1830) he found that the sources of Elohistic fragments represent a completely unified and coherent thread of narrative, which he accordingly characterizes as the basic text, which was later enlarged by Jahwistic supplementation. His theories were taken up primarily by Franz Delitzsch.[11] In his further works he postulated a second Elohistic author and isolated Deuteronomy as a special source. The theory of four sources was thus essentially worked out.

E) THE MORE RECENT DOCUMENTARY HYPOTHESIS

This hypothesis is called more recent to distinguish it from

---

8. A. Geddes, *The Holy Bible* (1792); *Critical Remarks on the Hebrew* (1800).
9. Vater, *Kommentar über den Pentateuch* (1802-1805).
10. De Wette, *Beiträge zur Einleitung in das AT* (1807).
11. Delitzsch, *Kommentar zur Genesis* (1852).

the older form proposed by Astruc and Eichhorn. This hypothesis, in its essential characteristics, has remained in the ascendency. The modern position of scholarship on the question is best characterized by Sellin-Rost as follows: "Just as certainly as all subsequent scholarly judgment regarding the number, origin, and age of the individual sources will be nothing more than essential scientific hypotheses, this one scientific fact must be regarded as absolutely established: the Pentateuch was written only in the post-Mosaic era, and it was composed of a number of sources or strata written in Palestine. This is the one unshakable foundation upon which the whole structure of Protestant Pentateuchal criticism rests in perfect agreement today." [12]

The true founder of the new documentary hypothesis must be regarded as Hupfeld, who, in his book *Die Quellen der Genesis* (1853), promoted the eventual victory of this thesis by a new demonstration of the presence of two distinct Elohistic sources, such as Ilgen had first postulated. The third source was the Jahwistic. These three originally independent documents were worked together by a later editor. At almost the same time, Riehm's *Die Gesetzgebung Mosis Im Lande Moab* (1854) promoted the conception of Deuteronomy as an independent document. This development more or less settled the literary criticism problem. Since the one Elohistic source was identified as "the priestly code," the Pentateuch was held to be the combined editing of four sources: P E J D (Priestly code, Elohistic, Jahwist, Deuteronomist).

The Pentateuch question entered upon a new stage when literary criticism was coupled with historical criticism in scholarly investigation. The basic problem to be solved was a question in literary history: how are the sources to be dated. In the perspective of the supplementation hypothesis, and proceeding from the chronological ordering and clear structure of the priestly document, scholars had long been tending to regard P as the fundamental document and oldest of the sources, followed historically by the second Elohistic source E, then the Jahwistic J, and finally Deuteronomy D, as successive stages of development.

---

12. Sellin-Rost, *op. cit.*, 31.

It was the investigation of Graf, Kuenen, and Wellhausen that produced this change in emphasis. It is true that both Reuss and Vatke, some decades earlier, had spoken in favor of a relatively later dating of P, but the acceptance of this thesis had to wait for the scientific foundation first established by the works of Graf, *Die geschichtlichen Bücher Des Alten Testamentes* (1866), Kuenen, *Godsdienst Van Israel* (1869) and Wellhausen's brilliantly written *History of Israel* (I, 1878) (later: *Prolegomena Zur Geschichte Israels* — 1883, 1905). Wellhausen's "abiding merit" lies in his demonstration of the fact that the Mosaic Law belonged not to the beginning but rather to the end of the Old Testament religion, and that the Jahwistic source must be considered the oldest in the Pentateuch.[13] The datings are as follows: J — 9th century, E — 8th century, D — 7th century, P — 5th century. Higher dates and a different sequence are suggested by: Dillmann: E 900 — 850, J 800 — 700, D 650 — 623; König: E 1200, J 1000, D 700 — 650, P 500; Köhler: E 1200, J 1000, P 700, D 700 — 650).

These investigations completely reverse the whole traditional historical picture of the Old Testament. Nothing in the entire Pentateuch is the work of Moses. In the Mosaic era itself and in the centuries which immediately follow it there is not even a single mention of the Law, not even the actual occurrence of certain practices which later became a law. The legislation in Israel would, according to this hypothesis, have begun only with what is reported as the discovery, or perhaps better the "invention" of the law of Deuteronomy under Josiah around the year 621 (2 K 22). The prophets are not reformers who called the people back to a proper attitude towards the Law, but rather they are themselves the formers and precursors of the Law that is to come, the Law itself achieving its final form only in the post-Exilic era.

It is certainly not our purpose here to cast disparagement upon the great life's work of famous scholars, but, from the present-day point of view, we cannot avoid the impression that this whole process had embarked upon what has proved to be a colossally wrong direction. Wellhausen's contribution is that he applied the concepts of evolutionist history of religion to the development of the Old Testament. In this he was following closely upon the philosophy of Hegel. His division

---

13. S. Weiser, *Einleitung in das AT* (1949), 64.

of the Old Testament into three successive phases, animistic
(polydemonism), henotheistic (prophets), and monotheistic —
and the text of the present-day Old Testament is supposed to
exhibit traces of this development from primitive materialism
to ethical monotheism — is, seen from today's point of view,
quite untenable and is represented by no modern champions.
In Asia Minor there was, at the time of Moses, and in the
immediate vicinity of his activity, only a polytheistic form of
religion, neither an animism nor a fetishism. That Moses worshipped and heralded the existence of one single god as the
invisible creator of the universe can, by virtue of intensive
investigation, be considered as definitively established today.[14]
This demonstration completely invalidates the very foundation
upon which the *Prolegomena* explains the development of
Israelite history.[15]

The school of Wellhausen held the field at the end of the nineteenth
century and in the beginning of the twentieth. This source criticism also
spread to the other books of the Old Testament. It was particularly
traces of E and J that were followed through the later tradition of the
Books of Joshua, Judges, Samuel, and Kings. This idea, first outlined
by Budde in his *Commentary on the Books of Judges and Samuel* (1890),
led to the crystallization of the so-called Deuteronomic history, which
was supposed to have arisen from the older sources J and E, being
reworked, together with other historical sources, by a Deuteronomic
editor into a single literary unity.

F)   THE FORM HISTORY SCHOOL

The archaeology of the Ancient Near East led literary criticism to a new plane: excavations suggested the possibility that
the contents of the Old Testament must be older than their
literary recording. Scholarly interest thus began to focus upon
the pre-literary stage of the Old Testament writings. "It is the
unfading merit of H. Gunkel that, in his great commentary on
Genesis,[16] he developed and analyzed the original narrative

---

14. W. F. Albright, *op. cit.*, 271.
15. Fr. König, *Babel-Bibel, 50 Jahre später*, in "Wort und Wahrheit," VII
    (1952), 685.

units and thus was able to appreciate their setting in time and space. The individual traditions were quite different in kind. A number of them were cultic etiological narratives, while others arose from the need to explain various characteristics in the circumstances of tribes and peoples; these are the traditions of ethnological etiology. Some narratives exhibit the form of creative development associated with the novel. But apart from recognizing the fact that these very ancient traditions are primarily sagas, we cannot push our knowledge further back into antiquity."[17] Gunkel had thus overtaken the historical conception promoted by the school of Wellhausen and demonstrated the greater age of the Old Testament in many points. But he was severely criticized for the fact that, by introducing the concepts of saga, folktale, and legend, he completely destroyed the historical character of the Biblical narratives. G. v. Rad, however, has more recently defended Gunkel's position by pointing out that the concept of saga does not exclude the possibility of historical genuinity, but merely represents one specific form of historical presentation.

The saga is not to be considered the product simply of poetic imagination; it comprises, rather, the sum total of living historical tradition in a people; it serves as the mirror of the facts and truths of a nation's history. It is the form in which the people represents its own history.... Saga is something other than exact historical writing. Moreover, it dates from a quite different era in the people's history. It lives and grows at a time in which the capacity of rational and logical historical knowledge has not yet been completely developed, an era in which, however, there is all the more uninhibited scope for the energies of an understanding that can be qualified as intuitive or even prophetic . . . . In order to understand such saga properly, we must achieve a broader and deeper concept of "history" than is commonly the case today. At the beginning of saga there is almost certainly an "historical" fact, serving as the proper point of crystallization.[18] If we understand "saga" in this light, then we are truly approaching the faithful tradition of an historical content. This, however, is not the common meaning of saga and thus, even

---

16. H. Gunkel, *Genesis übersetzt und erklärt* (1922).

---

17. G. v. Rad, *Das erste Buch Mose* (1950), 22.
18. *Ibid.*, 23ff.

in the judgment of G. v. Rad, the word should be avoided as conducive to misunderstanding.

G) THE TRADITIONAL HISTORICAL SCHOOL

Even though the majority of Protestant scholars still hold fast to the classical document hypothesis, such as Hölscher (*Die Anfänge der hebräischen Geschichtsschreibung,* 1942), more and more critical voices are being raised against it. First comes the attempts to further subdivide the sources. Eissfeldt finds, in the Jahwistic tradition, a separate thread of narrative which he calls the "lay source" (L); it is practically equivalent to the *Se'ir* source postulated by Pfeiffer, so named from the fact that its narrative derives from the mountains of *Se'ir,* east of the Sink of the Arabah.[19] Volz and Rudolf undermine the foundation of the Elohistic source by demonstrating that the criterion of the various names for God is unsuitable for the determination of distinct sources.

"The change in the name for God does not need to be taken as a principle for distinction, and the name for God cannot be a criterion for this distinction, since one and the same narrator (whom we call the Jahwist) uses both divine names. The Jahwist uses Yahweh and Elohim both and, moreover, he uses the form Elohim sometimes from general objective grounds, and sometimes for an artistic purpose.... No one would maintain that the change of divine name in the Pentateuchal narratives is a simple matter or that the difficulty occasioned by such a variety of evidence in the text itself can be completely solved: we are faced with a problem that has not been completely explained.... But one thing we can say with certainty, and it has become a point of more and more universal conviction: the change in the divine name cannot possibly be advanced as a sufficient criterion for determining among the various sources. But once this primary support of Pentateuchal literary criticism has been shattered, the entire edifice must appear to be severely shaken." [20]

What we have said on the subject of the divine name is also valid for the linguistic differences exhibited by the so-called sources. "The course of scientific investigation has increasingly undermined the founda-

---

19. A. Bentzen, *Introduction to the OT,* II, 18.
20. Volz-Rudolph, *Der Elohist als Erzähler, ein Irrweg der Pentateuch-kritik,* BZATW 63 (1933), 15-16.

tion; it would be good to let the foundation simply collapse in its entirety, and, as in the case of the divine name, so with all the linguistic evidence, to refrain from seeing the tabulation of supposed differences as evidence for distinguishing among the sources." [21]

As a result, A. Bentzen, after investigating the present status of the Pentateuchal question, arrives at the conclusion that "the younger generation is filled with a very pronounced scepticism with respect to the documentary hypothesis. We are living in an age in which new theories are being born." [22] Among the more recent streams of influence we might isolate two particular lines of development which are united in the stress they place on tradition:

1) THE SCANDINAVIAN SCHOOL: Nyberg, Widengren, Engnell, Danell and other scholars attempt to demonstrate the relative insignificance of source distinction by calling attention to the incomparable importance of the oral tradition. It is not the written word that primarily determines the text, but the oral handing down of the tradition that precedes it, a process which can spread over many generations. Thus a relatively recent literary text can well contain a very ancient corpus of tradition. [23] The bearer of these traditions is primarily the cult.

2) THE CULT-HISTORICAL INTERPRETATION: After being set free from the written word and its rigid formulation, scholarship looked further into the uncertainties of the pre-literary stage, and was now forced to seek here for the point at which the ancient traditions had crystallized. It was primarily the ancient cult, with its variety of liturgical practices, that suggested itself as just such a point. G. v. Rad reconstructs the origin of the Pentateuch (Hexateuch) in the following manner:

a) *The cultic creed*: "Our narrator (Jahwist) had at his disposal the ancient cultic creed, that canonical outline of salvation history which

---

21. *Ibid.*, 19.

22. A. Bentzen, *op. cit.*, 23: "Especially among scholars of the younger generation there exists a definite scepticism towards the Documentary Hypothesis . . . we are living in an age, where new theories are about to be born."

23. Engnell, *Gamla Testamentet, en traditionshistorisk inledning*, I, (1945). — Bentzen, *op. cit.*, II, 19. Sellin-Rost, *op. cit.*, 33.

ranges from the fathers to the possession of the promised land. (Cf. the text that was to be spoken on the occasion of the delivery of the first fruits at the sanctuary: Deuteronomy 26, 5-9; or the historical retrospect of Joshua at the assembly in Shechem: Josh 24, 2-13.) He had at his disposal, on the other hand, a large number of disparate individual narratives, some of which perhaps had already grown into small bodies of composition, although in their sum total they were certainly unconnected and of very modest scope. It is an accomplishment of remarkable creative power that he succeeded in forging this considerable mass of narrative units into a fundamental tradition that could support them and give them unity; and this he did by the simple outline of a salvation-history creed . . . . This creed gradually assimilates the Sinai tradition, the patriarchal narratives, and, finally all of prehistory . . . . The particular characteristic of the Jahwist is certainly his interest in the *how* rather than in the *what* of things past; that is, in the theological work of composition with which he has put together the raw material of the individual traditions and cycles of tradition to form one organized whole, all aiming at one great final purpose." [24]

b) *Cultic-sacral lectionaries*: Artur Weiser discovers the original form of the Pentateuchal sources not in the cultic creed of a layman, but in the official recitation by a cult person (priest or prophet; cf. Josh 24, 1; 1 S 12; Ps 78, 5; 81, 6ff.; 105, 5ff.) on the occasion of a covenant festival of the sacral community of the twelve tribes. These are to be understood as a sort of lectionary, that is, the written fixation of the traditions of salvation history common to the alliance of the twelve tribes, material which had previously been handed down in the form of oral tradition. The activity of the source authors was thus less a matter of collection and literary preservation of the ancient ethnic traditions (Gunkel) as rather the reforming and transforming — and eventually the organization into a festival cult — of already available materials and traditions. The Pentateuch that proceeds from this festival cult is thus something more than a literature of history in the more or less modern sense. Rather, the presentation of salvation history in cult like the theophany itself with which it is related, is the real actualization of salvation history in which the community, on the occasion of the festival, means to have an immediate participation. The Pentateuch thus takes on a sacral, in fact

---

24. Gerhard von Rad, *op. cit.*, 13, 14. — A. Weiser, *op. cit.*, 69. The cultic creed is too uncertain a basis for the construction of a grandiose system. According to E. Robertson, *The Old Testament Problem* (1950), there were various different traditions at the individual sanctuaries, all of them dating back to Moses, and these were perhaps gathered together under the direction of Samuel at a sort of Ecclesiastical Council of scribes, and edited in the unit we know as the Torah.

a "sacramental" character and is thus to be distinguished from every other historical tradition and literature. The individual strata of the Pentateuch are, accordingly, steps and types of the salvation-history tradition which had its origins in the cult of the alliance of the twelve tribes, and maintained itself in a sacral recital, even throughout the era of the political separation of the tribes, as the living heritage of the whole community, until the time that the Torah was read in the synagogue.[25]

The great merit of this hypothesis is the fact that it rescues the Pentateuch from the writer's studio and restores it to the midst of the religious life of the people. As a result, the liturgy, for want of a better word, the "living church of the Old Testament," becomes, by virtue of its cult, the true bearer and former of the Pentateuch.

H)   THE CLASSICAL RESULTS OF PROTESTANT PENTATEUCHAL CRITICISM

Retrospect and synopsis: For a century and a half, Biblical criticism has worked at the problem of the development of the Pentateuch with stubborn tenacity and inexorability. The final result of this labor is not in the form of any guaranteed result; we see rather that the hypotheses of the classical criticism are today more questionable than ever. Nonetheless, the reconstruction of the religion-history evolution of the Pentateuch has yielded one abiding fruit: the knowledge that the Pentateuch has undergone a highly developed process of evolution which we cannot successfully investigate down to its last detail. "A true understanding can be achieved only by the scholar who looks upon the Hexateuch (Pentateuch) not simply on the surface, but is willing to read it with an awareness of its deeper dimensions; who recognizes the fact that the revelations and lived experiences of faith from many eras are speaking to him here. For none of the stages in the infinitely long process of this work's evolution is ever really supplanted by its successors; something of every phase has survived and, as an abiding concern for every age, it has been preserved in the final form of the Hexateuch as

---

25. A. Weiser, op. cit., 78-79.

we know it. Only with this knowledge can a scholar possibly be prepared to appreciate the whole wealth of evidence encompassed by this work." [26]

In order to give a fuller appreciation of the individual peculiarities of these four sources (J E P D), we follow the description given by G. v. Rad.[27]

1) THE JAHWIST SOURCE (J):

"The natural genius of the Jahwist narrative can only be wondered at. The artistic mastery of this narrative has justly been acclaimed as one of the greatest accomplishments of literary productivity for all times. Wonderful clarity and final simplicity characterize the presentation of the individual scenes. Truly remarkable is the economy of media, and still it is the entire life of man, with all its heights and depths, that the narrator's purview embraces . . . . He is the great psychologist among the Biblical narrators; but really it is not the human person who believes himself to be alone in this world with his aspirations and despairs, but the human person to whom the living God has manifested himself, who is thus the object of a divine initiative, a divine activity, and thus also a divine judgment and a divine salvation.

"Thus, in the prehistory, it is the great human questions that he presents in the light of revelation: creation and nature, sin and suffering, man and woman, civil strife, the confusion in the world of the nations, etc. But it is primarily the ways of God in Israel's beginnings that he examines, in both their open wonders and their hidden mysteries. He sees the election of the Old Testament community in its full incomprehensibility . . . .

At the same time the Jahwist's narrative is full of the most ancient anthropomorphisms. Yahweh walks about the garden in the cool of evening, he himself closes up the ark, he comes down to earth in order to inspect the tower of Babel. But here there is something more than simply the native limitations of an archaic narrator that is at work here; much rather we must recognize that natural simplicity and directness which are really only the mark of a lofty and mature spirituality. This crystal-like transparency and fragile spirituality of the Jahwist narrative makes any attempt at explanation a difficult and almost insoluble objective." [28]

---

26. G. v. Rad, *Das Formgeschichtliche Problem des Hexateuchs* (1938), 72.
27. G. v. Rad, *Das erste Buch Mose* (1950), 16ff. (ATD).
28. *Ibid.*, 17.

The Jahwist source is, most probably, the oldest written presentation of the over-all history of the people of Yahweh and, at the same time, the oldest of the four so-called Pentateuchal sources; it developed in Judah, during the Davidic-Solomonic era.[29]

In general, it is the following sections that are ascribed to the Jahwist stratum (for more individual analysis, cf. the commentaries). The parentheses indicate a mixed source:

Gn: 2, 4b–4, 26; 5, 29; 6, 1–8; 7–8 (P); 9, 18-27; 10, 8–19, 25–30; 11, 1–9, 28–30; 12; 13 (P); 15 (E); 16 (P); 18, 1-19, 28, 30–38; 21, 1–7 (P); 32–33 (E); 22, 14–24 (E); 24 (E); 25 (P); 26 (P); 27 (EP); 28, 13–16; 29, 2–14, 31–35; 30, 9–16, 24–43 (E); 31 (EP); 32 (E); 33 (E); 34 (E); 36 (EP); 37 (EP); 38; 39 (E); 40–42 (E); 43; 44; 45 (E); 46 (EP); 47 (P); 48 (EP); 49, 1–27; 50, 1–11;
Ex: 1 (EP); 2–5 (EP); 7–10 (EP); 11, 4–8; 12, 21–27; 13–14 (E); 15, 22–27 (E); 15 (EP); 19, 20–25; 23–24 (EP); 32 (E); 34, 1–28;
Nb: 10, 29–32; 11 (E); 13–14 (EP); 16 (EP); 20–21 (EP); 22–24 (E); 25, 1–5 (E); 32 (EP);
Dt: 34 (EDP); 45.

2) THE ELOHISTIC SOURCE (E):

"The work of the Elohist is to be dated from one to two centuries later. It was at that time that an editor combined it very closely with the Jahwist stratum. Nonetheless, the differences between the two are quite obvious. In general, the Elohist does not achieve either the brilliance or the general mastery of the Jahwist's presentation; it is more popular; that is, it is the ancient sacral popular tradition which he has taken over with little alteration and far less spiritual development. Its connection with the popular tradition is particularly recognizable in an over-all outline. The Elohist begins with the story of Abraham, and thus presents no prehistory. He tells his story for the purpose of religious edification and instruction. Everywhere he stresses the divine guidance, the divine miracles, the divine plan for the people's destiny in the most explicit manner (cf. Gn 15, 6; 20, 11; 21, 17, etc.).

"The prophetic element is very much in evidence. The prophet is the one proper mediator called to stand between God and man; it is he who, as intercessor, brings man's concerns before God (Gn 20, 7, 17; Ex 15, 20; Nb 11; 12, 6). The Elohist's sympathy for the prophets and the prophetic mission is so strongly marked that there is much to

29. Sellin-Rost, op. cit., 47-53. Page 47 divides J. into ch. and v. / H. Schmökel, Zur Datierung der Pentateuchquelle J., ZATW 62 (1949/ 50), 319-321.
30. A. Weiser, op. cit., 89ff.

recommend the hypothesis that the entire work is the product of the ancient prophetic circles. But the interweaving of this tradition with the Jahwistic is so intimate that any distinction between the two involves a considerable loss in the sacred text." [31]

It is primarily the following sections that are ascribed to the E stratum:

Gn: 15 (J); 20, 21 (J); 22 (J); 24 (J); 27 (J); 28, 10–12; 29–34 (J); 35 (P); 36 (JP); 37 (JP); 39 (J); 40–42 (J); 45 (J); 46 (JP); 48 (JP); 50 (JP);

Ex: 1 (JP); 2–5 (JP); 7–10 (JP); 11, 1–3; 12 (JP); 13–14 (J); 15, 20; 16 (JP); 17–18; 19 (J); (20, 22–23, 19 = Bundesbuch); 23–24 (JP); 32 (J); 33 (J);

Nb: 10 (JP); 11 (J); 12; 13–14 (JP); 16 (JP); 20–21 (JP); 22–24 (J); 25, 1–5 (J); 32 (JP);

Dt: 31, 14; 32; 33; 34 (JDP).

3) THE PRIESTLY STRATUM (P):

"Quite different from the sources described above is the priestly stratum. The texts here cannot be understood by the lay person because of their strongly marked peculiarities in both form and content. This source cannot possibly be understood as a narrative. It is definitely a priestly writing, that is, it contains a doctrine, the precipitate of an intensive and theologically oriented reflection. In keeping with this objective, the manner of presentation is quite different.

"The language is concentrated and bulky, pedantic and unartistic. Only in the most important matters does the otherwise forced diction take on a more relaxed tone, and becomes broadly circumstantial in an attempt to express the subject matter in as complete and comprehensible a form as possible (Gn 1; 9; 17). If the Jahwist was characterized by a narrative of overpowering simplicity, without any didactic preoccupation, the priestly writing exhibits a minimum of intuitive narration and artistic movement. In this respect it has also renounced every claim to impressive ornamentation. On the other hand, it is precisely this renunciation that establishes its true grandeur; for this sober objectivity is, in reality, the supreme self-involvement, the supreme concentration upon the revelation from God. Everything is reflected, nothing is without its theological point of reference, for this work represents the essence of the theological concentration of many generations of priests.

"The 'composition' of such a work, because of the infinitely slow growth of such sacral traditions, cannot be determined in terms of years or even centuries. Though it probably took on its final form only in the time after the Exile, it has certainly combined a more recent and strongly

---

31. G. v. Rad, *op. cit.*, 16ff.: "die drei Erzählerquellen."

theologized and thoroughly reedited material side by side with more ancient traditions, in one and the same almost indistinguishable highly archaic form. As a general rule, the priestly texts have been taken into the composition of the Hexateuch (Pentateuch) without admixture. In Genesis, for example, it is only in the deluge narrative that the editor was forced to combine the traditions of P and J into a single text." [32]

The following concordance shows the sections assigned to P:

Gn: 1, 1–2, 4a; 5, 1–28, 30–32; 6, 5–9, 19 (J); 9, 28f; 10 (J); 11, 10–
   26, 27, 31–32; 13, 6, 11; 16, 1, 3, 15; 17; 19, 29; 21, 3–5; 23; 25,
   7–20; 26, 34; 27, 46–28, 9; 31, 18; 35, 9–13, 15, 22–29; 36 (EJ);
   37, 1–2; 46, 6–27; 48, 3–6; 49, 28–33; 50, 12f;
Ex: 1, 1–5, 7, 13f; 2, 23–25; 6, 2–30; 7, 1–13; 8, 1–3, 12–15; 9, 8–12;
   11, 9–12, 20, 28; 12, 40–51; 16 (JE); 24, 16–18; 25–31; 34, 2ᴼ–35;
   35–40;
Lv: entire.
Nb: 1–10; 13–14 (EJ); 15; 16 (JE); 17–19; 20 (JE); 25, 6–31, 54;
   27, 12–23; 32 (JE); 33-36 (sekundäre Zusätze).

4) DEUTERONOMY (D):

The name of the fifth Book of Moses goes back to a misunderstanding of Deuteronomy 17, 18, where the LXX misreads the words *"mišnê hattôrâ,"* which actually means "copy or transcript of the law," and translates them as *deuteronomion* (second law, repetition of the law). As opposed to the other Pentateuchal sources, D represents an independent literary unit; its style and language, its ideology, and its relatively compact outline clearly set the work off from the other strata of the Pentateuchal writings.

The situation of Israel before the death of Moses comprises the entire Book of Deuteronomy, making it a sort of legacy of the dying Moses. The central nucleus consists of chapters 12–26, which contain the "laws and precepts" of the covenant at Moab, while chapters 1–11 form an introductory speech, which serves as preparation for the legislation and exhortation to follow the precepts, and chapters 27–30 which are concluding exhortations to keep the law, with a clear reference to the consequences that will follow upon obedience or disobedience. Apart from the historical appendix (chapters 31–34), where there are clear traces of the other pentateuchal strata, Deuteronomy, taken as a whole, is a compact unit.[33]

The question as to the author of this work has occasioned the most divergent hypotheses. One element is, however, common to all attempts

---

32. *Ibid.*, 17ff.
33. A. Weiser, *op. cit.*, 99ff.

at solution, that is, some connection with the law discovered under King Josiah in the year 622 (2 K 22ff.). Wellhausen and his school see this narrative as a sort of pious fraud, which was deliberately perpetrated by the high priest Helkiah in order to force a reform of the cult. The law fabricated by him was a precursor of our present-day text of Deuteronomy and is thus referred to as Ur-Deuteronomy.

This hypothesis, however, has been almost completely given up today. Excepting for Hölscher who dates Deuteronomy in the post-Exilic era by reason of what he considers its "Utopian character," recent scholarship has stressed primarily the relatively early date of the Deuteronomic precepts. A brief study of the content clearly reveals the fact that we are here dealing with what is largely a very ancient popular body of material.[34] (For the relationship with the Book of the Covenant cf., chs. 22–25.) Sellin-Rost maintains that one cannot exclude the possibility that, from very ancient times, the Levites had brought with them from Kadesh the concept that Yahweh could be officially honored by the public cult in only one place, no matter how strong the opposition to this practice might have proved. This would shatter the most important argument for a later dating of Deuteronomy, namely the centralization of the cult under Josiah. His cultic reform would thus no longer take on the character of "invention" of a new law of centralization of cult, but appear rather as a "revival" of cultic precepts which had been enunciated before but had fallen into oblivion.

"This book of the law discovered in 622 can, however, not possibly have been an ancient Mosaic or even a Solomonic code. It would seem, rather, on the basis of its language and ideas, to have been composed shortly before the time of its alleged discovery and, as was customary for the publication of laws, to have been deposited in the Temple, before the face of Yahweh. It represents the crowning glory of King Josiah's reform activity and proceeds from the combined efforts and interests of prophets and Levites, the leaders of the 'am haares, the landed nobility of Judah (2 K 21, 24; 23, 30; Dt 11, 18, 20). Its precepts were influenced by both religious and social-political motives. It probably dates around 700." [35]

5) THE MOST ANCIENT MATERIALS:

Together with the four great source writings, criticism has also isolated numerous smaller segments as the most ancient materials in the Pentateuch. Among these are:

a) *The most ancient poetic fragments*: Lamech's sword-song (Gn

---

34. Sellin-Rost, *op. cit.*, 59ff.
35. Sellin-Rost, *op. cit.*, 61.

4, 23); the oracles of Noah (Gn 9, 25-27); the oracles of the patriarchs, Abraham (Gn 12, 2, 3; 13, 14-17), Isaac (26, 4), Jacob (27, 27-29; 28, 13f.), Esau (25, 23; 27, 39), and Joseph (48, 22); the blessing of Jacob (Gn 49), the blessing of Moses and the song of Moses (Dt 32; 33).

b) *The most ancient legislative elements*: the decalogue (Ex 20, 1-17; Dt 5, 6-18); the Book of the Covenant (Ex 20, 23 — 23, 19); the so-called Jahwistic decalogue (Ex 34, 10-27); the twelve commandments of Shechem (Dt 27, 15-26); the law of holiness (Lv 17 — 26).

c) *Among the most ancient narrative fragments* we might number the account of Abraham's campaign against the kings from the East (Gn 14), which was deposited in the archives of Jerusalem probably around the year 1500 B.C. and later discovered by David upon his conquest of the city.[36]

I) CATHOLIC PENTATEUCHAL CRITICISM

As we have seen above, Pentateuchal criticism is not the sole prerogative of enlightened rationalism. The literary problems of the books of Moses have claimed the attention of Catholic scholars as early as the sixteenth and seventeenth centuries, men like Masius, Pereira, Bonfrère. In fact, the prime movers and fathers of all Pentateuchal criticism can only be the Catholic physician J. Astruc and the Oratorian Richard Simon. Catholic Scriptural exegesis became largely a matter of representing the opposition only when literary criticism committed itself irrevocably to the evolutionary outlines proposed by the comparative study of religion, thereby bringing the whole of Biblical criticism into disrepute. The reaction was not, however, restricted to Catholic circles; it also sprang up among wide circles of conservative Protestants and Jews.[37]

---

36. K. Galling represents the thesis that the community law in Dt 23 develops from the border sanctuary at Beer-sheba and is proclaimed at the amphictyonic sanctuary at Gilgal in three phases: a. West-Jordanian tradition, b. East-Jordanian tradition: Moab-Ammon Laws, c. Edomite-Egyptian legal practices. Fs. Bertholet (1950), 176-191. / Sellin-Rost, *op. cit.*, 34-47.

37. A. Bentzen characterizes the situation thus: "The name of Wellhausen is sometimes named in tones as if he were Antichrist himself." *Op. cit.*, II, 16. — Especially argumentative is W. Möller, *Die Einheit und*

But after the evolutionist movement had run its course, there was once again room for an objective form of Pentateuchal criticism. Thus it is not surprising that critical Protestant and critical Catholic scholarship have, in many respects, proceeded hand in hand. All this only goes to strengthen one's confidence in the objectivity and reliability of Pentateuchal criticism.

Common to the Catholic authors is the unerring commitment to Mosaic authorship. Within this framework, however, there has been room for the most divergent hypotheses as to the proper solution to the Pentateuchal problem. The most important of these can be briefly characterized:

1) *The restoration hypothesis*: According to A. Scholz (*Zeit und Ort der Entstehung der Bücher des AT* — Würzburg, 1893) what was originally one single book of law was divided into individual sections in its transcription, according as the objective was the recording of laws or narratives. The 900 years of development, up to the time of the exile, have left their mark upon this book and its individual sections. The final redaction created a product in which the available material was simply taken up without alteration, without any attempt at comparing the individual elements. The restoration of the Pentateuch, as well as the composition of the remainder of the sacred text is, according to Scholz, the work of the schools in Babylon, produced by the 70 elders, the men of Hezekiah, and the 120 sages. For Scholz, the origin of the present-day Pentateuch is simply the restoration of the work previously composed by Moses.

Another form of this restoration hypothesis is represented by F. v. Hummelauer (*Commentary on Genesis, Cursus Scripturae Sacrae*, Paris, 1895). In the royal era, especially under Manasseh (698 — 643), the sacred writings were persecuted; they suffered serious damage and gradually fell into oblivion. Shortly after Manasseh, the pious Israelites began to collect the scattered fragments and put them back together.

Echtheit der fünf Bücher Mosis (1931). / On the Jewish side: Orientalist Halévy, Recherches bibliques I-II (1895-1901) and Cassuto, *La questione della Genesi* (1934). / Jülicher sums up his counter-argument in one sentence: "The most misleading and dangerous of all the Pentateuchal hypotheses that have appeared since Astruc is the mechanical application of the Mosaic hypothesis." (Jahrbücher f. prot. Theol. [1882], 102). — On Simon's significance for Catholic criticism, cf. R. Deville, R. Simon, *Critique catholique du Pentateuch*, NouvRevThéol. 83/73 (1951), 723-739.

This process was continued during the Exile and finally concluded by Ezra.

2) *The tradition hypothesis*: P. Vetter (1906) derives the pre-Mosaic history through the time of prehistory and the era of the patriarchs on the basis of family oral tradition, which, at the beginning of the written form which dates from the time of Joshua and the judges, was characterized by at least two distinct forms (P and JE). From Moses come the precepts, the chronological data regarding the trek through the wilderness, and the songs commemorating famous events. The priests took over the laws of Moses, further developed them through their casuistry, and published special collections of law, one of which is extant in Deuteronomy, which dates from the end of the era of the judges. About the time of the building of the Temple, the available materials, the narrative and legal traditions, were fused into the Pentateuch. The text, however, remained in a state of considerable flux, both in its content and in its scope, until it was given its final form under Ezra.[38]

3) *The source theory* of J. M. Lagrange attempts to establish some point of contact with the critical school insofar as Lagrange recognizes in Genesis the three sources J, E, and P.[39] Of these, E is supposed to have been composed by Moses himself, or upon his command, and consists of a collection of pre-Mosaic traditions which were not yet familiar with the divine name Yahweh. Together with this collection of already finished materials and traditions, Moses then either composed by himself or had composed by someone else (Joshua) a new presentation of the tradition (J), beginning with the creation of man; this new tradition was characterized by the use of the newly revealed name for God Yahweh. P was, in its original nucleus, a collection of Mosaic and partially also pre-Mosaic laws, to which, in the post-Mosaic era, a brief historical introduction was prefixed. The tradition of the Mosaic origin of the Pentateuch is, accordingly, firmly defended by Lagrange.

In his last article, which appeared shortly before his death,[40] Lagrange pictures the origins of Genesis as follows: Moses collected the patriarchal histories and composed them in their present form (E), in order to inspire the Hebrews in Egypt to undertake both the Exodus and the conquest of Palestine. After the legislation on Sinai he ordered someone else to collect the material in J, whereupon he himself reedited both

---

38. Cf. (1 and 2) Goettsberger, *Einleitung in das AT* (1928), 76ff.
39. *La méthode historique en son application à l'étude de l'Hexateuque* (Compte rendu du 4ème Congr. Scient. des Cath., II), Fribourg (1898), 231-265.
40. *L'authenticité mosaïque de la Genèse et la théorie des documents,* RB 47 (1938), 163-183.

the Elohistic and the Jahwistic narratives into one common form (JE), so that he is both editor and author. P is the result of later additions.

4) *The decision of the Pontifical Biblical Commission*: On June 27, 1906, the Pontifical Biblical Commission entered the field of Pentateuchal criticism with its statement: *"De Mosaica authentia Pentateuchi,"* and set up the following guidelines for further Pentateuchal criticism:

a) The arguments so far adduced by Pentateuchal criticism are insufficient to introduce any doubt as to the Mosaic authorship of the Pentateuch.

b) The Mosaic authorship is not to be understood in terms of literal dictation. Moses may have had help. But he must be considered as the primary author.

c) In the Pentateuch both written and oral sources have been combined by Moses to conform to the primary thesis of his work.

d) In the post-Mosaic era the Pentateuch underwent further alterations and additions.

5) *The recension hypothesis* attempts a compromise with the source hypothesis. It was first developed by Vaccari.[41] The original Pentateuch of Moses has achieved its present-day form only by the combined efforts of two different recensions. In northern Israel and in Judah two forms of the text gradually developed, distinguished primarily by their use of a different name for God. After the destruction of the Northern Kingdom, the two were fused into a single unified text.

6) *The organic development of the Pentateuch* is stressed primarily by the commentaries of H. Heinisch (Genesis — 1930, Exodus — 1934, Leviticus — 1935, Numbers — 1936, —— *Bonner Bibel*). Moses, according to this hypothesis, made use of written sources for recording his work, and also used scribes for this purpose. The laws first proclaimed by Moses were, in keeping with the needs of later times, further developed. The later laws are "Mosaic" in the sense that they are composed in the spirit of the great law-giver and based upon his original work. In the course of time, many other elements grew up about the Mosaic *oeuvre*: historical, geographical, and archaeological records, additions to the narratives, marginal glosses and new legal provisions. The present form of the Pentateuch dates only from the time of Ezra.

The same general approach, though with greater reservation, is proposed by the commentary of A. Bea (Institutiones Bibl. II, 1: *De Pentateucho,* Rome, 1933, 121-133). For the narrative sections, Moses had at his disposal both written and oral traditions, and likewise for the legislative

41. *Verbum Domini* 17 (1937), 371-373.

sections, which he filled with the spirit of the new divine revelation. The most personal characteristics of Moses are to be found in the priests' and cultic laws (P). The Books Exodus — Numbers were edited in their present form at the end of the 40 years' wandering in the wilderness, working from notes and records that had been made earlier. Bea admits certain editorial alterations for the post-Mosaic era, historical and geographical marginal glosses, the continued development of the laws, etc.

7) *Mosaic original and post-Mosaic final composition*: Whereas the above hypotheses all make Moses himself responsible for the essential formation of the Pentateuch, Junker sympathizes with the position that the Mosaic era is responsible only for individual sections, partially historical and partially legislative in their content, which he himself or, at his instigation and upon his authority, others composed for him, this material serving for the later formation of the coherent presentation characteristic of the present-day Pentateuch. This theory can claim as evidence the fact that, for example, in the case of the Book of the Covenant, Scripture itself expressly mentions a special composition and promulgation (Ex 24, 4-7), and that the almost universally accepted position of present-day Old Testament scholarship regards the "Book of the Law" discovered in the year 621 B.C. to be simply the Book of Deuteronomy, so that this legal text existed prior to that time, only as a separate book.[42]

The origins of the Book of Deuteronomy are best explained by reference to the Deuteronomistic sermon on the law. The preacher did not simply invent his material, but rather drew upon the Mosaic traditions. For Deuteronomy is not to be understood as a new entity; it is much rather a large-scale actualization of the most divergent ancient norms. Even the law of the centralization of cult is not an unheard of innovation; it is the eventual self-assertion of a cultic tradition that dates from the most ancient times of Israel but was long repressed by the actual development of the chosen people's history. It is only in this direction that it is possible to attempt a solution to the problem of Deuteronomy which takes proper account of the earlier traditions and still leaves open the possibility of a proper and unprejudiced historical understanding of the tradition.[43]

J) THE PENTATEUCH AS A DOCUMENT OF THE ANCIENT NEAR EAST

By way of introduction one might say that, within the circles

---

42. H. Junker, *op. cit.*, 7.
43. H. Junker, *Deuteronomium* (*Echter Bibel*) 1952, 1-7. — Cf. Rad, *Deuteronomium Studien* (1948).

of Catholic exegesis, there is real unity only with respect to the Mosaic origins of the Pentateuch, whereas, in other areas, an abundance of more or less tenable hypotheses have been advanced for the solution of the riddle. Today, the work of Moses is no longer viewed as a two-dimensional phenomenon; it has taken on a third dimension. In a statement from the Secretary of the Pontifical Biblical Commission, January 16, 1948, we find the following statement: "Today there is no longer anyone who could doubt the existence of such sources or contest a gradual development in the Mosaic law (*un accrois- sement progressif des lois mosaiques*), which has its basis in the "changing" social and religious situations of a later era, a continuing development, which is also to be observed in the historical narratives." [44]

Despite this statement, even today we have not yet reached the point at which we can give a simple and definite state- ment to the problems posed by the origins of the Pentateuch, as Goettsberger is forced to admit in his introduction to the Old Testament (1928, p. 112). "It would rather seem to be the objective of further criticism and scholarship, instead of tabulating and forcing the individual texts into some system that serves as a demonstration for preconceived explanations, to examine them without any prejudice whatsoever, to see if perhaps here or there they might themselves offer some hint as to the time and manner of their origins. It is only the final summation of such patiently worked out individual studies that can hope to explain how the text of the Pentateuch has come into such a peculiar and disunited state. Only so can we suc- ceed in properly comparing the arguments adduced for and against the concept of Mosaic origin in the Pentateuch, without arbitrarily rejecting one witness from antiquity while acknowl- edging the validity of another." [45]

With all due caution, it would seem to me, however, that today that hypothesis can claim the highest degree of probability which is most in harmony with the facts unearthed by arch-

44. *Acta Apostol. Sedis* (1948), 45ff.
45. Goettsberger, *op. cit.,* 112.

aeology. When Wellhausen began his criticism, the Ancient Near East was essentially an unknown quantity. Since that time, the spade of archaeology has hardly paused, and strata after strata of vanished culture and literature have come to light. We thus can recognize the fact that the Bible as a whole, and especially the Pentateuch, is a literary product of the Ancient Near East, and must thus follow the literary laws and traditions of the Ancient Near East.

The most important hallmarks of the Ancient Near Eastern literary tradition have been characterized by W. F. Albright in the following words: "A principle which must never be lost sight of in dealing with documents of the Ancient Near East is that instead of leaving obvious archaisms in spelling and grammar, as later became the fashion in Greece and Rome, the scribes generally revised ancient literary and other documents periodically. This practice was followed with particular regularity by cuneiform scribes. As a result scribes of the Middle-Babylonian age nearly always revise Old-Babylonian texts, substituting current grammatical forms and even contemporary phraseology. Neo-Babylonian recensions of the same texts are still further modernized." [46]

This knowledge which derives from the history of Egyptian and Babylonian literature [47] casts considerable light upon the fate of the Pentateuch.

"The divergences between narratives in the parallel documents J and E should not be considered as average variation, i.e., as typical of the differences between the documents, but rather as maximum variation; the real difference between the narratives of J and E was thus materially

---

46. Albright, *op. cit.*, 68ff.
47. Succeeding editions of the Egyptian texts in the Book of the Dead illustrate this process of enlargement by addition, especially in the case in which a particular text can be clearly followed from the pyramids of the 6th dynasty through the sarcophagus texts of the 12th dynasty down into the recensions of the Book of the Dead from the 18th century, and even into the Hellenistic-Roman era. In such cases the later recensions often contain commentaries and glosses of the original texts and frequently additional commentaries upon the commentaries.

smaller than is commonly supposed. Some of the most striking variations may probably be due to divergent traditions which were both incorporated into either J or E, as the case may be. It also means that much of the expansion evident in legal and liturgic passages is not due to literary doublets but to the normal swelling of the text by the accretion of commentaries or of subsequent court decisions, etc. Driver and Miles have shown that many of the divergences between the Code of Hammurabi and the Assyrian laws of about 1100 B.C. may be explained in this way.... As critical study of the Bible is more and more influenced by the rich new material from the Ancient Near East we shall see a steady rise in respect for the historical significance of now neglected or despised passages and details in the Old and New Testaments." [48]

Does such a position necessarily abandon the fate of the Pentateuch to the whims and awkwardness of Ancient Near Eastern scribes and redactors? Not at all. This difficulty is obviated primarily by the cult-historical line of investigation which locates the development of the Pentateuch in the very middle of Israel's religious and cultic life. The responsible bearer of the tradition is thus not some private *littérateur,* but the Old Testament "Church" as such. Thus, when, in the course of long centuries, the successive layers of Old Testament history form around the central work of Moses, these are not an arbitrary growth; they are the expression of a healthy vitality which handed down the ancient heritage not in the dead letter, but, "in spirit and in truth." It would be a miracle indeed if the great historical experiences of Israel, which were at the same time a powerful awareness in the life of the people, had left no trace whatsoever in the Pentateuch: the era of the conquest of Palestine, the era of the judges, in which Israel gradually asserted her sovereignty over the land promised her by Yahweh, the zenith and decay of the monarchy, down to the eventual demise of political independence and the reestablishment of the community of God after the Exile under Ezra. Truly a long and eventful route, that stretches over half a millennium.[49]

---

48. Albright, *ibid.,* 69.
49. In this respect, cf. v. Soden (Deutschen Orientalistentag, Bonn, July

Modern critical exegesis is more and more concerned with demonstrating the great age of the traditions handed down to us in the Pentateuch. We do not, therefore, hesitate to make Moses responsible for the origin of this work. It is not from some unknown narrator or editor that we have this tremendous spiritual effort encompassing the many centuries of the Old Testament, but only from the liberator, leader, law-giver, and prophet Moses, called by Yahweh himself. Why should we not suggest that, behind the Jahwist, this grandiose narrator, this magnificent psychologist, this revealer of Yahweh's abiding intervention in the life of his people, we might recognize the personality of Moses himself?

"The Jahwist is the great architect who selects his stones from many sources to construct an edifice of great compactness and perspicuity. Everything else is only an addition or a renovation, such as the artisan might, over the course of the centuries, add to a splendid building that is entrusted to his maintenance. Among these too there are very able men, but they are not compared to the old master who first outlined the sketch of the old construction, and our judgment over their work must be restricted to the decision as to whether or not they were true to the spirit of their master and his plans. Both of them, however, the creator of the edifice and those who preserve it, are in the service of the spirit." [50]

29, to August 2, 1952) on the problem of the historical sequence in the Akkadian literary texts: he demonstrates the independence of the later developments in the tradition. Literary works were never handed down verbatim, but always with some greater or lesser degree of revision.

50. W. Rudolph, Der "Elohist" von Exodus bis Josua (1938), 262-263.

THE CONQUEST OF CANAAN

CHAPTER XV

THE TAKING OF THE LAND
UNDER JOSHUA

LITERATURE

A. Schulz, *Das Buch Josue* (BB), 1924. / Alt, *Das System der Stammes-grenzen im Buche Josua*, Fs. Sellin 1927, 13. / Volz-Stummer-Hempel, *Josua* (in Werden und Wesen des AT), BZATW 1936, 13. / Möhlenbrink, *Die Landesnahme des Buches Josua*, ZATW 1938, 238. / M. Noth, *Das Buch Josua*, (HAT), 1938, — *Geschichte Israels*, 1950, 121, BBB 1, 1950, 152-167. / F. W. Albright, *The List of Levitical Cities in Jos 21*, (Fs. Ginzburg 1945, 49). / S. Mowinkel, *Zur Frage nach dokumentarischen Quellen in Josua*, 1946 — *The Westminster Historical Atlas to the Bible*, 1947, 39. / P. Auvray, *Josué*, DBS V, 1948, 1131-1141. / A. Gelin, *La Sainte Bible*, III, 1949. / Fr. Nötscher, *Josua* (EB), 1950. / F. M. Abel, *L'Anathème de Jéricho et la maison de Rahab*, RB 57, 1950, 321. / G. v. Rad, *Der hl. Krieg im alten Israel*, Abh. Theol. AT und NT 20, 1951. / E. North, *The 1952 Jericho-Sultan Excavation*, Bibl 34, 1953, 1-12.

AFTER Moses' death, it was Joshua, son of Nun, from the Tribe of Ephraim (1 Ch 7, 27) who succeeded to the leadership of the chosen people. Already during the lifetime of Moses, he had proven himself to be a clever, brave, and resourceful leader. Moses had entrusted him with the war against the Amalekites (Ex 17, 9). Furthermore, he had already taken part in the reconnaissance of the holy land from the base at

Kadesh and had taken exception to the deceitful reports brought back by the other spies (Nb 14, 6-38). He figures as Moses' confidant, and was considered to be, like Moses, filled with the spirit of Yahweh (Ex 24, 13; 33, 11).

The conquest of Canaan took place in several stages. After the crossing of the Jordan, the first objective was the capture of the key fortress city of Jericho. From this vantage point Joshua attempted to force his way across Ai and Bethel into the central mountain country. The march was facilitated by the treaty with the Gibeonites. The campaign threw the entire south into unrest. A coalition of kings attempted to break Israel's penetration, but they were defeated. The conquest and occupation of the south was thus well in hand. A further military action was directed against the north. The decisive confrontation occurred at the Waters of Merom, and after this victory the occupation of Galilee encountered no further resistance. It is surprising to note that there is no proper military action directed against the middle of the country, in the direction of Shechem.

The three stages of the conquest, middle, south, and north, must now be examined in greater detail:

1) *The conquest of Jericho*: The plan for the march into Canaan was developed by Joshua across the Jordan, at the last Israelite campsite at Abel Shittim (Acacia Wells), perhaps modern Tell Kefren on the eastern rim of the Jordan Plain, about six miles from the river at the same elevation as Jericho (Josh 3, 1; Nb 33, 49). From here Joshua sent spies out; for even though he was very conscious of Yahweh's abiding direction, his faith certainly did not release him from the need to employ every conceivable human medium as well. The house of Rahab, situated in the city walls, was a most advantageous position for the reconnaissance party. In ancient Babylon, public houses were also maintained by women. All kinds of people gathered there, and such houses were frequently the scene of business dealings and even political meetings, frequently of the type that needed to avoid open publicity and should, by rights,

have been reported by the proprietress. Such establishments have always figured prominently as nests of espionage.[1]

Despite the unsavory reputation of her profession, Rahab comes in for honorable mention in the New Testament, by reason of her faith and willingness to help (Heb 11, 31; Jm 2, 25), and her name is found in the genealogy of Christ (Mt 1, 5). The obvious presupposition is that, once she was saved, she espoused the religion of Yahweh.

The departure from the camp at Shittim took place in the sign of Yahweh. Joshua ordered the people to sanctify themselves, because "Yahweh would work wonders in their midst" (Josh 3, 5). The campaign is not conceived of as a profane event, but as a religious undertaking. Hence the precept of sexual abstention and proper clothing, since the people were to experience the wonders of Yahewh (Ex 19, 10, 14; Nb 11, 18). The war is a holy war. Its most characteristic expression is the *herem*, the ban, which decreed that the conquered city, with everything in it, humans, animals, and treasures, was to be dedicated to Yahweh by being completely destroyed. "To ban" (*haharêm*) and "to sanctify" (*hiqdîš*) have the same meaning.

The concept of the military ban is not a practice peculiar to Israel; it is attested to, for example, in the inscription of King Mesha of Moab (AOT, p. 440), and also among the Arabs, the Germanic tribes, the Indians, etc. By being declared holy or consecrated, the enemy becomes inviolable to all human claims of possession, and thus the renunciation becomes irrevocable. There is no question that this strict form of the ban (Josh 6, 17; 8, 24ff.; Jg 20, 48; 21, 10ff.; 1 S 15; 22, 11ff.; Dt 13, 16; 20, 16) was designed to prevent the undertaking of a war simply for purposes of acquisition or greed for booty, and that on occasion the victor himself fell under the ban if he had proved guilty of some transgression; in fact, it was invoked upon Yahweh's own people (Jg 20, 48; 21, 10ff.).

Just as the other ancient Semitic customs were somehow transformed by the Yahweh religion, so too the military ban. It became the ex-

---

1. Cf. Code of Hammurabi §108. / Nötscher, *Joshua*, 10. / W. Kornfeld, *L'adultère dans l'Orient Antique*, RB 57 (1950), 92-109. / F. M. Abel, *L'Anathème de Jéricho et la maison de Rahab*, RB 57 (1950), 321-330.

pression of unreserved submission to the demands of Yahweh. Young Israel felt itself to be the instrument of God's judgment. Since the Canaanites are ripe for judgment (Gn 15, 16; 9, 22; 19, 5), and since the Amalekites are merciless robbers (1 S 15, 2, 33), or also because the idolatry practiced by her enemies might prove to be an obstacle to Israel's fidelity to Yahweh, they are all given over to annihilation. The ban thus becomes an instrument of punishment in the hand of Yahweh. Yahweh himself, through the military ban, takes vengeance upon his enemies (Jer 50, 13); to ban and to punish is one and the same thing.

Despite this fact, the military ban could not be an abiding institution. In time it undergoes considerable transformation itself, since the cattle and booty, as well as women and children, are excepted from the ban. Israel's waging of war was, on the whole, rather inclined towards mercy, and her kings stand out as merciful kings (1 K 20, 31). The shedding of blood just for its own sake, as we frequently see it expressed in the Assyrian inscriptions, is an unknown phenomenon. Neither do we find any mention of the fact that the Israelite warriors are accused of the rape of captive women, and, in their military law, fruit trees are accorded a special protection (Dt 20, 19). In the later royal era, the practice of the ban seems to have entirely disappeared.[2]

On Joshua's march towards the city of Jericho, the Israelites were greatly assisted by either a natural phenomenon or a miracle. Just as in the crossing of the Red Sea, so too in the case of the Jordan crossing, unexpectedly favorable natural conditions prevailed at precisely the proper moment. The crossing of the Jordan took place during the harvest time. In Palestine, the harvest time, approximately April/May, is regularly dry, since there is little rainfall around this season. But the water level of the Jordan River, which is determined by the melting of the snows on Hermon, is frequently somewhat delayed, so that the harvest, in the hot Jordan Valley towards the end of April, can also be involved in the flooding. In purely human terms, the selection of this time for crossing the Jordan was the

---

2. W. Eichrodt, *Theologie des AT*, 1, 60. / G. v. Rad, *Der hl. Krieg im alten Israel*, Abh. Theol. ANT 20 (1951): "This is not so much as a religious war in the modern sense of the word as it is rather a battle for the political existence of Israel with the personal help of the God Yahweh. But since Israel's political existence was completely dependent upon her religious existence, the national battle fought by Israel must necessarily also become a battle against the Canaanite gods and cults" (Ex 23, 24; Dt 7, 5, etc.).

most unfavorable of the entire year. But then came a "happy accident." The Book of Joshua describes the event in the following sober words: "The Jordan overflows all its banks throughout the time of harvest.... The waters stood still. The waters coming down from above stood and rose up in a heap far off, at Adam, the city that is beside Zarethan, and those flowing down towards the sea of Arabah, the Salt Sea, were wholly cut off" (3, 15, 16).

The city of Adam, modern ed-Damijeh, lies approximately 18 miles above the place of crossing, in the vicinity of the confluence with the Jabbok. Zarethan (1 K 4, 12; 7, 46), perhaps the Qarn Sartabe, can no longer be identified with certainty. In this vicinity, in December of 1267 A.D., the Jordan's course was blocked for half a day by a landslide, an historical event which has frequently been advanced as an explanation of this miracle. We have seen, in the wonders related from the career of Moses, that the natural events also have a most significant role to play; in crossing the Jordan the same thing would appear to be true. After crossing the river, Joshua had erected a monument with twelve stones, according to one tradition at the Jordan itself (Josh 3, 12; 4, 4-7), according to another tradition at Gilgal (Josh 4, 2ff.); apparently two ancient traditions, each of which recounted the story of one monument, have been fused into one.[3] In Gilgal, which probably means "a circle of stones" — Hirbet Mefjir, about a mile northeast of ancient Jericho, the paschal festival was celebrated (Josh 5, 10, 12), and those of the people who were not yet circumcised underwent this ritual. Thus the "reproach of Egypt" was "rolled away" (5, 9). We have here a popular etymology and explanation of the name Gilgal, derived from the verb *galal* (to roll away). But this does not necessarily mean that the narrative of the circumcision was simply invented as a later addition designed to explain the enigmatic name of Gilgal; it was rather the reverse: the historical event was identified and explained in terms of the ancient name.

The crossing of the Jordan River and the first camp at

---

3. Nötscher, *op. cit.*, 14ff.

Gilgal had closed a significant chapter in the history of God's chosen people. The Exodus from Egypt had achieved its first goal. Israel was no longer wandering through the wilderness; its foot had entered the "land flowing with milk and honey" (Josh 5, 6). The rhetorically exaggerated description of milk and honey, regularly applied to Palestine (Ex 3, 8, 17; Nb 13, 13; 14, 8; Jer 11, 5), but also referred to Egypt in Numbers 16, 13, presents the picture of a cultivated country with its vegetation, its agriculture and viniculture, and its flocks, as opposed to the barren wilderness with its almost complete lack of vegetation, even though the figure is probably a reference to the honey produced by wild bees.[4] The promises made of old to the fathers are now to be fulfilled. Yahweh had proved himself faithful to his servants. The entry into the promised land was initiated by an apparition to Joshua of an angel of Yahweh, the "prince of the host of Yahweh," with a drawn sword, not as a sign of threat, but as a powerful encouragement; what was destined to happen in the following chapters is not simply a matter of profane history; the powers of heaven are also at work in determining the events that take place on earth. Only thus was Joshua able to undertake the march against the fortress city of Jericho. Since it was a holy war, the priests carried the Ark of the Covenant and circled the citadel of the city. The priests blew upon their trumpets. When the surrounded fortress did not surrender, its doom was sealed on the seventh day. The fortress city's walls were shaken and collapsed. Israel entered through the breaches and carried out the terrible ban.

The excavations at Jericho: Despite a series of archaeological campaigns, the problem of Jericho is not yet completely solved. Few digs have cast more light upon the progress of archaeology in the last century, in fact in the last decades, than the great excavations at ancient Jericho. The history of excavation has been filled with surprises and new knowledge. The first investigators to examine the mound hardly thought that excavation would repay their efforts, but the more recent excavators have discovered the most ancient and longest series of cultural development and the clearest succession of strata so far encountered, so that

4. Nötscher, *ibid.*, 17.

today Jericho can be characterized as Palestine's oldest city. When he first visited the site in 1831, Edward Robinson thought that it was simply an ancient campsite. In the year 1869, Charles Warren recognized the remains of towers and walls in the small hill which towers over the magnificent spring of 'Ain es-Sultan, but doubted that this could be the site of ancient Jericho. It was only in 1894 that the true significance of the mound was realized. Professor Ernest Sellin, together with Dr. Karl Watzinger, undertook the first great excavation in the years 1907 — 1909, the results of which were published in 1913 in a magnificent volume with painstaking descriptions, sketches, and figures. Their datings, however, did not remain unchallenged, and the problem called for further excavation. In January of 1929 Garstang, the director of "the Department of Antiquities of the Palestine Government in Jerusalem," once again undertook a systematic excavation, which continued, in six separate campaigns, until the year 1936. In the years 1953, 1954, and 1955, Kathleen M. Kenyon carried on three further excavations which considerably enlarged our knowledge of the archaeological history of Jericho.

The Archaeological History of Jericho:[5]

Scholars had formerly supposed that the most ancient settlement was located at the height of the tell, by reason of the favorable situation of the hill at whose foot flows a spring which is still in use today. This would correspond to the otherwise familiar outline of a Palestinian city plan: the city itself on the hill and the spring at the foot of the mountain. The excavations of 1954 showed, however, that the whole hill was artificial. The first settlement was on the same plane as the spring and was not at all raised above the level of the surrounding country. Were these primeval hunters who settled around the spring? In Jericho, at all events, we note the early advent of agriculture and city settlement. And that is not all. In order to secure themselves against enemy attack, they surrounded their settlements with powerful stone walls. Their houses, reminiscent of the round Beduin hut, were built in circular form, of sun-dried bricks, while the city walls were constructed of unhewn stone, the blocks laid regularly one on top of the other. The original level of the wall is almost 50 feet below the

---

5. Excavation account in Sellin-Watzinger, *Jericho* (1913). / John Garstang, *Annals of Archaeology and Anthropology XIX-XXIII* (1932-36). / *Story of Jericho* (1948). / G. E. Wright, *Epic of Conquest,* BiblArch 3 (1940), 25-40. / Chester C. McCown, *The Ladder of Progress in Palestine* (1943), 68-84. / Kathleen M. Kenyon, *Excavation at Jericho,* PEQ 84 (1953), 81-96; 85 (1954), 45-63; 86 (1955), 108-118. / Claus Schedl, *Stand der Ausgrabungen in Jericho,* Bibel u. Liturgie 22 (1955), 172-176.

present level and, at some places, the walls are still standing at a height of nearly 20 feet. The ancient walled city enclosed a population which was not yet familiar with the use of pottery. The stone vessels which were used for eating are strikingly simple.

Jericho in the recent Stone Age (8,000 — 4,500 B.C.) exhibits the following strata: 1. The first settlement with round houses; 2. The building of the stone fortress walls; 3. Transition to a square house construction with paved floors; 4. The appearance of the first pottery. Level three yielded an unexpected discovery. Several prepared skulls were discovered. The hollow of the skull was filled with earth, while the face was sculpted to present a true-to-life portrait. In the eye sockets, for six of the skulls, flat mussels had been inserted, which present a surprisingly accurate imitation of the eyelids. The top of the skull was not covered, and, in one case, it was painted. Whether these are victory trophies or some form of ancestor cult cannot be determined.

Between the recent Stone Age and the beginning of the Bronze Age there is a layer of humus attesting to the lack of settlement, and suggesting a destruction of the city during the recent Stone Age, following which the tell remained unsettled for 300 — 400 years. With the help of carbon testing, this stratum can be dated to the year 3260 B.C., with a greater or lesser degree of certainty.[6]

Jericho in the Bronze Age emerges from the dim light of history as a practically impregnable fortified city, surrounded with walls and moats. The attacking enemy would first have to carry the broad moat; once across the moat he would have to mount an escarpment with an elevation of 25 degrees, almost 40 feet high, surmounted in turn by a brick wall about eight feet high. But even this early Bronze-Age fortress was destined for destruction. Not only Jericho, but other settlements in the Jordan Trench were also suddenly destroyed. In the year 1954 in connection with preparations for a series of locks and dams, 24 sites were explored in the Jordan Valley. They all yielded remains from the Copper-Stone Age and the early Bronze Age. Then the history of settlement abruptly ends, apparently in connection with the second great wave of Semitic invasion, the Amurru.

It may not have been too long a time before the Amurru Beduins had assimilated civilized life. But they continued to lead their nomadic existence, living in tents, in the Jordan Plain. But the Middle Bronze Age (2000 — 1600 B.C.) is, for Palestine, the era of the city. Jericho, too, arose from its ruins, more defiant than before. This era is known, from Palestinian archaeology, as the period of fortress construction with glacis works. This Middle Bronze Age city has a double significance for the Biblical historian, because it is here that the first appearance

---

6. F. E. Zeuner, *The Neolithic-Bronze Age Gap on the Tell of Jericho*, PEQ 85 (1954), 64-68.

of the patriarchs must be fitted in. The excavation yields provide a very
vivid picture of the everyday life. The climate of Jericho is dry, just
as that of Egypt. Wooden objects have thus been preserved up to the
present day. It seems that the dead man was supplied with all the
normal household utensils upon his burial. At his lips stood a clay pitcher,
so that he would not thirst, as well as a basin and a bowl. At his side
stood a wooden table, upon which stood another large earthen bowl.
Beside the table, on the floor, stood a plaited basket. It is certainly
possible that the patriarchal family made use of similar vessels. The
narrative of the sacrifice of Isaac takes on a new immediacy against the
background of Jericho. In the early Bronze Age, in the foundations of
a rather large house, which has been identified as a temple, the bones
of a child were found interred, a clear example of the practice of
foundation sacrifices, also attested from other sources.

But even this flourishing city fell before the destructive violence of
her enemies. This time it may have been the Egyptians, who, in their war
of liberation against the Hyksos, pushed into Palestine where they conquered the fortified cities and even occupied them with their garrisons
(c. 1580 B.C.).

The Jericho of the time of Joshua must have belonged to the late Bronze
Age. Whereas the excavations have yielded unexpected new historical insights into the recent Stone Age and the early and middle Bronze Ages,
for the late Bronze Age they have uncovered practically nothing. Earlier
excavations had identified the middle Bronze Age city as the settlement
conquered by Joshua.[7] But the pottery remnants are a clear argument
against this position. After the campaign of 1953, scholars went so far
as to suggest that, by reason of the lack of late Bronze Age yields, the
Jericho of Joshua must be located on a different mound. But the excavation of 1954 has shown that there was no need to depart from the
traditional site. After its destruction at the end of the Hyksos period,
the city remained in ruins and was given over to the destructive power
of weathering and erosion in the time from 1580 to around 1400 B.C.
The sparse remnants which have been unearthed testify to its later re-
settlement. Immediately under the present surface of the mound the walls
of the city's fortification can still be recognized; close nearby is a section
of the contemporary ground level, only about 10 feet square. A small
oven (tabun) was found here and, beside it, a late Bronze Age pitcher.
On the basis of the sparse remains we can hardly expect that the city
of Joshua will still be discovered. It has apparently fallen victim, in its
entirety, to exposure and erosion.

Even though, despite the curse upon the city, Hiel of Bethel once
again rebuilt Jericho (1 K 16, 34), sacrificing his first-born upon the

---

7. On the earlier scholarship, cf. Albright, *From the Stone Age to
Christianity.*

laying of the cornerstone and his last-born upon the completion of the building, this Israelite Jericho never attained the glory of the Jerichos of ages past. The Tell es-Sultan had already played its role in history. The Roman and Byzantine Jericho and the Jericho of the crusades was built upon a more favorable location on the level ground, where the present-day Arab settlement of Eriha is to be found.

Still, the excavations of the older levels may yield some key as to the possible manner of Jericho's destruction under Joshua. No storming trumpets were found, nor any other signs that would attest to an extraordinary and miraculous conquest of the city. The miracle is to be explained, as so often in the Old Testament, on the basis of the historical and geographical data characteristic of the area in question. Jericho lies in the Jordan Trench. Already in the most ancient levels evidence of earthquake activity can be established. From the recent Stone Age, sprung walls and ripped up floors are not a rarity. A worker from Eriha, modern Jericho, who lived in a house built from clay bricks, said, during the excavation of the walls of Jericho: "These walls look just like our house did after the earthquake."

In connection with the earthquake in 1927, the banks of the river, in the vicinity of ed-Damijeh, fell into the stream and blocked the course of the water for some time. A similar occurrence is recorded by the Arabian scribes for the year 1267 A.D. We can well imagine that the Israelites, who were camped across the river in the "Fields of Moab," where the brooks from Transjordania join the river and make a camp possible, were filled with eager anticipation to cross the stream. Then the power of heaven comes to their aid. Suddenly the waters of the Jordan cease to flow: the camp is hastily broken and the Israelites pass across the dry river bed and suddenly confront the astounded fortifications of Jericho, which are subsequently captured with the help of Yahweh.

2) *The March into the Mountain Country*: The most advantageous route leading from Jericho into the Palestinian mountain country does not lie in the direction of Jerusalem; much easier is the route actually chosen by Joshua, through Ai and Bethel, which lie open to the Jordan Plain by a valley. In the exultation of his victory, Joshua sent a small band against Ai in the hope of capturing the city by a surprise attack. But the attempt was a failure. Even worse than the loss of his forces was the damage suffered by the morale. Joshua's troops lost their self-confidence and the enemy, after their initial terror (Josh 2, 9-11; 6, 27), took on new courage (7, 9). Joshua tore his clothing and cast dust upon his face and lamented before Yahweh. The existence of Israel, and the authority of Yahweh

himself, hung in the balance. How could Yahweh have permitted such a disaster. The primary cause of the catastrophe was discovered in Israel's sin (Josh 7, 10). Achan had kept for himself some of the prey of Jericho which had fallen under the ban, and thus involved the entire community in curse. After judgment had been passed upon him and his family (7, 10-26), Joshua prepared for a new attack upon Ai. This time he employed the military strategy of an ambuscade. The attacking force appeared to execute a retreat and thereby enticed the defenders outside the fortress. When they had gone far enough from the city, the ambuscade charged out of its hiding, overpowered the enemy, set fire to the city, and carried out the ban (Josh 8).

Israel thus stood upon the heights of the middle Palestinian mountain country and had achieved a key position for her further operations, as the course of events will clearly demonstrate. Archaeological investigation has shown that the middle Palestinian mountain country, in the Bronze Age, was either unsettled or very sparsely settled. The Canaanite cities were located primarily along the edge of the mountain slopes. It is thus hardly surprising that the occupation of this territory, since it was seen as something non-essential, is hardly mentioned at all in the Book of Joshua. It is quite within the range of possibility that the Israelite raids were able to proceed, without any major resistance, as far as Shechem, where Joshua renewed the covenant and public obligation to the law on Mt. Ebal (Josh 8, 30-35).

The excavations at Ai pose an archaeological puzzle. In the years 1933 — 1935 Judith Marquet-Krause, with support from the Rothschild Foundation, explored the ruins of et-Tell situated in the vicinity of the Arabian city of Beitin, Biblical Bethel, where the ancient Ai was supposed to be located. The excavation proved that an ancient Canaanite city had actually existed on the mound, but that it had been destroyed already around the year 2000 B.C. and subsequently left unsettled, as witness the name Ai, that is, "ruins." [8]

---

8. "Les Fouilles de 'Aj, la resurrection d'une grande cité biblique," Paris (1949). — Cf. Noth, PJ 31 (1935), 7-29, for the story of the excavation: it would be an error to abandon the certain data of archaeology in favor of literary-historical reconstructions.

How are we now to explain the problem posed by Joshua 7, 1-8, where there is explicit mention of a conquest of the city of Ai? Three possibilities must be considered: *a.* Vincent claims that the ancient mound had been hastily refortified by the Canaanites living in the vicinity as a defense measure against the possibility of Israelite attack. *b.* Albright, on the other hand, represents the view that the destruction of Ai should more properly be referred to the city of Bethel, which, on the basis of excavations conducted there, was settled from 2200 — 1300, and then lay in ruins only to be resettled around 900 B.C. *c.* Kopp suggests a variation upon the solution proposed by Vincent, claiming that the people generally dwelt outside the city and only in times of crisis sought refuge within its walls. Thus, the true relationship of the ruins at Ai to the Biblical narrative awaits a satisfactory solution.

3) *The Conquest of the South*: This first successful attack by the Israelites was followed by an organized resistance on the part of the native population. Canaan was divided into several city states which, although they were otherwise independent of each other, formed a common alliance in times of crisis, for their mutual defense. It was to Israel's advantage that she never had to face a coalition of the entire country, but simply partial alliances of various Canaanite cities.

The first group to approach Joshua were the people from Gibeon, most likely *ed-gib,* about 6 miles northwest of Jerusalem. Instead of attempting armed resistance they sought an understanding with Joshua in some form of agreement. They pretended to be an embassy which had just arrived from a great distance, seeking a treaty with Israel. Joshua received them and solemnly swore a treaty with them. But when the deceit was revealed, acting upon the advice of the elders of the assembly, Joshua pronounced a curse upon the Gibeonites and, though he could not hand them over to absolute annihilation, he did impose a sort of servile existence upon them, by condemning them to a slave's work in the sanctuary of Israel (Josh 9). The three Havite cities of Chephirah, Be-eroth, and Kiriath-Jearim (wood city, *der el-azhar*) were joined by treaty to Gibeon and thus shared the same fate.

The defection of the Gibeonites provoked the united resistance of all the Canaanite kings. The leadership of the coalition was undertaken by Adoni-zedek of Jerusalem. Their first objective was to take revenge for the defection of the Gibeonites. They in turn called upon Joshua for help. Now Joshua was forced, even against his will, to enter into the contest. Chapter 10 of the Book of Joshua presents a detailed description of the campaign that followed. It is testimony to Joshua's strategic skill. After the defeat of the five Canaanite kings at Aijalon (stag city), Joshua turned to the south, into the Shephelah, carefully avoiding the strong fortress city of Geser, which came under Israelite control only under the reign of Solomon. First he conquered the city of Makkedah in the vicinity of Beth-shemesh (house of the sun), and then he attacked Libnah, at the entrance to the Valley of Elah (oak valley), where David later killed Goliath. From here he made a bold attack upon the strongly fortified city of Lachish.[9] Excavations have shown that this city, as demonstrated by the hieratic inscription on a pot found in 1937, was violently destroyed around 1230 B.C. Finally, the last city in the plain which he captured was Eglon which, on the basis of excavations, was destroyed at the same time as Lachish.

Joshua had thus won control over the south country and could now attempt to approach the isolated central fortress in the Judaean mountains, Hebron. After the capture of Hebron it was a simple matter to take the frontier fortress of Debir or Kiriath-sepher (city of the scribes). The Israelite invasion made a profound impression even on the Egyptians, as we can deduce from one strophe in the triumphal poem of Pharaoh Merneptah, dated in 1229 B.C., excepting that here the complete collapse of Egyptian power in Palestine has been transformed into the victory over Israel: "The people of Israel is without consolation, they have no more seed. Palestine has become a widow for Egypt." [10]

Archaeological excavation and investigation is casting considerably more light upon the character of the Israelite conquest around the year 1200 B.C. The first point to be noted is the

9. W. F. Albright, *A Case of Lèse Majesté in Pre-Israelite Lachish, with Some Remarks on the Israelite Conquest*, BASOR 87 (1944), 32-38.
10. Galling, *Textbuch zur Geschichte Israels* (1950), 34.

fact that the conquerors immediately settled in the captured cities. The Israelites were no longer typical nomads and not even semi-nomads; they had reached the stage of sedentary development, tilling the soil and living in stone houses. Secondly, the Israelite settlement was considerably denser than that of the Canaanites who preceded them. Throughout the entire hill country we find the remains of Iron Age villages dating from the twelfth century, but, in the late Bronze Age, they were not inhabited at all in many cases. Thanks to the rapid spread of cisterns which were covered on the inside with the hitherto unknown limestone plaster, the settled territory rapidly expanded and the Israelites began to turn the woodland into arable, and settled in inaccessible areas [11] (cf. Josh 17, 15).

Joshua and the miracle of the sun: After the victorious battle against the Canaanite coalition of the five kings, Joshua was afraid that he would be unable to follow up his advantage because of the approach of evening. He thus spoke the following incantation:

"Sun, stand thou still at Gibeon,
     and thou, Moon in the Valley of Aijalon.
And the sun stood still,
     and the moon stayed,
     until the nation took vengeance on their enemies" (10, 12-13).

The explanations offered by modern exegetes are many: "Only a variety of hailstorm," "a meteor shower followed by an extraordinarily bright night," "the refraction of the rays of the sun," "a period of darkness caused by a hailstorm, as though the sun had set, so that after the storm had passed the sun once again appeared as if at the beginning of a new day, and thus the story that Joshua won a miraculous victory over his enemies is simply a poetic elaboration of the natural facts" — none of them very satisfying explanations. At all events, our narrator, following the popular style, means to recount a miracle. How it was

---

11. Albright, *op. cit.,* 277. — Chester C. McCown, *The Ladder of Progress in Palestine* (1943), 85: Tell beit Mirsim (Kirjath-Sepher) 133: "Border Cities of the Shephelah." This is the precise point at which to observe the transition from the Canaanite to the Israelite period. The Canaanites built strong and sturdy buildings, while the Israelites put up very hasty structures. The Canaanite culture was mature and developed, while the Israelite was still poor and primitive.

possible and how it actually happened is not the object of his text.[12]

4) *The Conquest of Northern Palestine*: Disturbed by the Israelite successes in the south, King Jabin of Hazor [13] (probably Tell Wakkas or Tell el-qedah, 4 miles west of the Lake of Huleh), organized a resistance similar to that called together by Adoni-zedek in the south. We do not know whether Joshua made his way northward through the Jordan Trench or over the mountain country. The Canaanite cities numbered in Joshua 11, 1ff., are also partly found on the city lists of Thutmose III (1501 – 1447). The northern coalition was far superior to Israel in the technology of war, since they were equipped with horses and war chariots, – a form of armament Israel could hardly command. And yet the younger invading nation won a decisive victory at the Waters of Merom, by which we are to understand probably not the Lake of Huleh (Merom), but rather the headwaters of a place called Merom (Egyptian Marama) situated in Upper Galilee in the vicinity of Safed. As frequently in the Ancient Near East, one single battle decided the entire campaign. The adversary fled and scattered in all directions, to the northwest towards the Phoenician coast (Sidon), to the west towards Acco, and into the east.

This temporary quelling of the resistance did not make Canaan Israel's uncontested property. This would require a long series of battles and confrontations, continuing into the royal era. But the battles had, at all events, made it possible for Joshua to proceed to the division of the country, assigning each tribe its territories which still needed to be won, in part, by force of arms.

At the end of his work, Joshua convened an assembly of the people at Shechem, the elders of Israel, the heads of the families, the judges and the directors, in the presence of Yahweh (Josh 24, 1ff.), in order to proclaim his testament. Looking back upon the history of Israel, he once again appeals to the

---

12. Nötscher, *op. cit.*, 33. / D. I. Alfrink, *Das "Still-Stehen" von Sonne und Mond in Jos 10, 12-15*, Nimwegen (1949).
13. Hazor is familiar from the Mari texts as an important Canaanite city. Correspondence is still extant. Or 19 (1950), 509.

great deeds worked by Yahweh. Israel's whole existence is the work of God. It was Yahweh who called them from across the river, when they were still serving foreign gods (24, 2); it was Yahweh who saved them from Egypt and led them into the promised land. If they were to survive as a nation, it can only be in virtue of their allegiance to Yahweh. But it is a difficult thing to be faithful to Yahweh. The demands that he makes upon his worshippers are not slight. To fulfill them requires sacrifice. Infidelity and defection after their solemn acceptance of responsibility is a worse sin than original paganism. Yahweh's goodness and clemency are bounded by the holiness of his very essence, in virtue of which he cannot let infidelity or injustice go unpunished. Revolt from Yahweh means the end of the people and the loss of the promised land. In the face of this far-reaching commitment, the people answer as with a single voice: "We will serve Yahweh" (24, 21). Joshua thus renews the covenant for the people and enacts laws for them at Shechem.

He also recorded the events in the book of the law of God. Then he took a huge stone and set it up there under the terebinth at the sanctuary of Yahweh, while speaking to the assembled people: "Behold, this stone shall be a witness against us; for it has heard all the words of the Lord which he spoke to us; therefore it shall be a witness against you, lest you deal falsely with your God." Then Joshua dismissed the people, each into his own inheritance. He himself withdrew into his own territory, at Timnath-serah in the mountains of Ephraim, where he died at the age of 110 years. So ended the life of one of Israel's great heroes, a man whose memory could not ever be erased in Israel's history. At the same time, his passing marks the decisive moment for the course of history to follow. For Israel's history in Canaan is not simply a matter of profane politics, but rather a history of her relationship with or opposed to Yahweh.

5) *The Literary Problem of the Book of Joshua:* The Book of Joshua begins the second half of the Jewish canon, which is called "prophets," and contains eight books. The first four

are: Joshua, Judges, Samuel, and Kings. They bear the name *nebi'im ri'šônim*, the "first, earlier prophets," as opposed to the *nebi'im 'aharônim*, the "later prophets," which include the Books of Isaiah, Jeremiah, Ezekiel, and the twelve "minor prophets." The distinction between "first" and "later" probably develops from the actual ordering in the canon. The "earlier prophets" have one common characteristic: they all record the course of Israel's history and thus many scholars consider them together with Deuteronomy as the "Deuteronomic history."

The 24 chapters of the Book of Joshua can be divided into three sections: 1, 1 — 12, 24 describes the conquest of Canaan under the leadership of Joshua; 13, 1 — 21, 42 follows the division of the land according to tribes; 21, 43 — 24, 33 contains Joshua's final discourse at the assembly at Shechem, together with a brief notice of his death and burial.

The name of the author is unknown. We are told in 24, 26 that Joshua recorded some events, but not that he actually composed the book named after him. This claim is made first by the Talmud (*Baba bathra* 14b), but this can hardly be correct. The frequently recurring remark (which can hardly be evaluated as anything other than a later addition) that things and circumstances have continued "to the present day" clearly points to a later era (4, 9; 6, 25). Whether this is before the time of the kings or in the early royal era itself remains a matter of conjecture. The city of Gezer is, for our author, still a Canaanite city (16, 10); it became Israelite only under Solomon (1 K 9, 16); in much the same manner Jerusalem is still Jebusite (15, 63; 18, 16, 28); it was conquered by David (2 S 5, 6). One could conclude on the basis of this evidence that the author lived before the time of David and Solomon, but it is also possible that it is simply the sources of the tradition he uses that date back to this earlier era.

The sources could very well date back to the time of Joshua himself, since Rahab is still alive (6, 25), and this could hardly have been true for the time at which the author actually lived. It is thus the sources of the tradition which the author uses, and not necessarily the author himself that stands so close to the events described that in many cases the freshness and vitality of the presentation is clearly in evidence. Thus the formula quoted in 10, 13 (sun, stand still) might well come from the same "Book of the Just" which contains David's lament for Saul and Jonathan (2 S 1, 18).

This combination of various ancient oral or written traditions accounts for the manifold stylistic failings, peculiarities, and inconsistencies of the book which, in the work of an individual author, would certainly be most remarkable. When the Book of Joshua took on its definitive form is difficult to determine, and the question is, moreover, of only secondary importance with respect to the book's credibility.[14]

Since the Pentateuchal sources JEDP as such represent a questionable hypothesis, their extension to the Book of Joshua is an even more contested hypothesis. Martin Noth concludes that there are too few positive arguments to warrant any identification of the "anthology" with any of the narrative strains in the Pentateuch, either with certainty or even with a high degree of probability. He thus attempts to put the problem on a quite different basis by assuming two documents as the primary sources: one of them is a listing of tribal frontiers which, on the basis of the actual holdings of the tribes in the cultivated land, outlines an ideal geography and lays claims to territories which were actually never possessed by the tribes in question. The second document is a list of sites in the Kingdom of Judah after its division into twelve districts, which are thus made to derive from the time of Joshua.

These two documents would then have been used retrospectively, in an effort to establish the lands actually held by the twelve tribes on the occasion of the original division. These two documents would also have been enlarged by the addition of etiological sagas.[15] But this tribal geography involves some untenable theses and is quickly lost in a hypercritical reevaluation of the sober historical facts recorded in the book.

If the Book of Joshua does leave many points obscure — the course of the conquest is drawn in very brief and sketchy strokes; a faithful reconstruction of the actual course of events is beyond the scope of even the most astute criticism — still the religious line of the book is clearly and powerfully worked out. The author is not writing history for the sake of history; he uses the source material available to him — and it is a material of quite unequal historical value — in order to chart the supra-historical course of history that stands in the background of the conquest of the Holy Land, a history which is just as real as the destruction of the city of Jericho. Israel's history is a history for or against Yahweh; that was the purpose of his "anthology."

The text is well preserved. The Septuagint, however, frequently departs from the Hebrew; it is somewhat shorter and smoother. Whether this is to be explained by the stylistic liberties of the translators or the use of a different Hebrew source remains to be decided.[16]

---

14. Nötscher, *op. cit.*, 6.
15. M. Noth, *op. cit.*, VIIff. History of the tradition of the second half of the Book of Joshua, BBB 1 (1950), 152-167.
16. Nötscher, *op. cit.*

CHAPTER XVI

THE ERA OF THE JUDGES

LITERATURE

Zapletal, *Das Buch der Richter,* 1923. / O. Eissfeldt, *Die Quellen des Richterbuches,* 1925. — Fs. Beer 1935, 19. / A. Schulz, *Das Buch der Richter und das Buch Ruth,* BB 1926. / O. Pretzl, *Septuaginta-Probleme im Buch der Richter,* Bibl 7, 1926, 233, 253. / J. Garstang, *Joshua-Judges,* 1930. / G. E. Wright, *Archaeological observations on the Period of Judges and the Early Monarchy,* JBL 60, 1941, 27-42. / W. Rudolph, *Textkritische Anmerkungen zum Richterbuch,* Fs. Eissfeldt 1947, 199-212. / H. Cazelles, *Le livre des Judges,* DBS IV, 1949, 1394-1414. / H. H. Rowley, *From Joseph to Joshua,* 1950. / J. Soisalon-Soininen, *Die Textformen der Septuagintaübersetzung des Richterbuches,* 1951. / M. Noth, *Das Amt des "Richters" Israels,* Fs. Bertholet (cf. Bibl 33, 1952), 420.

Introductions: Höpfl-Miller-Metzinger: *Introductio specialis in VT,* 1946, 137-146, (includes earlier literature). / A. Weiser, *Einleitung in das AT,* 1949, 223-225. / Simon-Prado, *Praelectiones biblicae VT,* 1949, 33ff.

In terms of Israel's overall history the Book of Judges is treated in: P. Heinisch, *Geschichte des AT,* 1949, 120-128. / M. Noth, *Geschichte Israels,* 1950, 120: "Die Selbstbehauptung der Stämme im Kulturland." — The Westminster Historical Atlas: "Palestine during the Period of the Judges," 1947, 43.

IN the Book of Joshua the conquest of Canaan is narrated with such a height of national and prophetic enthusiasm that, upon superficial reading, one might easily get the impression that Israel had already taken firm control of the country. But this is not the case. The Book of Judges supplies ample evidence to the contrary. We see the tribes who had made their way from across the Jordan in a state of constant struggle for existence. The Canaanite city-states and city alliances continued to exist and they represented not only a political danger for Israel, but also a religious peril. Then there were the foreign robber hordes that swarmed over the country, making their way from east and west and plundering the loosely organized tribal alliances of Israel to the point where they could hardly be borne. It was in such hours of crisis, that, in one or another of the tribes, one powerful figure would regularly arise, a judge who, relying upon the support of his own tribe and sometimes with the assistance of brother tribes, succeeded, by reason of his charismatic powers, in "judging," Israel, that is, saving Israel from her crisis.[1]

The social and political system of the new nation was extremely simple. Even after the conquest of the country the patriarchal family and clan formed the backbone of the national life. The Israelites were too freedom-loving and too particularistic to submit, under normal circumstances, to the head of a different tribe, even for a very brief time. This naturally weakened the young nation's power whenever unified action was necessary. On the contrary, Israel's enemies — Moab, Ammon, the Philistines and Canaanites — were all, at that same time, organized about a tightly structured central leadership, administered by kings or princes, and this proved to be a further disadvantage for Israel.

---

1. M. Noth, *Das Amt des "Richters Israels."* Fs. Bertholet (1950), 404-417. The word *šôphet* (judge) is an Old Canaanite word which is found in the Phoenician and Carthaginian records in the sense of "judge, civil magistrate" (*suffete*). The official powers of this "judge" comprise not only the dispensation of justice as such, but extend much further. "Judge" means "savior from crisis." In this sense we are also to understand the "justice of God" in the psalms, as Yahweh's saving and justice-creating intervention in history.

A simple examination of the map for the era of the Judges[2] reveals the fact that the territories settled by Israel contained many Canaanite cities. Then Gezer was not taken by the Israelites until the time of Solomon, and Jerusalem was conquered only under David (Jg 1, 21; 2 S 5, 6ff.). The tribe of Judah controlled the southern mountain country, but it was unable to drive out the inhabitants of the plain country with their iron war chariots (Jg 1, 19). This means that the coastal plain from Gaza as far as Ekron, and inland as far as Gath remained outside the Israelite sphere of power. The situation was even more desperate for the tribe of Manasseh, which was almost completely divided from the Galilean territory by a belt of Canaanite cities: Beth-shan, Jibleam, Taanach, Megiddo, and Dor. The control over the great and fertile plain of Jezreel remained in non-Israelite hands.

Archaeological investigation has, today, supplied us with considerable material for exploring the cultural situation of the era of Judges. Since the Israelite culture, at the time of the conquest of Canaan, was, in many respects, not very well developed, we might expect that the Israelites would have been strongly influenced by the culture of their Canaanite predecessors. But excavations in the Palestinian hill country have shown a sharp break between the Canaanite culture of the late Bronze Age and the early Iron Age of Israel. Ancient Israelite strata do not point to a situation in which the wealth and power were concentrated in the hands of the few; the palaces of the Canaanite cities have been replaced by big and little peasant enclosures. In place of the massive Canaanite fortresses we now find thin walls of the new casemate type. Forced labor was apparently unknown in every era of Israel's history, unless perhaps it was imposed occasionally by foreign conquerors. The word which, in Canaanite documents (Amarna, Ugarit) means "serf" takes on the meaning of "free man" (*hophši*) apparently because the peasant to whom the word most regularly referred is now no longer a Canaanite serf but rather a free-born Israelite.[3]

---

2. *Westminster Atlas,* map VI.

Nonetheless, one must certainly suppose that after the conquest of Canaan a gradual reorientation of Israelite thinking must have taken place. It is true that Israel at this era was not a pure nomadic tribe; the patriarchs were already semi-nomads, practicing some agriculture. The same is true for the sojourn in Egypt. But after Israel became a sedentary people, we note a change in attitude. Since Yahweh, for the Israelites, and Baal for the Canaanites, represents the lord of heaven and the sender of rain, the storm god and the giver of fertility, it is no wonder that the two peasant religions gradually began to fuse into one. Purely external evidence for this is the occurrence of personal names compounded with the word Baal, dating to the beginning of the royal era. Furthermore, the great cultic agricultural festivals of the Canaanites could not have been without their influence upon the strict and imageless Yahweh cult. The religious fate of the era of Judges consists in the danger of creeping Canaanization. In many popular circles we note a mixture of the Yahweh faith and the Canaanite Baal cult. This is the point at which the theology of the Book of Judges takes a stand. The Canaanite syncretism is the one real cause of national disaster for Israel. It is because of their revolt from Yahweh that the individual tribes are given over into the hands of foreign conquerors and raiders. The rhythm of history is determined by defection, punishment, conversion, and salvation. The purpose of the Book of Judges is thoroughly religious; it is an appeal to the national conscience to learn from its past history and be converted to Yahweh (Jg 2, 11-20). The material for this call to repentance has been taken from the stories of the great heroes which were available to our author. From these popular traditions he chose six "greater" and six "lesser" judges who brought their people help and salvation in the hour of supreme peril. Since the hostile threat generally did not involve the entire land, the influence of these

---

3. Albright, *op. cit.*, 284. / G. E. Wright, *Archaeological observations on the Period of the Judges and the Early Monarchy,* JBL 60 (1941), 27-42.

judges generally does not extend beyond their immediate tribal territories.

1) *The judge Othniel* (Vulg: *Othoniel*): "And the people of Israel did what was evil in the sight of the Lord, forgetting the Lord their God, and serving the Baals and the Asheroth. Therefore the anger of the Lord was kindled against Israel, and he sold them into the hand of Cushan-rishathaim" ("Moor of the double wickedness," Jg 3, 7-11, a popular equivalent of the man's real name, which can no longer be determined). According to the present Hebrew text, this oppressor is supposed to have come from Aram-Naharaim, that is, Mesopotamia, so that it would perhaps be better to read Edom for Aram.[4]

The weakness of primarily the tribe of Judah was seized upon by the Edomites who shared the southern frontier with Judah. Against this oppression Yahweh raised up the judge Othniel, son of Kenaz, the younger brother of Caleb. The spirit of Yahweh came upon him and he went out to battle and drove the enemy from the land. "Spirit of Yahweh" is here not to be understood as the third person of the Trinity, but rather a sudden, energetic, and most effective divine power which comes upon a weak human person, "falls upon him," "invests" him, and makes him capable of super-human acts of heroism. The era of Judges is, in truth, the supreme era of the spirit of Yahweh, Israel's heroic age, produced by Yahweh.

2) *Ehud* (Vulg: *Aod*) *and the oppression of Moab*: The Moabites were settled east of the Dead Sea, between the Zered and the Arnon; but throughout their entire history they were possessed of the desire to acquire the fertile plains north of the Arnon. It was in this direction that lay their only potential for enlarging their agricultural land, and it was in this area that they frequently came into contact with the Israelite tribes. On the trek through the wilderness the Israelites made their way around the Moabite territory to the east. The then king

---

4. Aram and Edom are often confused because of the similarity in the letters R and D: cf. 2 Sm 8, 12; 4 K 6, 16; Ezek 16, 57.

Balak attempted to break their power through a curse spoken by the seer Balaam. The Moabite territory must thus have extended as far as the northern end of the Dead Sea. Since Israel, after the conquest of Canaan, was entirely without any central administration, it was an easy matter for the well organized Moabites, who had long been under the control of a king, to assert themselves successfully. Thus it happened that they were able to exert their power even across the Jordan, and, in the city of Jericho which Joshua had destroyed, to establish a point of support from which to levy tribute upon the Israelite tribes in the vicinity.

It was primarily the tribe of Benjamin that was oppressed under Eglon (bull), until a savior arose for them in the person of Ehud, a "left-handed man," who enticed Eglon into his upper chamber under the pretence of having some secret message for him and there killed him. The Book of Judges does not mean to pass any judgment on the subject of tyrannicide. As a military expedient against the enemy of the country the deed is not condemned, and it would seem to have been not too unusual for that era.[5]

3) *The battle against the Canaanite chariots*: A much greater threat now faced Israel in the form of a growing alliance of Canaanite cities. This oppression was directed primarily against the northern tribes in Galilee, but must also have made itself felt in the Ephraimite mountains in middle Palestine. The course of this battle is recorded in two separate forms, one in prose (Jg 4), and the victory song of Deborah (Jg 5). The present-day state of the text leaves many things unexplained.[6] But the course of the decisive confrontation must have been something like the following:

If scholarly judgment is correct in assuming that the name of the Canaanite general Sisera is Illyrian in origin,[7] this means

---

5. Nötscher, *Richter* 16.
6. In the text we have today, the Jabin tradition from the era of Joshua has been worked into the original, apparently going back thus to a later revision of the text. This results in some confusion in the text.
7. Noth, *op. cit.*, 129.

that elements of the sea peoples had established themselves in the Canaanite cities, after the manner of the Philistines in the south, had seized control of the government, and were now attempting to extend their sphere of power into the mountain territories. In this venture they were considerably aided by the fact that Israel was not in a position to offer any genuine resistance. The center of the hostile forces was in Harosheth (*Tell 'amr el-hâritiye*) on the northeastern end of the Plain of Jezreel, eight miles southeast of Haifa.

In this time of national crisis the initiative for the resistance proceeds from the prophetess Deborah ("bee"), who spoke judgment in the mountains of Ephraim between Rama and Bethel. She called Barak (lightning) from the Tribe of Naphtali and ordered him, in the name of Yahweh, to undertake the battle. Barak's call was followed by his tribe of Naphtali and the neighboring tribe of Zebulun. From Kedesh in Galilee, where the forces were assembled, he made his way to Mt. Tabor, from where he marched against the chariot forces of Sisera which had meantime gathered in the Plain of Jezreel. He won a complete victory over the feared adversary, a victory which the Israelites could attribute only to the direct intervention of Yahweh. Sisera himself, after his chariot forces were shattered, was forced to flee on foot. In the tent of a nearby Kenite he was murdered by Jael.

Excavations have yielded considerable evidence on the constantly fluctuating battles between Israel and the Canaanites. Bethel, for example, was destroyed between 1200 and 1000 B.C., on four separate occasions.[8]

The fortress of Megiddo, which guarded the pass across Mount Carmel, was destroyed by the Israelites either around 1150 or 1100 B.C. Some years passed before it was resettled. In this interval we might well date the battle against Sisera's chariot forces which, according to the Song of Deborah (Jg 5, 19), took place "near Taanak by the waters of Megiddo." The fact that the site can be identified only by reference to the city of Taanak already presupposes the fact that Megiddo lay

---

8. Albright, *op. cit.*, 286.

in ruins at the time in which the account was first recorded. This would mean that the battle of the Northern Tribes against the Canaanite cities would have to be dated around the year 1100 B.C.[9]

The Song of Deborah, with its alternation of dramatically vivid scenes, filled with plastic strength, beauty, and immediate appeal, is a good example of how a prosaic event can be recast into poetic form. The fresh and living poetry mirrors an originally popular conception which still required some sort of religious purification. The basic theme which pervades the entire composition is the praise of Yahweh, to whom the war, the victory, and the ensuing peace era are all ascribed.[10] It is no wonder that, in situations such as this, Israel should have developed a warlike conception of her religious commitments, and that Israel's God becomes "Yahweh, the God of hosts." [11]

4) *Gideon* (Vulg: *Gedeon*) *and the Midianite attack*: The Midianites lived as camel-nomads on the Sinai Peninsula (Ex 2, 15-22), but were centered in north-western Arabia, inland of the Gulf of Elam, and were thus separated from Israel by the territory of Moab. Their radius of activity must have been considerable, since despite this separation they attacked the territories west of the Jordan. According to Judges 6, 3 there were "sons of the east" (*benê qedem*) among them, that is, other east-Jordanian Beduin tribes.[12] As nomads they were not attempting to occupy any country; they were content with booty and pasturage. With their great herds of camels, which had just been domesticated around this time, they spread considerable panic. The Israelites fled before them and sought refuge in the mountain caves. With their camels, the enemy were able

9. *Westminster Atlas* (1947), 44.
10. Nötscher, *op. cit.*, 21. / P. R. Ackroyd, *The Composition of the Song of Deborah*, VT 2 (1952), 160-162.
11. Albright, *op. cit.*, 286. Cf. Ex 15, 3, 6: "Yahweh is a warrior . . . . Your right arm shatters the enemy."
12. Perhaps it is also true that all robber hordes are referred to as Midianites since it was first under this form that they became known to the Sinai Peninsula.

to undertake lightning-like raids, plundering the western sea coast (Jg 6, 4). When the crops were ripe, they descended like a flock of locusts and devoured all the produce of the country. For the peasants this meant the loss of their daily bread and the crisis to their continued existence.

In this time of crisis Yahweh once again intervened to save his people. He sent down his spirit upon Gideon (the name means apparently "feller," from the verb *gader* — to fell) from the clan of Abiezer in the Tribe of Manasseh. He had his home in Ophra, whose location can no longer be precisely determined. Gideon raised the standard of revolt in the cause of Yahweh by tearing down the altar his fathers had erected to Baal, and chopping down the asheras. The national liberation thus begins with a religious act. Apparitions by angels and the miracle of the dew [13] confirm the divine origins of his mission. He calls up a military levy. But from the many forces who gather in answer to his call, he selects only 300 men, by the test at the stream, supplies them with pitchers, torches, and trumpets, and then launches a surprise attack upon the Midianites encamped in the Plain of Jezreel. The surprised enemy fled in confusion. Before they could reach the Jordan, they were overtaken by the Ephraimites who were hurrying after them. They cut them off from the horde and the two princes Oreb (Raven) and Ze-eb (wolf) were taken prisoner. They were killed at the "rock of the raven" and at the "wine-press of the wolf." Gideon himself continued the pursuit into Transjordania, where he exacted blood vengeance for his brothers who had been murdered on Tabor, striking the Midianites Zebah and Salmunna (Jg 8, 18) and carrying out a terrible verdict upon the cities of Succoth and Penuel which had mocked him upon his march into the country.

After the victory Gideon was offered the position of king, but he refused it, remarking that Yahweh alone should be their king (Jg 8, 23). It is possible that Gideon was here employing simply a polite expression that he did not actually mean. Subsequent developments suggest the possibility (Jg 9, 2) that he actually did establish a sort of monarchy as Jephthah later expressly demands for himself.

---

13. Supposedly a fleece of wool (such as was customarily worn for a coat) was laid upon the threshing floor, a flat piece of ground stamped hard which lay just outside the village gates. Cf. Ps 72, 6. The mystical interpretation, referring the miracle to the Blessed Virgin, is pure accommodation. Nötscher, *op. cit.*, 30.)

The extent to which power can blind even a hero of religious liberation is demonstrated by the fact that Gideon had an ephod [14] made for himself from among the booty, apparently an image of God. It was meant to promote the worship of Yahweh, but it clearly involved the danger of confusion with the Baal cult. That is why history's verdict upon Gideon is a doubtful one. On the other hand the "day of Midian" had become the type of the messianic victory at the end-time (Is 9, 3), but on the other hand Gideon is a man of his time, quite subject to the temptation of the Canaanite religion.

5) *Abimelek's fortune and end*: The monarchy which Gideon had refused with his polite formula was coveted by his son Abimelek ("my father is king") with a bloody insistence. He was the result of Gideon's marriage with a Shechemite and was thus not accepted as a full brother by his 70 brothers. In the battle which now begins, the rivalries between the ancient sedentary population of Shechem, the Hivites, and the Tribe of Ephraim which enjoyed the supremacy, must have had a great role to play. A native tyrant is easier to bear than a foreign ruler. Thus Abimelek insinuates himself into the favor of the ruling clique at Shechem. The people are prepared to make him king instead of one of the 70 sons of Gideon. He then proceeds to murder his brothers. Only the youngest of them, Jotham, escapes the blood bath (Jg 9, 7ff.).

Raised by the aristocracy to the position of city-king at Shechem, the young tyrant does not rest content with the position of petty Canaanite city-king, in the traditional manner. Instead — apparently with more or less pressure and force — he extended his power to the clans of Manasseh and Ephraim that were established upon the mountains around Shechem.[15] His rule

---

14. The *ephod* is generally the official garment of the highpriest (Ex 28, 6-30; 29, 5; 39, 2-21). Here it refers not to a garment, but to a cult object (cf. Jg 17, 5; Ex 32, 5).

15. In the Amarna era the city king Labaya of Shechem had already extended his rule far beyond the mountains of Middle Palestine. Cf. M. Noth, *op. cit.*, 132. / A. Alt, *Die Landnahme der Israeliten in Palästina* (1925), 18ff.

thus turned into an unorganized hybrid and quickly collapsed. During the days in which he had hoped to be not only city-king of Shechem but also to extend his rule as far as possible over the Israelite tribes, Abimelek had moved his residence to Aruma (perhaps *Tell el-'ormel*, about 6 miles southeast of Shechem), in Ephraimite territory. In Shechem he installed an "official" (*paqîd*) as his representative. The Shechemites who had raised him to this position of power took offense at this move. They let themselves be provoked into a rebellion, where-upon Abimelek quickly attacked the city with his mercenaries and destroyed it. The foundation of his kingship was thus destroyed, and he himself perished with it. In the later battles around the city of Tebes, (modern Tubas, some nine miles east of Shechem) the tyrant came to a disgraceful end: a woman threw a millstone down upon him and mortally wounded him, whereupon he had his arm-bearer deliver the final blow.

Abimelek's appearance was only a single episode, his per-sonal work, which was not destined to achieve any permanent institution. Still it is worth noting that Abimelek — from his mother's side he is certainly a mixture of Israelite and Can-aanite blood — was the first to call himself "king." [16]

6) *Jephthah and the Transjordanian peril*: The danger to the Transjordanian tribes arose from the Ammonites; it may even have been a joint Moabite-Ammonite action — the text is unclear on this point.[17] The Ammonites were centered around the city Rabba (the "great," that is, the "great city of the sons of Ammon," also called Rabbat-Ammon). The name has been preserved in the modern capital city of Jordan, Amman. These people too had a monarchy from very early times, certainly before the Israelites, and had formed a minor state. From their tribal territories they were attempting to extend their control

---

16. M. Noth, *op. cit.*, 132.
17. Jephthah's dealings with the adversary bent upon attack is directed against Moab rather than Ammon (Jg 11, 12-28). The territory in question had never been Ammonite: also, Chemosh is the principal god of the Moabites.

in a northwesterly direction. Here lay a fertile plain, which, in modern times, is called *el-buqe'a*. In this plain the Ammonites firmly established themselves and began to spread northward into the territory of Gilead. They also attempted a direct attack which succeeded in reducing Gilead to a position of subjection (Jg 10, 6 — 12, 6).

In this time of crisis the men of Gilead sought a helper. Since they could find no other man in their ranks they turned to a certain Jephthah (*Yapthah* — may he [Yahweh] open), the illegitimate and unacknowledged son of a man from Gilead who had, as a result of his situation, been thrown out of his family and now lived in "the land of Tob" at the head of a band of freebooters. Freebooting, in the ancient and even the modern Oriental way of seeing things, is not a dishonorable profession (cf. David, 1 S 22, 2). Jephthah was willing to take charge of the situation only on condition that, after his victory he be given full royal power in the country. Pressed by necessity, the people promised him this request. While the other judges were all called charismatically to their office of liberation, by the "spirit of Yahweh," Jephthah is invested with his power by the people (Jg 11, 1). After receiving his mandate from the elders of the people, Jephthah made his way to Mispah in Gilead, where he mustered the troops. There the "spirit of Yahweh" also came upon him (Jg 11, 29) and made him a charismatic leader as well. He conquered the Ammonites in battle and drove them from the land. The possession of the land of Gilead was thus secured for Israel.

Jephthah was forced, however, to pay a very high personal price for the victory he won. Before the campaign he had made a vow that whatever he encountered at the door of his house upon his return from the victory he would sacrifice. What he, and everyone else, expected was that an animal suitable for sacrifice would be found somewhere along his homeward path. The story does not, accordingly, involve a deliberate vow of human sacrifice. Jephthah's deed cannot be judged by the criteria of the high prophetic ethics; Jephthah was a fighting man and neither a religious nor a theological authority. The wording of the text makes it clear that it was a human sacrifice, as was the case in the human sacrifice offered by Hiel of Jericho and the king of Moab, or in the case of Isaac (1 K 16, 34; 2 K 3, 27; Gn 22). Until the twelfth Christian century translators and exegetes have explained this oath in precisely this way, and thus accused Jephthah of rashness and lack of proper reflection.[18]

7) *Samson's adventures and the Philistine crisis*: The story of Samson is the most explicitly recorded of all the Judges, and at the same time the most personal. It is the popular hero himself, and not the crisis of his country, which is prominently in the foreground (early history and birth Jg 13, dealings with the Philistines 14ff., capture and death 16), much more so, and in a much different manner, than in the case of the other "great Judges." The fight against the dangerous public enemy, the Philistines, only serves as background against which to portray the person of Samson. He did not, like his predecessors, muster up a great army from among the people and face the enemy in a great battle. His is a private war against the Philistines, without any visible effects upon the situation of his country, a war entered upon from motives of personal revenge and advantage.

It is true that this confrontation with the Philistines is "arranged" (14, 4) by Yahweh, and the Biblical presentation lays considerable stress upon the serious moral application of the story: uncontrolled passion destroys even the strongest hero, bringing death and destruction even to the champion whom God's anointing had called to greatness. Despite these failures, Samson, in ancient Israel, by reason of his tremendous strength, his droll humor, and the almost grotesque pranks that he executed against the greatly feared traditional enemy of his people, and also on grounds of national pride, became a favorite figure of the popular tradition.

The author of the Book of Judges, without destroying the tone and coloring of the popular narrative and partially folklore character of his sources, and without interjecting too much

---

18. Nötscher, *op. cit.*, 50.

in the way of praise or blame, has taken over the oral or written traditions and, with only a few notes of his own (13, 1-5; 15, 20; 16, 31), fitted it neatly into the framework of his own composition.[19]

Samson (from *shemesh* — sun, "sun hero"?) is from the tribe of Dan. His mother was informed by an angel that her son should be dedicated to Yahweh throughout his entire life, that he should be a Nazirite, and that, as a sign of his dedication, his hair should never be shorn. In the narratives that follow, Samson always appears as a man of extraordinary physical strength, which he owes to his consecration to Yahweh. His hostility towards the Philistines began when he had fallen in love with a Philistine girl in Timnath, in the Shepelah, 3 miles southwest of his native city of Zorah. On the occasion of the wedding he offered a riddle for solution. His bride, with tears and entreaty, managed to entice the answer from him. Samson thereupon killed thirty Philistines and gave their clothing to the wedding guests as their prize for solving the riddle. In his anger he also left his young bride who was then taken by one of the wedding guests for his own wife. When Samson learned this, he avenged himself by capturing 300 jackals and tying them together, two by two, by their tails, together with a burning torch, and then driving them into the Philistines' grain fields. He then withdrew into Judaean territory. The Philistines demanded his extradition, a demand to which the Judaeans shamefully acquiesced. They bound Samson, but he burst his bonds and killed 1000 Philistines with the jawbone of an ass.

Another gallant adventure led him into the city of Gaza where he spent the night with a prostitute.[20] The Philistines planned to kill him the following morning. But at midnight

19. *Ibid.*, 53. The Greek Heracles legend and the Babylonian Gilgamesh Epic exhibit so many serious points of distinction that there can be no possibility of interdependence.

20. The establishment visited by Samson in Gaza was not necessarily a house of ill repute. As in Josh 2, 1, where Rahab maintained a public house, in Babylonia too, "prostitutes" were really innkeepers, who did not enjoy the best reputation.

he carried off the city gates and brought them as far as Hebron, 36 miles from Gaza. A third gallant adventure, with Delilah, proved to be his undoing. The prostitute succeeded in wheedling from him the mystery behind the hero's great physical strength, which lay in his long hair, the symbol of his being a Nazirite, a man dedicated to Yahweh. Following an amorous hour with the hero, when he had fallen asleep with his head on her lap, Delilah cut off all his hair. The Philistines captured him, put out his eyes, and condemned him to a slave's labor, turning the mill. On the occasion of a victory festival in honor of the god Dagon, Samson was brought out as an object of mockery. Then the power of Yahweh suddenly came down upon him. The blind hero ripped the wooden columns upon which the pavilion rested from their stone foundations, so that the entire edifice collapsed, killing many of the spectators together with the great hero.

8) *The six "lesser judges"*: The Book of Judges mentions little more than the names. Shangar killed 600 of the Philistines with an ox-goad (3, 31), Tola was from Issachar (10, 1), Elon from Zebulun (12, 11), Jair was prominent for his wealth and his numerous posterity. He came from Gilead (10, 3-5), Ibzan from Bethlehem in the territory of Zebulun (12, 8-10), and Abdon from Ephraim (12, 13-15).

9) *Appendices to the Book of Judges*: The history of the Judges is followed by two appendices. In the first (17 and 18) are recorded the wanderings of the tribe of Dan which was forced to abandon its hereditary possessions along the western slope of the Judaean hill country by attacks from the Philistines, whereupon they migrated northward to the sources of the Jordan in search of a new home. Their migrations led the Danites over the mountains of Ephraim where they took possession of the private sanctuary erected by Micah, violently seized the divine image (perhaps the figure of a bull as in the case of the golden calf; Ex 32, 4) as well as the ephod for inquiring the will of Yahweh, and thereby established an illegal cult in Dan.[21]

---

21. A. Murtonen, *Some Thoughts on Judges* XVII, VT 1 (1951), 223.

The second appendix (19 — 21) records the particularly brutal rape of a woman by the Benjaminites of Gibea. The outrage prompted almost all of Israel to undertake a united action which almost completely wiped out the Tribe of Benjamin: after the battle only 600 men survived. In order to provide wives for them, a strong force, which had not taken part in the campaign of vengeance against Benjamin, set out for the city of Jabesh in Transjordania, conquered the city, killed all the men and women, but gave over the maidens to the Benjaminites. Since there were still not enough wives, it was decided that at the festival in Shiloh the Benjaminites would be allowed to carry off wives from among the pilgrims.

10) *The literary problems of the Book of Judges*: The 21 chapters of the Book of Judges apparently exhibit a very definite outline. 1, 1 — 2, 5 is an introduction which takes up the events from the conquest of Canaan and partially overlaps with the Book of Joshua. 2, 6 — 16, 31 then presents the real substance of the text, the story of the six great Judges, with the brief record of the six lesser Judges added to it. 17 — 21 finally contains the two appendices on Dan and Benjamin.

But despite this division, the Book of Judges is not a compact or self-contained unit; it is rather a collection of the most divergent narrative materials, held together only by their incorporation into an outline provided by the theology of history (2, 11-19). The book is named from its primary material. It does not include all the judges. Heli (1 S 4, 18) and Samuel (1 S 7, 15-17), who are also characterized as judges, are not even mentioned.

The author has thus collected the available narrative material, which is not identical with the Pentateuchal sources JEDP,[22] and, without working it over very much, has raised it to the level of a theology of history, thereby transforming the popular traditional material into a prophetic warning to the entire nation. The actual date of composition cannot be determined with certainty. From the repeated notice (17, 6; 18, 1; 19, 1; 21, 25) that there was "at that time no king in Israel and that every man did what he wanted," one might conclude that the author lived in the more ordered circumstances of the royal era. The

---

22. Bentzen, *op. cit.*, II, 86ff.

conclusion that the author had also experienced the captivity of the northern tribes, in the years 733 or 722, could be substantiated only if we presume that the remark "until the day of the captivity of the land" (18, 30) is clearly the work of the author himself and not a later hand. At all events, the book does contain ancient traditions; whether they took their final written form in the early or late royal era is of much lesser significance.[23]

The author does not consider it his objective to fit the stories of the Judges into the broader context of world history. The non-Israelite peoples and events enter into his purview only insofar as they come into contact with Israel or have influenced the life of his nation. This failure to consider the larger picture also explains why the chronology of the book contains so many riddles.

a) According to the chronology of the Book of Kings (1 K 6, 1), 480 years separated the Exodus from Egypt and the building of the Temple under Solomon. It would appear that the numbers in the Book of Judges contradict this statement.

b) The total number of years in the Book of Judges, including the years of oppression, yields a total of 410 years. To these must also be added the 40 years of wandering in the wilderness, the time of Heli (according to 1 S 4, 18, 40 years, according to LXX, 20 years), as well as the time of David's reign (40 years according to 1 K 2, 11) and the first three years of Solomon: this would be a total of 123 years. We must also include the careers of Samuel, Saul, and Joshua, which are not given in terms of years. We thus reach a sum total of 533 (according to LXX 513) + x + y + z years, and not the 480 years demanded by the Book of Kings. The riddle can be solved perhaps to some degree by identifying the 40 years of the Philistine crisis with the careers of Samson and Heli (20 + 20) and subtracting these 40 years, together with the years of the "lesser judges" (753) from 513 (LXX). We thus get a total of 400 years, and can divide the remaining 80 years among the careers of Joshua, Samuel, and Saul. These presuppositions do much to explain the chronological structure of the book, but it presupposes the insertion of the "lesser Judges" as a later addition, by which the essential harmony of the numerical structure, no longer properly understood, was destroyed.[24] The meaning of the 480 years is to be explained by numerical symbolism. 480 = 12 x 40, that is, the time from the Exodus to the building of the Temple forms a self-contained unit of 12 generations. The number is meant to suggest the closing of one epoch in salvation history: another "world year" has come to an end.

---

23. Nötscher, op. cit., 6.
24. Bentzen, op. cit., 89.

c) Archaeological facts which have been supplied by excavation open the way for an admissible "profane chronology." The conquest of Canaan under Joshua should be assigned to the years 1250 — 1200 B.C., and the era of the Judges from 1200 — 1020 B.C. It was during this period of 200 years that the loose confederation of twelve tribes was welded together into the united people of Israel, in the course of serious internal and external struggles. The common experience of crisis and danger had bound the people tightly together.

CHAPTER XVII

THE BOOK OF RUTH

LITERATURE

Commentary: Gunkel, *Ruth*, Reden und Aufsätze, 1913. / A. Scholz, *Das Buch Ruth* (Bonner Bibel), 1926. / P. Joüon, 1924. / W. Rudolph, KAT, Leipzig 1939. / M. Haller, *Megilloth*, HBAT 1940. / A. Vincent, *Le livre de Ruth*, Jerusalembibel 1952. / H. H. Rowley, *The Marriage of Ruth*, Harvard Theol. Rev. 40, 1947, 77-99. / Einleitungen: Simon-Prado, 1949, 342. / Weiser, 1949, 223ff. / Bentzen, 1948, II, 182.

THE Book of Ruth presents a family story from the era of the Judges, and is, accordingly, placed immediately after the Book of Judges in the Septuagint translation and in the other versions dependent upon the Greek. According to the Rabbinic tradition it is also supposed to have been written in the era of the Judges. The Massora, however, places the small book among the contents of the Megillot.

Contents: The very compact introduction (1, 1-6) tells how a Jewish family was forced by famine to leave Bethlehem and move to Moab. After the death of the father Elimelech, his two sons Mahlon and Chilion marry Moabite girls, but soon die themselves, so that their mother Naomi (Vulg: Noemi) wishes to return to her native country.

In 1, 7-22 we learn how Naomi attempts to persuade her two daughters-in-law, who are accompanying her, to remain in their country, and how finally the one, Orpha, does in fact return while the other, Ruth, goes with her: "Where you go I will go" (1, 16). In chapter 2 the somewhat more expanded narrative continues to follow the career of the energetic and virtuous Ruth, who, while gleaning in the fields of Boaz, finds favor with the owner who is a relative of her husband. According to the custom of the levirate marriage, in which the closest blood relative has the obligation to marry the wife of the man who died childless in order to provide him with children, Ruth, advised by her mother-in-law, throws herself at Boaz' feet to await his decision in this question (ch. 3). After another man, who had a prior claim to the levirate, renounced his opportunity, Boaz himself takes Ruth as his wife. She becomes the mother of a son who is adopted by Naomi and given the name Obed; Obed is the grandfather of David. In 4, 18-22, an appendix presents the genealogy of David.[1]

In terms of literary genre, the story of Ruth is best characterized as a novel. Gunkel and Gressmann see it simply as a novel meant to glorify the fidelity of a woman, without any historical basis. Rudolf objects that this explanation turns the ancient text into a too modern outline. Other scholars have seen the book as a polemic against the overly rigorous policies against mixed marriage as promoted by Ezra and Nehemiah, and, accordingly, date the book in the post-Exilic era. But probably the most accurate interpretation of the book is the one which regards it as a free novel-like reworking of historical material dating from the era of the Judges. The names and traits of the figures of the book, Elimelek, Naomi, Boaz, all point to an historical tradition. On the other hand, the names of the sons Mahlon (sickness) and Chilion (consumption) give the impression of poetic invention. The name Orpha (turning the back) and Ruth (the traveling companion) have symbolic value. The interpretation which sees the names of persons and places as references to an ancient cultic myth that originated in Bethlehem[2] is, according to Rudolf, a relapse into the best days of Pan-Babylonianism.[3]

The time of composition cannot be far removed from the era of the Judges. The rabbinic tradition claims Samuel as the author (*Baba bathra* 14b). Since the book is written primarily to glorify the ancestress of King David, it is quite possible that it should be dated in the Davidic or post-Davidic era.

The book is a splendid testimony to God's providence and direction and thus has an abiding religious value. Ruth achieves her greatest nobility by her incorporation into the genealogy of Christ (Mt 1, 5). But its artistic qualities, too, assure the Book of Ruth of a place of honor in the abiding monuments of Old Testament literature. No less a critic

---

1. Based on A. Weiser, *op. cit.*, 223.
2. W. E. Staples, JSLL (1936), 145. / Bentzen, *op. cit.*, II, 184.
3. Rudolph, *Ruth* (1939), 8.

than Goethe referred to it as "the loveliest little volume that has been ethically and idyllically handed down to us." [4]

RETROSPECT AND CONCLUSION

With the conquest of Canaan the drama of salvation that is the divine and human history of the world has entered upon a decisive stage. What God had promised to the fathers of old has now become reality. He has laid a new foundation in Abraham, in order to transform the catastrophic history of humanity into a salvation history, through the call of Abraham. The will of God intervening in history, with its constant demands and new creations, takes on a more and more concrete form. God reveals a new name, with signs and wonders he frees his enslaved people from Egypt, he sets up a covenant in blood, he leads the rebellious and obstinate people to the very gates of Canaan, and finally gives them their promised heritage.

It is not a fairy tale that we have studied here: God and nature do not love "tenderly" and "unrealistically." The history of Israel, in all its phases, is part and parcel of the Ancient Near East; the chosen and selected people are not an ideal example of a people, without flesh and blood; they are young and rebellious people with a stiff neck that answered God's call with defiance and defection. If, despite the advent of God's judgment, the tents of Israel are established on the mountains of Canaan, this can only be the miracle of Yahweh's grace, for his mercy is without measure.

The circle of God's deliberate activity becomes more and more well defined. The patriarchal blessing already separates those who are unworthy. The bearer of the blessing becomes, finally, the tribe of Judah, from between whose feet the sceptre will not ever depart. The ancestress of the future Messiah already appears in the Book of Ruth, and thus the national history of the people is expanded into the universal context of the history of all humanity. The heroic battles, the heroes

---

4. Weiser, 225.

upon whom the spirit of Yahweh descended in the era of the Judges — these all look to the future ruler who will encompass all Israel's political power, to shatter the enemies of God's people and establish the great world empire. Thus a new epoch begins in Israel's history.

Just as the external course of history is the real story of the Ancient Near East, so literary analysis has demonstrated that the books in which this history of God have been handed down are perfectly faithful to the stamp of their time. Revelation and inspiration never take place in an unhistorical vacuum. God does not annihilate the human agent when he makes him the organ and mouthpiece of his will. Neither does God simply dictate the work of human history, although he does not hesitate to inspire a human author to create such a work in keeping with his own talents, his own source material, and his own appreciation of history, always in such a manner that, despite all human frailty, the traces of divine inspiration are clearly evident. Scripture thus becomes a constantly progressing "incarnation of the word," which has considered it not beneath its dignity to put off the divine glory and appear as human speech.

INDEX

GEOGRAPHY OF
THE OLD TESTAMENT

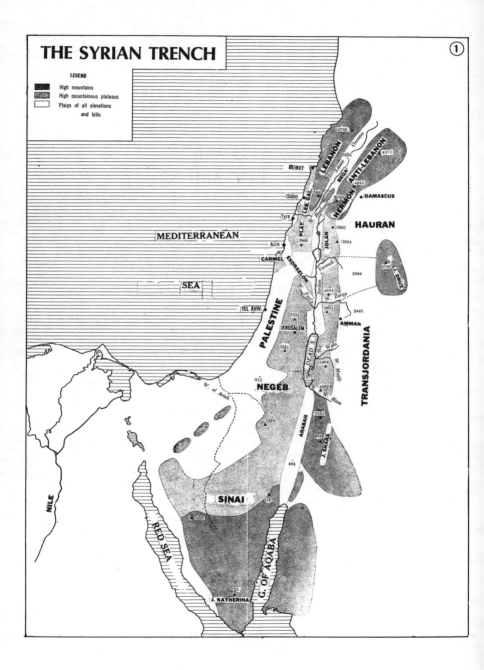

THE SYRIAN TRENCH

LEGEND

High mountains
High mountainous plateaus
Plains of all elevations and hills

①

MEDITERRANEAN

SEA

BEIRUT

Sidon

Tyre

Acre

CARMEL

TEL AVIV.

JERUSALEM

NILE

RED SEA

SINAI

J. KATHERINA

NEGEB

PALESTINE

ESDRAELON

DEAD S.

ARABAH

G. OF AQABA

LEBANON

ANTI-LEBANON

LEB. GAL.

PLAT.

HERMON

BUQA'

Litani

Orontes

N. Hasbani

Hasbani

Yarmuk

Jordan

W. Faria

W. Zarqa

W. Wala

W. Mujib

W. Hasa

W. el Arish

GOLAN

HAURAN

DAMASCUS

AMMAN

TRANSJORDANIA

J. DRUZ

J. SHARA

10700

3259

8572

4092

589

9232

3907

3024

3960

2604

5750

4054

3651

2443

3333

3221

3464

1277

1660

4860

913

3464

5353

6048

494

3183

8505

494

8733

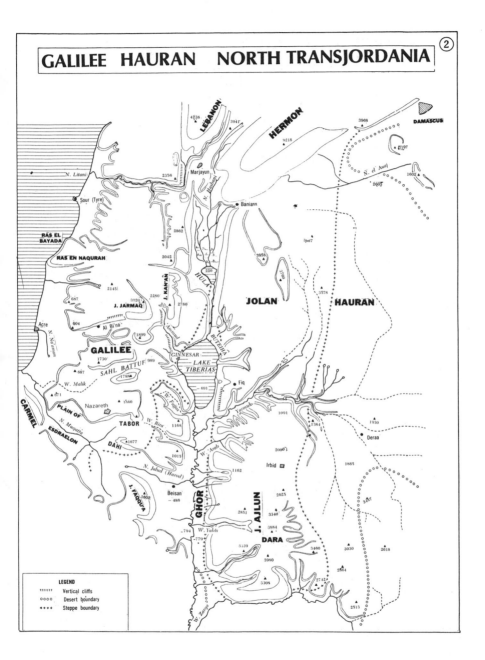

GALILEE HAURAN   NORTH TRANSJORDANIA

LEGEND
'''''' Vertical cliffs
ooooo Desert boundary
++++ Steppe boundary

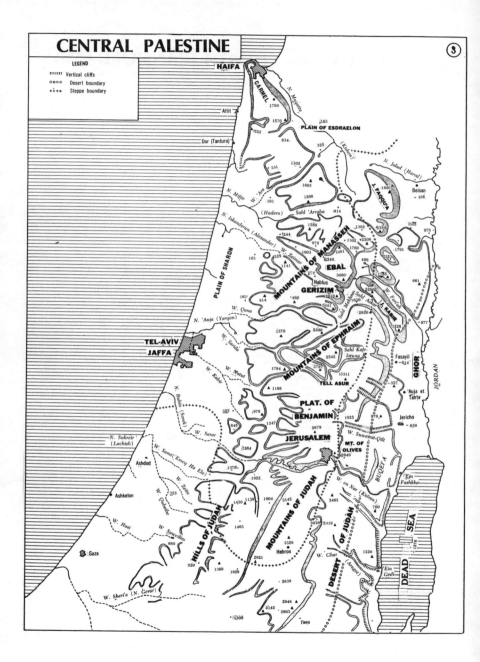

CENTRAL PALESTINE

③

HAIFA

CARMEL

N. Miqatta

Atlit

1780

1570

522

Dor (Tantura)

834

PLAIN OF ESDRAELON

325

(Kishon)

N. Jalud (Harod)

351

1302

1685

1268

391

N. Mifjir

W. 'Ara

(Hadera)

Sahl 'Arraba

814

N. Iskanderun (Alexander)

1588

1244

976

1302

1620

Beisan
-488

975

J. FAQUA

MOUNTAINS OF MANASSEH

EBAL

GERIZIM

Nablus

1603

325

1141

163

678

814

1480

2910

3041

2850

3060

2208

2481

1760

488

4240

163

W. Zeimat

W. Fār'a

J. KABIR

1791

2327

661

1370

2300

N. 'Auja (Yarqon)

W. Qana

W. Sa'īda

2542

Sahl Kafr
Istuna

Sahl Makhna

Sahl Asur

1620

2286

977

1228

1225

MOUNTAINS OF EPHRAIM

TEL-AVIV
JAFFA

W. Natuf

1784

3787

13311

TELL ASUR

Fasayil
814

GHOR

JORDAN

1188

N. Rubin

976

1247

PLAT. OF
BENJAMIN

1922

979

-337

'Auja et
Tahta

325

845

JERUSALEM

2879

W. Succeinit-Qilt

Jericho
-839

N. Sukreir
(Lachish)

W. Samt('Emeq Ha Ela)

W. Sarar

1264

MT. OF
OLIVES

2649

BUQE'A

'Ein
Fashkka

Ashdod

W. Zeita

1370

1923

Ashkelon

325

W. Qubeibe

1430

1138

1904

3142

2463

W. en Nar (Kidron)

760

'Ein
Gedi

DEAD SEA

-2276

W. Hasi

W. Succeilim

1463

3038

2019

MOUNTAINS OF JUDAH

680

HILLS OF JUDAH

920

1389

1629

3329

Hebron

2921

W. Ghar
(Arugot)

1220

DESERT OF JUDAH

Gaza

W. Sheri'a (N. Gerar)

2639

1300

2142

2948

2803

980

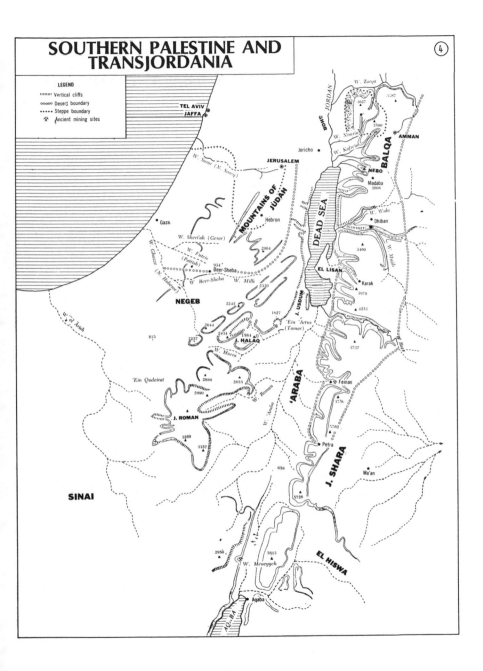

SOUTHERN PALESTINE AND TRANSJORDANIA

LEGEND
- """""" Vertical cliffs
- ooooo Desert boundary
- ••••• Steppe boundary
- ⚒ Ancient mining sites

④

TEL AVIV
JAFFA

W. Zarqa

3627   3587

W. Nimrin   3500

BALQA

W. Kafrein   AMMAN

Jericho

JERUSALEM   NEBO

W. Sarir (N. Sorey)   Madaba
2608

MOUNTAINS OF JUDAH   W. Wala

Gaza   Hebron   Dhiban

W. Sheri'ah (Gerar)   DEAD SEA   3460

W. Futeis   2964   W. Mujib
(Pattish)

934   EL LISAN

Beer-Sheba   J. USDUM   Karak

W. Ghazze (N. Habeon)   W. Beer-Sheba   W. Milh   2339   3979

NEGEB   4231

2243

1827   'Ein 'Artuz   5737
(Tamar)

W. el 'Arish   2044   2434   1584
813   2227   J. HALAQ

W. Murra

'Ein Qudeirat   2880   Feinan

2990   2633   1736

W. Roman   3702

J. ROMAN   W. 'Araba   Petra

3269   J. SHARA

3337   658   Ma'an

SINAI   3726

2950   3615   EL HISWA

W. Meneyyeh

AQABA   Aqaba

ROADS BETWEEN BEER SHEBA AND SHECHEM

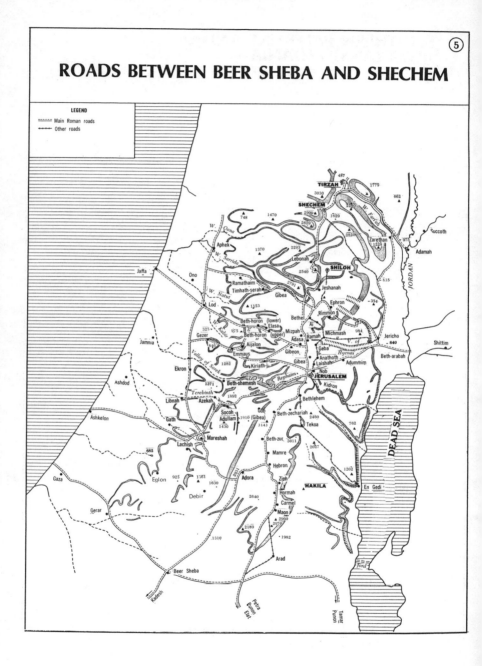

LEGEND
===== Main Roman roads
←←← Other roads

ROADS OF SAMARIA AND GALILEE

⑥

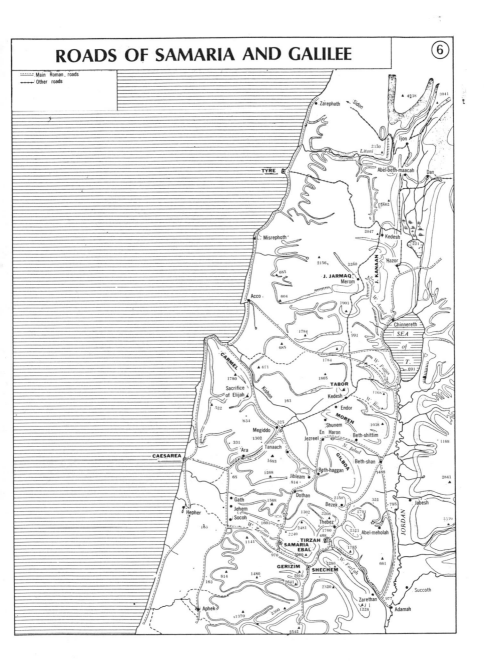

Main Roman, roads
Other roads

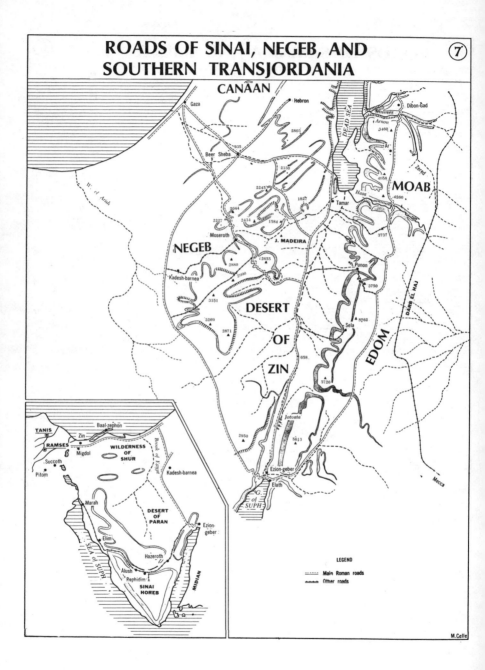

ROADS OF SINAI, NEGEB, AND SOUTHERN TRANSJORDANIA

⑦

CANÃAN

Gaza • Hebron • Dibon-Gad

DEAD SEA

2801 3460 ▲

Ar •

Beer Sheba • 935

2330

Zared

2245 4058 ▲ MOAB

1827 Hasa 4260

2044 Tamar •

2227 2434 1584 ▲

Moseroth

J. MADEIRA 3737

NEGEB

2880 ▲ 2655 Punon •

Kadesh-barnea • 2090 3750

3351 3762 ▲

3269 DESERT Sela •

2871 OF EDOM

ZIN DĀRB EL HAJ

658 •

3726 ▲

Jotvata

2950 5613 ▲

Ezion-geber •

Elath •

G. of SUPH

Mecca •

W. el Arīsh

Brook of Egypt

TANIS Baal-zephôn

Zin

RAMSES Migdol WILDERNESS OF SHUR

Succoth

Pitom Kadesh-barnea •

Marah DESERT OF PARAN

Ezion-geber

Elim

SEA of SUPH Hazeroth

Alush MIDIAN

Rephidim

SINAI HOREB

LEGEND

----- Main Roman roads
━━━ Other roads

M.Celle

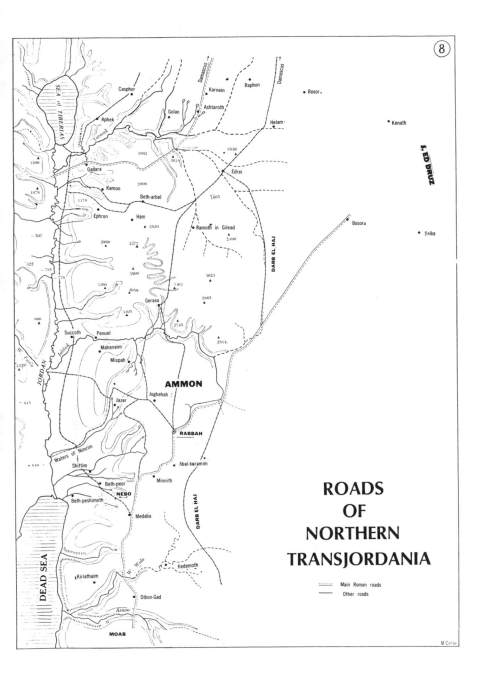

ROADS
OF
NORTHERN
TRANSJORDANIA

- - - - - Main Roman roads
———— Other roads

M Celie

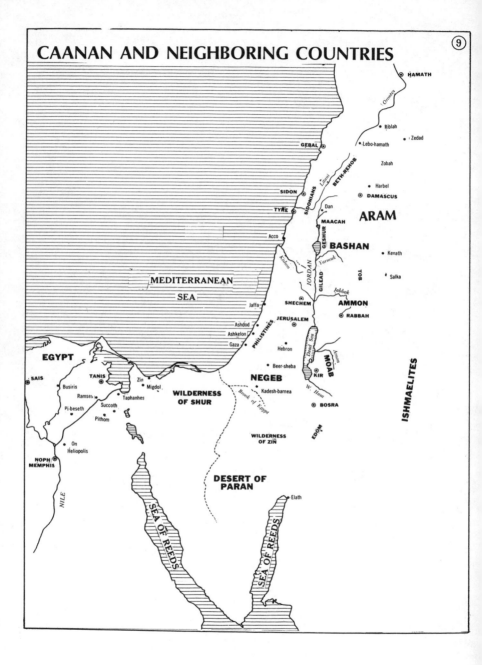

CAANAN AND NEIGHBORING COUNTRIES

⑨

HAMATH

Riblah
Zedad
Lebo-hamath

GEBAL

Zobah

BETH-REHOB

Harbel

SIDON
DAMASCUS

SIDONIANS
TYRE
Dan
ARAM

MAACAH
Acco
GESHUR
BASHAN
Kenath

Kishon
Yarmuk
TOB
Salka

MEDITERRANEAN
JORDAN
GILEAD
Jabbok

SEA
Jaffa
SHECHEM
AMMON

JERUSALEM
RABBAH

Ashdod
PHILISTINES

Ashkelon
Gaza
Hebron
Dead Sea
Arnon

ISHMAELITES

EGYPT
Beer-sheba
MOAB

SAIS
NEGEB
KIR

Busiris
TANIS
Zin
Kadesh-barnea
W. Hasa

Ramses
Migdol
WILDERNESS
OF SHUR
Brook of Egypt
BOSRA

Pi-beseth
Taphanhes
Succoth

Pithom

On
Heliopolis
WILDERNESS
OF ZIN
EDOM

NOPH
MEMPHIS

NILE
DESERT OF
PARAN

SEA OF REEDS
Elath

SEA OF REEDS

TRIBES AND DISTRICTS UNDER SOLOMON, NEIGHBORING PEOPLES

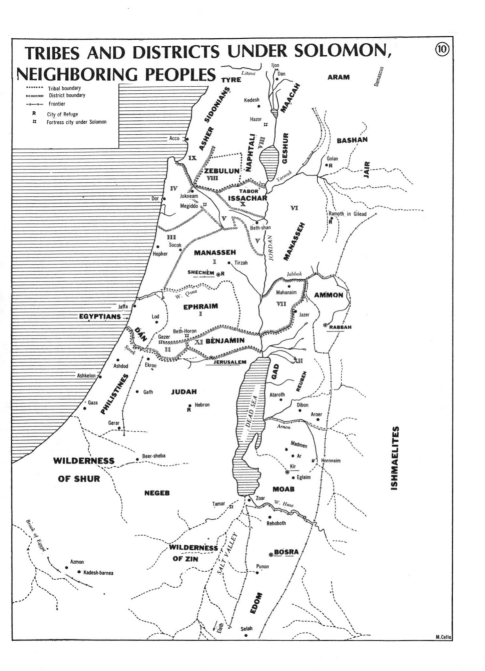

(10)

Tribal boundary
District boundary
Frontier

R   City of Refuge
⊓   Fortress city under Solomon

TYRE
Litani
Ijon
Dan
ARAM
Damascus

SIDONIANS
Kedesh
MAACAH
GESHUR

Acco
ASHER
Hazor ⊓
NAPHTALI VIII
BASHAN

IX
ZEBULUN VIII
Golan • R
JAIR

IV
Jokneam
TABOR
ISSACHAR X
Yarmuk

Dor
Megiddo ⊓
V
VI
Ramoth in Gilead R

III
Socoh
Beth-shan
V
MANASSEH

Hepher
MANASSEH I • Tirzah
JORDAN
Jabbok

SHECHEM ⊙R
Mahanaim
AMMON

Jaffa
W. Qana
EPHRAIM I
VII
Jazer

EGYPTIANS
Lod
Beth-Horon
RABBAH

DAN
Gezer
XI BENJAMIN
Sorek
II
JERUSALEM
XIII
GAD
REUBEN

Ashkelon
Ashdod
Ekron
Ataroth
Dibon

Gath
JUDAH
DEAD SEA
Aroer

Gaza
Hebron R
Arnon

Gerar
Madmen

WILDERNESS
OF SHUR
Beer-sheba
Ar
Horonaim
Kir ⊙ Eglaim

NEGEB
MOAB
ISHMAELITES

Tamar ⊓
Zoar
W. Hasa

Rehoboth

Brook of Egypt
WILDERNESS
OF ZIN
BOSRA

Azmon
Punon
SALT VALLEY

Kadesh-barnea

EDOM
Elath
Selah

M.Celle

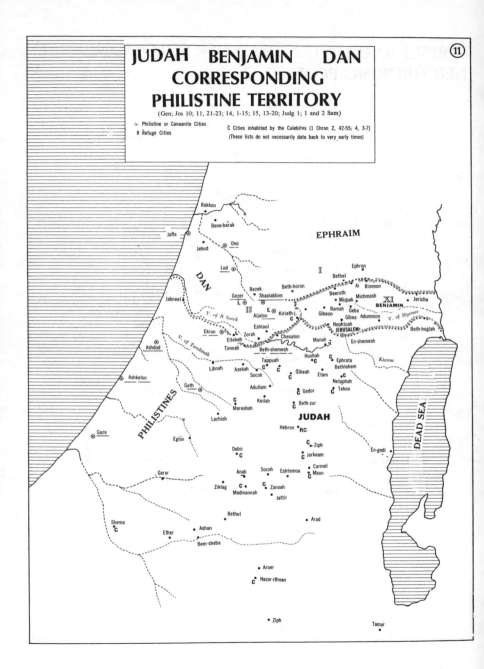

JUDAH   BENJAMIN   DAN
CORRESPONDING
PHILISTINE TERRITORY
(Gen; Jos 10; 11, 21-23; 14, 1-15; 15, 13-20; Judg 1; 1 and 2 Sam)

⊙ Philistine or Canaanite Cities
R Refuge Cities

C̄ Cities inhabited by the Calebites (1 Chron 2, 42-55; 4, 3-7)
(These lists do not necessarily date back to very early times)

⑪

EPHRAIM

DAN

BENJAMIN

JUDAH

PHILISTINES

DEAD SEA

Rakkon
Bene-berak
Jaffa
Jehud
Ono
Lod
Ephron
Bethel
Ai   Rimmon
Bezek
Beth-horon
Beeroth   Michmash
Jericho
Gezer   Shaalabbim
Jabneel
Mizpah
Ramah   Geba
V. of R Surek
Aijalon   Kiriath-j.
Gibeon   Gibea   Adummim   V. of Hyenas
Eshtaol
Nephtoah
JERUSALEM   Beth-hoglah
Ekron
Zorah   Chesalon
Ashdod
Eltekeh
Manah   En-shemesh
V. of Terebinth
Timnah   Beth-shemesh
Hushah
Tappuah   C̄   Ephrata   Kiaron
Ashkelon
Bethlehem
Libnah   Azekah
Gibeah   Etam   C̄
Socoh
Netophah
Gath
Adullam   C̄   Gedor   Tekoa   C̄
Keilah
Beth-zur
Mareshah   C̄
Lachish
Hebron   RC
Gaza
Eglon
Ziph   C̄
Debir   C̄
Jorkeam   C̄
En-gedi
Gerar
Anab   Socoh   Eshtemoa   Carmel
Maon   C̄
Ziklag   C̄   Zanoah
Madmannah
Jattir
Bethul
Arad
Shema   C̄
Ether   Ashan
Beer-sheba
Aroer
Hazor-ithnan   C̄
Ziph
Tamar

NORTHERN AND CENTRAL TRIBES
CORRESPONDING DISTRICTS

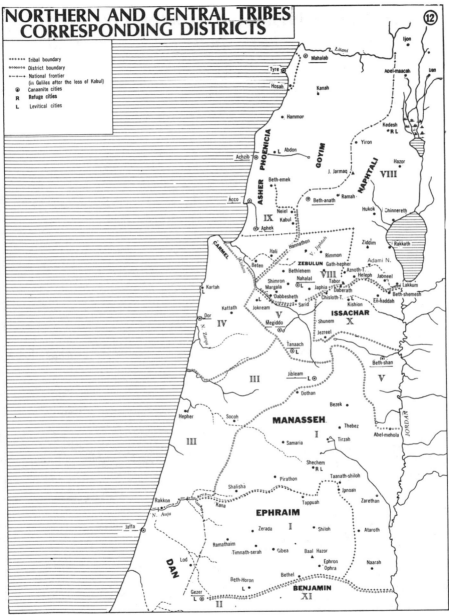

①②

- ••••••• Tribal boundary
- ○○○○○○○ District boundary
- •—•—•— National frontier
  (in Galilee after the loss of Kabul)
- ⊚ Canaanite cities
- R Refuge cities
- L Levitical cities

THE TWO DIVISIONS OF TRANSJORDANIA

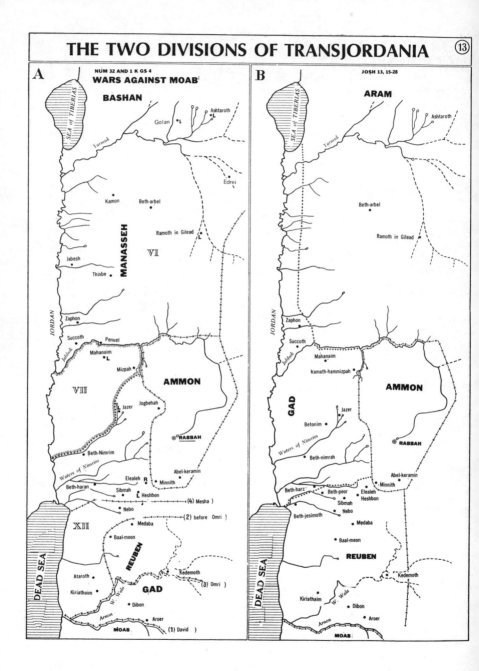

A — NUM 32 AND 1 K GS 4 — WARS AGAINST MOAB

B — JOSH 13, 15-28

Panel A labels: SEA of TIBERIAS, BASHAN, Golan, Ashtaroth, Edrei, Kamon, Beth-arbel, Ramoth in Gilead, MANASSEH, VI, Jabesh, Thisbe, JORDAN, Zaphon, Succoth, Penuel, Mahanaim, Mizpah, AMMON, Jabbok, VIII, Jazer, Jogbehah, RABBAH, Beth-Nimrim, Waters of Nimrim, Elealeh, Abel-keramin, Beth-haran, Sibmah, Minnith, Heshbon, (4) Mesha, Nebo, (2) before Omri, XII, Medaba, Baal-meon, REUBEN, DEAD SEA, Ataroth, Kedemoth, Kiriathaim, GAD, W. Wala, (3) Omri, Dibon, Arnon, Aroer, (1) David, MOAB

Panel B labels: SEA of TIBERIAS, ARAM, Ashtaroth, Yarmuk, Beth-arbel, Ramoth in Gilead, JORDAN, Zaphon, Succoth, Jabbok, Mahanaim, Kamath-hammizpah, GAD, AMMON, Jazer, Betonim, Waters of Nimrim, RABBAH, Beth-nimrah, Abel-keramin, Beth-haran, Beth-peor, Minnith, Elealeh, Heshbon, Sibmah, Nebo, Beth-jesimoth, Medaba, Baal-meon, REUBEN, DEAD SEA, Kiriathaim, Kedemoth, W. Wala, Dibon, Arnon, Aroer, MOAB

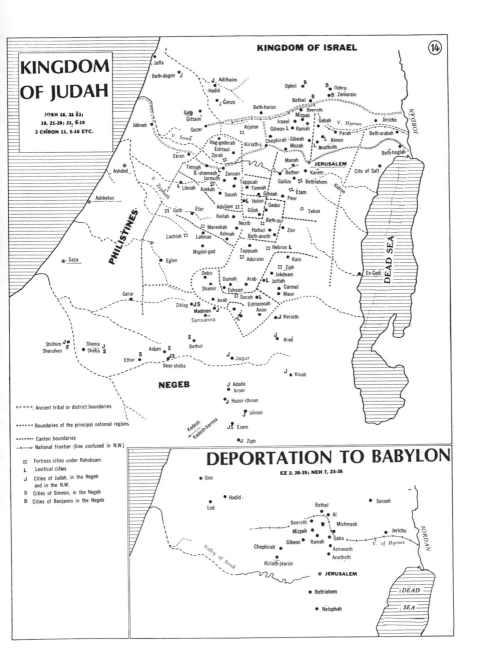

KINGDOM OF JUDAH

JOSH 15, 21 ඪ;
18, 21-28; 21, ⑨-19
2 CHRON 11, 5-10 ETC.

KINGDOM OF ISRAEL

⑭

Jaffa
Beth-dagon J
J Adithaim
Hadid
J Gimzo
Ophni B
Ophra
B Zemarain
Bethel
B
Beth-horon
Mizpah
Beeroth
Gath Gittaim
Irpeel
Gebah V. Hyenas
Jericho
Jabneh
V. Sorek
Gezer
Aijalon
Gibeon L Ramah
Parah
Beth-arabah
Hag-gederah
Chephirah Gibeah
L Almon
Eshtaol
Kiriath-j.
Mozah
Anathoth
Ekron
Zorah
Beth-hoglah
Timnah
Manah
JERUSALEM
Ashdod
B.-shemesh Zanoan
Bether Karem
City of Salt
Jarmuth
Tappuah
Gallim Bethlehem
Libnah Azekah
Socoh
Gibeah Etam
Ashkelon
Timnah
Peor
L Holon
Gath
Eter
Adullam
Gedor
Tekoa
Keilah
Giloh
Beth-zur
Mareshah
Nezib
Lachish
Lahmas
Ashnah
Beth-anoth
Zior
Migdal-gad
Tappuah
L Hebron
Gaza
Eglon
Adoraim
Kain
Debir
Ziph
Dumah
Arab
Jokdeam
En-Gedi
Shamir
Eshean
Juttah
Carmel
Socoh
Maon
Gerar
Anab
Eshtemoah
Ziklag JS
Anim
Madmen J
Sansanna
J Kerioth
Shilhim J S
Shema J
Bethul
J Arad
Sharuhen S
Sheba S
Ashan S
Ether
JS
J Jagur
Beer-sheba
J Kinah
NEGEB
J Adada
Aroer
J Hazor-ithnan
J Dimon
Ancient tribal or district boundaries
Kedesh
Kadesh-barnea
JS Ezem
Boundaries of the principal national regions
J. Ziph
Canton boundaries
National frontier (line confused in N.W.)

PHILISTINES
V. Zephath

DEAD SEA

JORDAN

Kidron

⊓ Fortress cities under Rehoboam
L Levitical cities
J Cities of Judah, in the Negeb and in the N.W.
S Cities of Simeon, in the Negeb
B Cities of Benjamin in the Negeb

DEPORTATION TO BABYLON

EZ 2, 20-35; NEH 7, 23-38

Ono
Hadid
Lod
Bethel
Senaah
Ai
Beeroth
Michmash
Mizpah
Jericho
Chephirah
Gibeon
Ramah
Geba
V. of Hyenas
Azmaveth
Kiriath-jearim
Anathoth
⊛ JERUSALEM
Bethlehem
Netophah

JORDAN

DEAD
SEA

PALESTINE UNDER THE ASSYRIAN EMPIRE

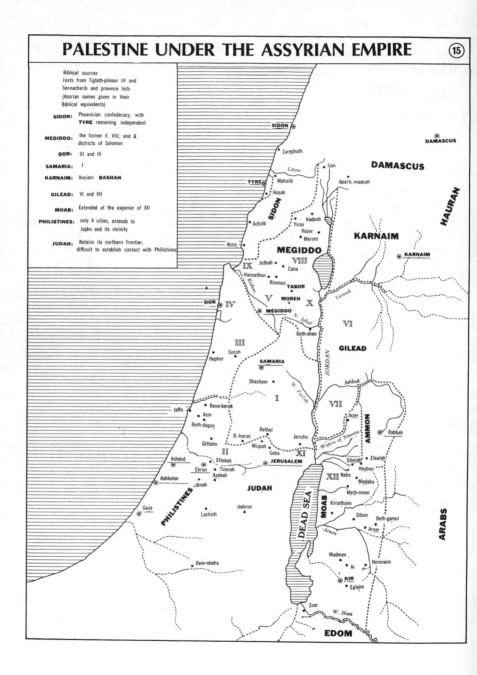

(15)

Biblical sources
Texts from Tiglath-pileser III and
Sennacherib and province lists
(Assrian names given in their
Biblical equivalents)

SIDON: Phoenician confederacy, with **TYRE** remaining independent

MEGIDDO: the former V, VIII, and X. districts of Solomon

DOR: III and IV

SAMARIA: I

KARNAIM: Ancient **BASHAN**

GILEAD: VI and VII

MOAB: Extended at the expense of XII

PHILISTINES: only 4 cities, extends to Japho and its vicinity

JUDAH: Retains its northern frontier; difficult to establish contact with Philistines

SIDON

DAMASCUS

DAMASCUS

Zarephath

HAURAN

Litani   Ijon

Mahalib   Abel-b.-maacah

TYRE

Hosah

Kedesh

Achzib   Yiron

Hazor

Merom

KARNAIM

Acco

KARNAIM

MEGIDDO

Kishon

IX   Jotbah   VIII

Hannathon   Cana

Rimmon   TABOR

V   MOREH

DOR   IV   X

MEGIDDO   N. Jalud   Yarmuk

Beth-shan   VI

III   Socoh   GILEAD

Hepher

SAMARIA   JORDAN

Shechem   Jahbok

I   W. Farah

Jaffa   Bene-berak   VII

Azor   Jazer   AMMON

Beth-dagon   Rabbah

II   B.-horon   Bethel   Jericho

Gittaim   Mizpah   Geba   Waters of Nimrim

Ashdod   Eltekeh   XI

Ekron   Timnah   JERUSALEM   Sibmah   Elealeh

Azekah   Nebo   Hesbon

Ashkelon   Libnah   XIII   Medaba

JUDAH   Meth-meon

Gaza   Hebron   Kiriathaim

Lachish   MOAB   Dibon   Beth-gamul

DEAD SEA   Arnon   Aroer

Beer-sheba   Madmen   Horonaim

Ar

KIR

Eglaim

Zoar   W. Hasa

PHILISTINES   ARABS

EDOM

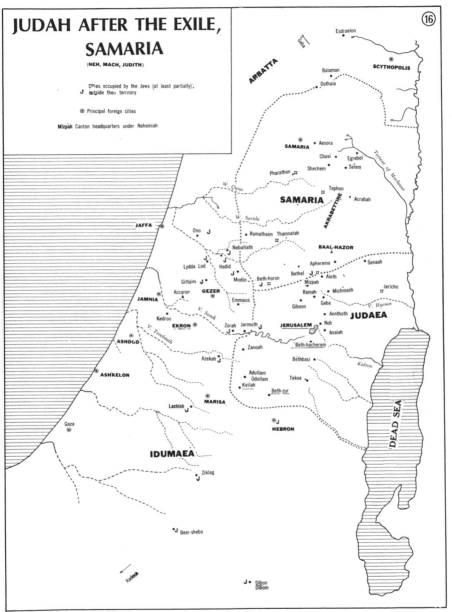

JUDAH AFTER THE EXILE, SAMARIA

(NEH, MACH, JUDITH)

Cities occupied by the Jews (at least partially); **J** outside their territory

⊛ Principal foreign cities

Mizpah Canton headquarters under Nehemiah

Esdraelon

Geba

ARBATTA

SCYTHOPOLIS

Balamon

Dothaia

SAMARIA
Aesora

Chusi
Egrebel

Shechem
Salem

Pharathon

Torrent of Mochmur

Tephon

Acrabah

W. Quun

W. Sarida

SAMARIA

AKRABBETTINE

JAFFA

Ono **J**

Ramathaim Thamnatah

Neballath

BAAL-HAZOR

Lydda Lod
Hadid

Apherema
Senaah

Bethel **J**
Aiath

Modin
Beth-horon **J**
Mizpah

Jericho

Gittaim **J**

Accaron
GEZER

Ramah
Michmash

Emmaus

Gibeon
Geba

JAMNIA

V. Sorek

P. Hyenas

Kedron

Anathoth
JUDAEA

V. Terebinth

EKRON ⊛

Zorah Jarmuth

JERUSALEM
Nob

Anaiah

ASHDOD

Zanoah

Beth-hacherem

Azekah **J**

Béthbasi

Kidron

ASHKELON

Adullam
Odollam

Tekoa

Keilah

Beth-zur

Gaza ⊛

MARISA

Lachish **J**

⊛**J**
HEBRON

DEAD SEA

IDUMAEA

Ziklag **J**

J Beer-sheba

Kadesh

J • Dibon
Dibom

(16)

KINGDOM OF HEROD   NEIGHBORING COUNTRIES

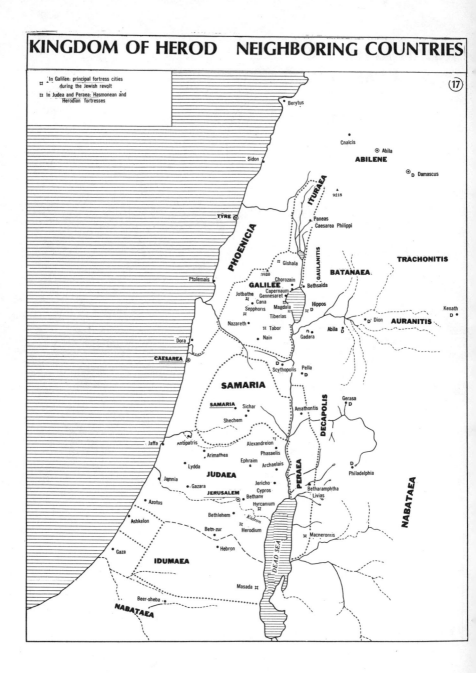

⊡ In Galilee: principal fortress cities during the Jewish revolt
⊠ In Judea and Peraea: Hasmonean and Herodian fortresses

Berytus

Cnalcis
⊙ Abila
ABILENE

⊙ D Damascus

Sidon

ITURAEA

9218

Paneas
Caesarea Philippi

TRACHONITIS

TYRE ⊙

PHOENICIA

⊡ Gishala

GAULANITIS

Ptolemais

3920

Chorozain

BATANAEA

Bethsaida

GALILEE
Jotbathe   Capernaum
⊠ Cana   Gennesaret
Sepphoris
Nazareth ·   ⊠ Tabor
Nain

Magdala
Tiberias

Hippos
D

Abila ⊡
D

D· Dion   **AURANITIS**

Kenath
D ·

Gadara

Dora

CAESAREA ⊙

D
Scythopolis   Pella
D

SAMARIA

SAMARIA   Sichar
Shechem

Amathontis

DECAPOLIS

Gerasa
D

Jaffa ·   Antipatris ·
Arimathea
Lydda ·
Jamnia
· Gazara

Alexandreion
Phasaelis
Ephraim
Archaelais

JUDAEA

JERUSALEM

Jericho
Cypros
· Bethany

D ·
Philadelphia

PERAEA

Betharamphtha
Livias

NABATAEA

Azotus ·

Hyrcanium

Ashkelon ·

Bethlehem ·

Kidron

Beth-zur ·   Herodium
⊠

⊠ Macnerontis

Gaza ·

IDUMAEA

· Hebron

DEAD SEA

Masada ⊠

Beer-sheba ·

NABATAEA